Robert Watts

The Newer Criticism and the Analogy of the Faith

A reply to lectures by W. Robertson Smith, on the Old Testament in the Jewish Church

Robert Watts

The Newer Criticism and the Analogy of the Faith
A reply to lectures by W. Robertson Smith, on the Old Testament in the Jewish Church

ISBN/EAN: 9783337241605

Printed in Europe, USA, Canada, Australia, Japan

Cover: Foto ©Lupo / pixelio.de

More available books at **www.hansebooks.com**

THE NEWER CRITICISM

AND THE

ANALOGY OF THE FAITH.

A REPLY

TO LECTURES BY W. ROBERTSON SMITH, M.A., ON THE OLD TESTAMENT IN THE JEWISH CHURCH.

BY

ROBERT WATTS, D.D.,

PROFESSOR OF SYSTEMATIC THEOLOGY IN THE GENERAL ASSEMBLY'S COLLEGE, BELFAST.

THIRD EDITION.

EDINBURGH:
T. & T. CLARK, 38 GEORGE STREET.
1882.

*Morrison and Gibb, Edinburgh,
Printers to Her Majesty's Stationery Office.*

In Memoriam.

To the Memory of DR. THOMAS CHALMERS, DR. WILLIAM CUNNINGHAM, *and* DR. CHARLES HODGE, *this Contribution to the Defence of the Faith for which they so mightily contended, is affectionately inscribed, by*

THE AUTHOR.

PREFACE.

THE present volume owes its origin to a course of lectures on Biblical Criticism by W. Robertson Smith, M.A., delivered in Edinburgh and Glasgow in the beginning of the current year, before audiences, as the author informs us, of not less than eighteen hundred, and given to the public afterwards in a volume of 446 pages. The object aimed at in the course, was to give the Scottish public "an opportunity of understanding the position of the newer criticism, in order that they might not condemn it unheard." Stated otherwise, the delivery of these lectures was simply an appeal from the decision of the Free Church Commission, in the previous October, suspending the author "from the ordinary work of his chair in Aberdeen," to the general tribunal of "the Scottish public," who, of course, are presumed by the lecturer to be more competent than the Free Church Commission to sit in judgment on the claims of "the newer criticism."

The course professes to give "an outline of the problems, the methods, and the results of Old Testament criticism," and the lecturer claims that "the sustained interest with which his large audience followed his attempt is sufficient proof that they did not find modern Biblical science the repulsive and unreal thing which it is often represented to be." Other, and different, representations have been made regarding the sustained interest and the dimensions of the audiences; but neither the sustained nor the waning interest of the audience can be accepted as a proof or disproof of the science, or the soundness, of the doctrines propounded. Large audiences, in large cities, may be gathered and kept together to hear discussions much less complimentary to the Bible than the course in question. It is not by such tests as such gatherings furnish that systems of criticism are to be adjudged. These gatherings are now dispersed, and have, it would seem, given no verdict, so that the court appealed to has not pronounced judgment in the case. If we are to judge of the impression made, by the very decided action of the late Free Church Assembly, we cannot conclude that the appeal to the public has been a success. Either the six hundred requisitionists, at whose request the course was undertaken, have not proved true representatives of the estimate in which "the newer criticism" is held by the Free Church of Scotland, or else "the attempt to lay its problems, methods, and results before the public," has been made in such a way as to open the eyes of Christian men to its bearings upon the claims of the Old Testament to be any longer regarded as the word of God.

It is true the author of these lectures claims it as "the great value of historical criticism that it makes the Old Testament more real to us;" but if the reality be as it is represented in this "outline," we are brought face to face with the fearful alternative of accepting as the word of God a palpable forgery claiming to be divinely inspired, or of rejecting it as a mockery and a fraud. To use the language of the author (p. 309) in reference to the Mosaic authorship of the Pentateuch, "if we are shut up to choose between" such a theory of the origin and composition of the books of the Bible, "and the sceptical opinion that the Bible is a forgery, the sceptics must gain their case." The fact is, the theory leaves no room for choice; for, as it is set forth in these lectures, it is simply an elaborate and detailed account of the way in which a guild of men availed themselves of a meagre historical outline to give an air of antiquity and authority to practices and doctrines which were either unknown and unheard of within the historical limits to which they have been fraudulently referred, or were, in ruder forms, denounced by the prophets of Jehovah, who, after authorizing His prophets to utter the denunciation, reversed His judgment, and gave his sanction to the doctrines and practices previously denounced!

It is needless to say that there is no room for choice here. One cannot choose between such a theory and scepticism, for the simple reason that there is no difference between the two things. The fact that the theory has been espoused and advocated by a professor in a Christian Seminary does not alter its character. Whether it come from the pen of a Kuenen, or a Wellhausen, or a Smith, it is still the same faith-subverting theory, which no ingenuity of man can reconcile with the history or character of the Old Testament revelation; and no one can accept it and continue long to regard the sacred Scriptures as the word of God, or hold the system of doctrine exhibited in the Symbols of the Reformed faith. Under the deep and painful conviction that the principles, critical and theological, advocated by the lecturer, are subversive of all confidence in the Old Testament as a divine revelation, as well as of all faith in the fundamental doctrines of Christianity, the present Reply has been prepared. The ever-recurring principle, in obedience to which the whole Old Testament record is to be not only revised, but recast, is that the non-observance of a law proves its non-existence! Reversing the apostolic maxim, that "where there is no law there is no transgression," our critic proceeds throughout upon the assumption that where there is transgression there is no law. It were no exaggeration to say that, if the portions of his volume which rest on this assumption were removed, the book would be reduced to one-third of its present dimensions. Indeed, so all-pervading and regulative is this principle, from the beginning to the close, it soon becomes manifest that, without it, the author could not have given the faintest colour of plausibility to his theory of the post-exilic origin of the Levitical system, or of the all but exilic origin of the Deuteronomic code—in other words, could not have written his course of lectures at all. With regard to the other critical principles laid down by the author, suffice it to say that, where valid, they are either inapplicable altogether, or, if strictly applied, would only serve to embarrass and confute the theory he has sought to establish. For confirmation of this representation and estimate of a work which evinces extensive reading and the possession of literary ability, which, if regulated by sound judgment and a spirit of reverence toward the Holy Scriptures, might have contributed largely to the defence of the faith, the reader is referred, without further preface, to the volume herewith given to the public, and committed to the providence and grace of the Eternal Logos, who is the only Revealer of the Father under the Old Testament or the New.

ROBERT WATTS.

ASSEMBLY'S COLLEGE, BELFAST,
    Oct. 14, 1881.

PREFACE TO THE SECOND EDITION.

IT is extremely gratifying to find that the first edition has been exhausted within a few weeks, and it may perhaps be assumed without presumption, that this Reply has in some measure met a felt want. In this second edition the attempt is made, by a new division into chapters, by a slight alteration in the arrangement, and by other changes, to render the work more clear and effective.

In the meantime, the author of *The Old Testament in the Jewish Church* has been furnishing further proof, if further proof were needed, of the revolutionary and baneful tendencies of "the newer criticism." In the last volume of the *Encyclopædia Britannica* (vol. xiii.) there are articles from his pen on "Joel" and on "Judges." In the former a late date is assigned to the book, and one of the main arguments in support of this position is that the Levitical legislation is post-exilic; while in the latter, the theory by which Aaron and his sons have been reduced to a priestly guild is applied, under the inspiration of Nöldeke, to many of the minor judges of Israel.

Thus, with every new appearance, "the newer criticism" — octopus-like — reaches out still further its relentless arms, drawing into its deadly embrace priest and sacrifice, prophet and judge. Already the Pentateuch is dismembered; Joshua is assigned to a late date because of its relation to Deuteronomy, and because of its altar of witness, so fatal to the claims of "the New Apologetic"; Samuel is declared to be teeming with interpolations; the Chronicles are unhistorical; Isaiah and Zechariah are each rent asunder; Ecclesiastes proclaims a lie; and now Joel and Judges are discredited. Thus, with a persistency that will brook no repression, this school prosecutes its destructive task, rifling the Bible of pre-exilic times of its chiefest glory, and stripping it of every symbol and type that could signify or foreshadow the redemptive work of Christ.

Yet, bad as all this is, it does not approach in its spirit of irreverence an article entitled "Israel," from the pen of Wellhausen, one of the author's masters in criticism, which appears in the same volume of the *Encyclopædia*. This article is but fairly characterized when it is pronounced blasphemous. Critical it cannot be called by any one who has any regard to the right use of language. It challenges, and pronounces false and fraudulent, the leading historical incidents which are at once the credentials and the glory of the chosen race. The critical apparatus by which this degradation of the race and their history has been achieved is exceedingly simple. It is, in fact, reducible to the one fundamental of all rationalistic criticism, viz. the impossibility of the miraculous,—a principle which, carried out to its final and necessary consequences, involves the denial of the miracles of the creation of the universe, and of the incarnation and resurrection of Christ; and with these, of course, the denial of all evidence of the existence of an ante-mundane, extra-mundane, personal Creator, and all evidence of the fundamental facts of Christianity,—thus, at one fell swoop, destroying all theology, whether natural or revealed, and, with it, all possibility of religion among men!

Regard for the third commandment forbids extracts from this latest utterance of "the newer criticism;" and the apology for even referring to it, is that the representative of the school in Scotland is careful, after he has carried his pupils through the initial stages of its irreverent *curriculum*, to hand them over to Wellhausen for further guidance. The editor of the *Encyclopædia* has now unveiled to the English reader the goal of such guidance, and it is manifest that he who accepts it must, if divine grace prevent not, eventually take leave, not only of the Bible and its divine authorship and the redemption it reveals, but of the God of Creation and Providence, and settle down in absolute atheism, or in blank, unthinking agnosticism.

It is truly astonishing, as it is inexplicable, to find venerable Christian men, whose hoar hairs testify that they must have lived in the days of Chalmers and Cunningham, publicly proclaiming the introducer of Wellhausen as the only man "who can speak with the enemy in the gate!" The true historical precedent and parallel of such "speaking with the enemy" would certainly not be the conference held with Rabshakeh by Eliakim, and Shebna, and Joah, when they endeavoured to dissuade him from speaking his blasphemies in their own language in the hearing of the people that were on the wall. Wellhausen is subjected to no such restrictions; on the contrary, he is introduced to the people of these lands speaking in their own tongue wherein they were born, and is allowed, through the medium of a publication which professes to give the latest and most authoritative deliverances on all the subjects of which it treats, to associate the Jehovah of Israel with Baal, and to relegate the leading events in the history of the chosen race to the region of the purely mythical. The proper precedent for such "speaking with the enemy" would be the conference held by Lundy, governor of Derry, with the emissaries of King James, when he agreed to surrender to that monarch the Maiden City.

It is surely time for the Church of God, irrespective of denominational distinctions or national boundaries, to rise in arms against this deadly foe now welcomed to her gates. She cannot, without proving recreant to her trust, countenance or tolerate in any office-bearer, of whatever rank, doctrines, or actions, which are subversive of the very foundations of our common Christianity.

ROBERT WATTS.

Assembly's College, Belfast,
December 1881.

PREFACE TO THE THIRD EDITION.

THE prefaces to the first and second editions render it unnecessary formally to introduce the present issue. It is satisfactory to find that the book has met with such acceptance among the friends of reverent criticism and sound theology, on both sides of the Atlantic, as to demand a third edition. The Author avails himself of this opportunity to return his most sincere thanks to the many kind reviewers who have so cordially aided him, by their favourable notices, in his attempt to defend the fundamental doctrines of the Analogy of the Faith.

So far as the author has seen, no critic has questioned the justice of the grave, momentous charge, preferred on p. 147, that " God's grace from Adam to Ezra worked on the assumption that the sole obstacle in the way of forgiveness was to be found in the subjective state of the sinner himself; or, in other words, that during the whole history of our world, prior to the Babylonish exile, the grace of God was administered upon Socinian principles as modified by 'the newer criticism.'" So long as the friends of "the newer criticism" allow this and other kindred charges to remain unchallenged and unrefuted, their attempts at reply must be regarded as mere trifling. No one who believes that "without shedding of blood is no remission" can accept, as either scientific or Biblical, a system of criticism which teaches, that for more than three thousand years of the divine administration, salvation was neither by grace nor by blood, but by the deeds of the law.

ROBERT WATTS.

Assembly's College, Belfast,
   31*st March* 1882.

CONTENTS.

CHAPTER I.

	PAGE
THE NEWER CRITICISM AND THE HISTORY,	1
The Author's First Principle of Criticism,	1
Applicability of this Principle,	2
Trustworthiness of the Old Bridge questioned,	4
Trustworthiness of the Author's Judgment challenged,	6
Origin of the Esdrine Torah,	7
Author's Counsel accepted,	11
The Ezekielian Hypothesis of the Origin of the Levitical Torah,	14
Arguments from the History of the First Temple,	21
Argument from the Sin of Jeroboam,	26
Argument from Elijah's Sacrifice on Carmel,	27

CHAPTER II.

THE NEWER CRITICISM AND THE HISTORY (*continued*),	29
Argument from the Reformation of Josiah,	30
The Bearing of these Facts on the Author's Theory,	31
Author's Method of meeting the Argument from Josiah's Reformation unhistorical,	35
Ethical Difficulties in the way of this Deuteronomic Theory,	42
Argument from Ezekiel against a Pre-exilic Priestly Torah,	45
Ezekiel's New Ordinances,	47

CHAPTER III.

THE NEWER CRITICISM AND THE INTERPRETATION OF THE PROPHETS,	52
Consequences of denying a Levitical Torah under the First Temple,	54

xx   CONTENTS.

	PAGE
The Theory in Conflict with the Institution of the Passover,	56
Its Exegesis of Jeremiah places him in Conflict with the Institution of the Passover,	58
Boiling not inconsistent with Sacrifice,	61
Our Author cannot exorcise the Priesthood out of Jeremiah,	66
Recognition of Deuteronomic Code in Josiah's day creates a Difficulty,	68
Attempted Solution of this Difficulty,	70
Examination of the foregoing Solution,	71

CHAPTER IV.

THE NEWER CRITICISM AND THE INTERPRETATION OF THE PROPHETS (*continued*),	73
Theory of Religion in Pre-exilic Times,	74
Essential Elements of Religion as known in Pre-exilic Times,	75
Israel's Ignorance of the Doctrine of Atonement in Pre-exilic Times,	78
The Theory arrays the Pre-exilic Prophets against the Post-exilic Prophets,	83
The Author's Solution Suicidal and Inconsistent,	85
Rule for the Interpretation of such Passages,	87
Argument from such Passages proves too much,	89
"The Newer Criticism" and the Fifty-first Psalm,	91
Argument not met by proving the Psalm exilic,	92
The Difficulty of "the Newer Criticism" is not met by omitting the last two verses of this Psalm,	93
Author's Views of the Status of God's People in Pre-exilic Times,	94
His Doctrine Anti-confessional,	94
Doctrine of a Collective Organic Spiritual Inhabitation,	96
This Doctrine examined, and proved Unscriptural,	97
Romish Cast of the Doctrine,	98
Summation,	99

CHAPTER V.

THE NEWER CRITICISM AND THE TEXT,	101
Author summoned as a Witness to the Faithfulness of the Scribes,	101
Date of the Samaritan Pentateuch inconsistent with a Post-exilic Torah,	104
Author's Faculty of Generalization,	105
Author's Accusations of the Scribes met by himself,	106

Text to be transmitted was without Vowel-Points,	107
Vowelless Text all the easier of Transmission,	109
Ignorance of Import not a Foe to Accurate Transmission,	110
Competency of the Massorets to Vocalize the Record,	112

CHAPTER VI.

THE NEWER CRITICISM AND THE DOCTRINE OF SACRIFICE,	116
Worship by Sacrifice, and all that belongs to it, uncommanded prior to the Exile,	117
The Theory assumes the Human Origin of Sacrifice,	120
The Author's First Assertion,	122
Universal Prevalence of Sacrifice consistent with a Divine Origin,	123
Human Origin of Sacrifice not reasonable,	123
Argument from the fact that Sacrifice preceded the Use of Animal Food,	124
Argument for Divine Origin from Abel's Offering,	125
Argument from Noah's Sacrifice,	126
The Author's Second Assertion,	128
The Author's Third Assertion,	129
Argument confirmed by the Epistle to the Hebrews,	129
Wherefore then serveth the Law?	131
Uncommanded Worship Unconfessional Doctrine,	133
Uncommanded Worship a Breach of the Sinaitic Covenant,	134

CHAPTER VII.

THE NEWER CRITICISM AND THE DOCTRINE OF SACRIFICE (*continued*),	138
Exposition of the Author's Theory of Forgiveness,	141
Estimate and Classification of the Author's Theory of Forgiveness,	142
Simply one of the many Subjective Theories of Salvation,	146
Gravity of the Question thus raised,	146
Author's Theory of Pre-exilic Grace seems to determine his Theory of the Date of the Pentateuch,	147
The Theory denies what the Confession affirms,	148
The Theory omits what the Confession asserts,	150
Further Justification of this Charge,	151
The Confession does not admit the Author's Distinction of the Economy into Pre-exilic and Post-exilic,	153
Meaning of the term Law in the Epistle to the Romans,	154
If Moses gave no Priestly Torah, how can the Levitical System be developed from Mosaic Principles?	156

Historical Deductions from the Ten Words of Moses, . . . 157
Other Arches of the Ceremonial Viaduct, ... 158
The Bridge does not reach all the way across, ... 159

CHAPTER VIII.

THE NEWER CRITICISM AND THE DOCTRINE OF SACRIFICE
(*continued*), ... 161

The Import of all this, ... 164
How does the Author know that Moses was a Priest, or that his
    Torah had Priestly Elements? 165
The Theory of Development demands what our Author cannot
    admit save at the sacrifice of his Fundamental, . . . 168
The Charge of Fraud still remains, ... 170
Principles at Stake in this Discussion, ... 171
The Theory Unreasonable, ... 174
Another Instance of the Author's Proclivity for Generalization, . 177
This Adverse Generalization becomes eventually adverse to the
    Author, ... 179
A Crucial Question to be answered by our Author, . . . 182
The only Theory of the Coincidence in Harmony with God's
    Attributes, ... 185

CHAPTER IX.

THE NEWER CRITICISM AND THE DOCTRINE OF WORSHIP, . . 187

The Theory tested by Historical Facts, ... 189
Arguments in support of the Theory based upon Erroneous Inter-
    pretations of Scripture, ... 191
As a Theory of Prayer the Doctrine is incredible, . . . 194
Argument from the Book of Jonah, ... 195
Argument from Psalm cvii., ... 196
Views of the Ancient Heathen on this Theory of Prayer, . . 197
Origin of this Conception, ... 199
The Theory implies Changeableness in Jehovah, . . . 200

CHAPTER X.

THE NEWER CRITICISM AND THE DESIGN OF THE MOSAIC
    ECONOMY, ... 202

Symbolic Import of the Passover, ... 203
Sacrificial Character of Paschal Lamb recognised by Christ and
    His Apostles, ... 205

	PAGE
Anti-Economic Separation of the Ceremonial from the Moral Law,	207
A Fundamental Economic Question,	208
The Moral Law states the Conditions of Life under all Dispensations,	209
The Moral Law applies to the Substitute as well as to the Principal,	210
The Ceremonial Law correlative to the Moral,	210
Arguments in support of this Position,	211
Reason of the Sacredness of the Ark,	213
Reason of the Appointment of the Ark as the Seat of the Divine Administration,	214
Bearing of these Facts upon the Character of the New Testament Dispensation,	215
Extent of the Typology of the Mosaic Dispensation,	216
Conclusion from the foregoing Facts,	218
Bearing of these Facts upon the Post-exilic Theory of "the Newer Criticism,"	218
Mediation in Pre-exilic Times is still found even in the Minimum of Record acknowledged by "the Newer Criticism,"	220
The Theory needs to rid the Pentateuch not only of Mosaic Authorship, but of Moses himself and his Mediation,	223

CHAPTER XI.

THE NEWER CRITICISM AND THE MOSAIC INSTITUTIONS—THE ARK, THE AARONIC PRIESTHOOD,	225
Ceremonies connected with the Ark unsanctioned until the Ark was lost!	227
The Theory in conflict with the References to the Ark in the Epistle to the Hebrews,	228
The Ark necessary from the time the Moral Law was given,	229
Question of Fraud raised again by the Post-exilic Theory,	231
Special Insuperable Difficulties of the Theory arising from the acknowledged Loss of the Ark during the Exile,	232
Aaron and his Sons,	234
Account of the Consecration of Aaron and his Sons pronounced not Historical,	236
The Theory assumes that there may be Regulative Precedents destitute of any Historical Basis,	238
The Theory attempts to shake Confidence in the Historical Character of the Narrative,	239

xxiv   CONTENTS.

	PAGE
The Tent pitched by Moses was not the Tabernacle,	240
The Context confirms this View,	242
The Charge of Falsifying the Record preferred again,	245
Extravagant Claim advanced in behalf of "the Newer Criticism,"	246
The alleged Historical Discrepancy examined,	247
The Assumption necessary to make out the Charge of Discrepancy,	249
Consequence of the Failure of this Impeachment of the Record,	251
The New Testament endorses this Impugned Record,	252

CHAPTER XII.

THE NEWER CRITICISM AND THE PRIESTLY OFFICE,	255
The Relation of the Priestly to the Prophetic Office,	256
Author's View of the Relation of Priesthood to Prophecy,	257
Analysis of the foregoing Assertions,	259
Is the Primary Function of a Priest Oracular?	260
The True Ideal of a Priest,	263
Definition not to be determined by mere Etymology,	264
Special Illustration from the Practice of our Missionaries in India,	265
The Nature of the Priestly Function determines its Relation to the Prophetic,	267
Relation of Christ's Priestly Functions to His Prophetic and Kingly Functions,	268
Relation of these Functions as foreshadowed in the Mosaic Legislation,	269
Argument from the Experience of God's People,	270
Importance and Gravity of this Question,	271
"The Newer Criticism" and Development,	273

CHAPTER XIII.

STRICTURES ON THE ARTICLE "BIBLE,"	277
Conclusion,	320
Appendix,	322
Index,	323

THE NEWER CRITICISM.

CHAPTER I.

THE NEWER CRITICISM AND THE HISTORY.

IN examining and estimating a system of Biblical criticism, it is but due to the system and its author to ascertain and consider carefully the principles on which the system depends, and by which the author is guided in his investigation of the Sacred Record.

The Author's First Principle of Criticism.

The first principle laid down in this course of lectures—a principle which our author must regard as vital to his theory, as he gives it precedence of all others, and builds a very large portion of his argument upon it—is thus stated on p. 23 : "The first principle of criticism is that every book bears the stamp of the time and circumstances in which it was produced. An ancient book is, so to speak, a fragment of ancient life ; and to understand it aright we must treat it as a living thing, as a bit of the life of the author and his time, which we shall not fully understand without putting ourselves back into the age in which it was written."

Applicability of this Principle.

As a general rule, this canon of criticism is perfectly fair, but only as a general rule can it be accepted. It is obvious that there may be books written in an age so remote from the time of the critic that he cannot "put himself back into it." This is pre-eminently true of most of the books composing the volume which our author has undertaken to criticise. They were written at dates so remote, that there is nothing that can be called literature wherewith to compare them. Indeed, the author himself, who on page 23 lays down the foregoing rule for the guidance of historical interpretation, has admitted a state of matters which should have made him very modest and backward in the application of it to Old Testament literature. On page 17 he writes: "In the study of the New Testament we are assisted in the work of historical interpretation by a large contemporary literature of profane origin, whereas we have almost no contemporary helps for the study of Hebrew antiquity beyond the books which were received into the Jewish Canon." In note 3 to Lecture I., the absence of the literary requisites for the application of this rule is still more explicitly acknowledged. "The Old Testament writers," he confesses, "possessed Hebrew sources now lost, such as the Book of the Wars of the Lord, the Book of Jasher, and the Annals of the Kings of Israel and Judah. But Josephus, and other profane historians whose writings are still extant, had no authentic Hebrew sources for the canonical history except those preserved in the Bible." Confirmatory of this confession is the testimony of Wellhausen in the article "Israel" (*Encyc. Brit.*, vol. xiii. p. 431): "For all that precedes the time of Alexander the Old Testament is the only native authority. Among foreign sources, besides the stone of Mesha, the Assyrian inscriptions hold the first rank; for the chronology they are of decisive importance. The Egyptian inscriptions, on the other hand, are of slight value. Besides these, mention must be made of the notices in the *Chronicon* of Eusebius, and in the *Contra Apionem* of Josephus (Manetho and Berosus)." Under such literary conditions it is difficult to see how the author can find his way back into the age in which each of the books of the Bible was written, and report to the Scottish public the literary canons by which the writers were guided, what documents the writer of a particular book had before him, how much he took from one and how much he took from another, and how he shaped and modified their contents by additions or omissions. One would think that the confession of the critic should have greatly moderated the tone of his criticisms, and have led him to speak with less confidence of the use and wont of pre-exilic times. Nor is the fact to be overlooked that the recent discoveries, mentioned by our author in the note referred to, do but serve to prove the trustworthiness of those historical writers whom he has assailed. In those instances in which their writings synchronize with the public records or cuneiform chronicles of Nineveh or Babylon, or with the hieroglyphs of Egypt, or with the inscription on the Moabite Stone, the result of a comparison has been such as to confirm our confidence in the trustworthiness and superiority of the sacred narratives, and in the inspiration of the sacred writers.

Now, while admitting this chronological literary difficulty, the author has overlooked it, and proceeded in his treatment of these most ancient records as if no such difficulty existed. He has acted throughout upon the assumption that he is in possession of materials for the construction of a literary critical viaduct, by which he has actually bridged the vast gulf of the intervening centuries; and that he has passed over it himself, and is now ready to convey all who will accept his guidance into the midst of the temporal circumstances, literary culture, and customs of the age, however remote, in which each portion of the sacred record was produced.

Trustworthiness of the Old Bridge questioned.

We are furnished with an account of the building of this bridge, and of the material employed in its construction. In the first place, the old structure, consisting, in the main, of Jewish traditions, had to be cleared away. The learning of the Rabbins was untrustworthy, and as "scholarship moved onwards, and as research was carried farther, it gradually became plain that it was possible for Biblical students, with the material still preserved to them, to get behind the Jewish Rabbins, upon whom our translators were still dependent, and to draw from the sacred stream at a point nearer its source," p. 47. A large portion of the lectures is spent in depreciating the scholarship of the Rabbins, and magnifying the ignorance and untrustworthiness of the scribes in the copying and transmission of the original records, whilst the most extravagant claims are set up for modern critical scholarship. The object of all this depreciation of Jewish scholarship is to shake confidence in Jewish testimony to the authorship and age of the books of the Bible, and especially to the authorship and age of the Pentateuch. Take the following as a specimen: "This, then, is what the scribes did. They chose for us the Hebrew text which we have now got. Were they in a position to choose the very best text, to produce a critical edition which could justly be accepted as the standard, so that we lose nothing by the suppression of all divergent copies? Now, this at least we can say,—that if they fixed for us a satisfactory text, the scribes did not do so in virtue of any great critical skill which they possessed in comparing MSS. and selecting the best readings. They worked from a false point of view. Their objects were legal, not philological. Their defective philology, their bad system of interpretation, made them bad critics; for it is the first rule of criticism, that a good critic must be a good interpreter of the thoughts of the author," pp. 76, 77.

Trustworthiness of the Author's Judgment challenged.

On this estimate of the scribes and their work it may be remarked, that they had not, at the outset, to choose, as modern critics have to do, either for themselves or for us a Hebrew text in the exercise of their own unaided powers as philologists. The chief object of our author is to disprove the traditional view of the age and authorship of the Pentateuch; and if it can be shown that he has failed in this, we may conclude that his book is a failure. Now, so far as the Pentateuch is concerned, he admits that " there can be no doubt that the law which was in Ezra's hands was practically identical with our present Hebrew Pentateuch," and that this " Pentateuch or Torah, as we now have it, became the religious and municipal code of Israel," pp. 56, 57. On page 158, the author ascribes the establishment of this Canon to Ezra, and says that he led " his people to accept a written and sacred code as the absolute rule of faith and life," and affirms that " this Canon of Ezra was the Pentateuch." Reference is here made to this representation of Ezra's relation to our Pentateuch, simply to show that, even on the author's own showing, Ezra's book is our Hebrew Pentateuch. We are thus, so far as the Pentateuch is concerned, carried beyond the scribes to "their father" Ezra, who imposed upon his successors, not the task of choosing a "text," but the task of a faithful transmission of *the recognised text* to posterity. If, then, there was any such thing as a choosing of a "text" to be transmitted, that choice was made by Ezra.

Origin of the Esdrine Torah.

The question, then, is, did Ezra find this Torah, or Pentateuch, in existence, or did he invent or develop it out of certain principles of a brief Mosaic legislation? As our author holds and argues that this complete Levitical system, given by Ezra, dates from the Exile, it must follow that Ezra or others are the authors of it; and that, as he or they could not have extemporized it amid the confusion and excitement connected with the execution of his mission in Jerusalem, the work must have been composed in the land of their captivity. If originated at all by Ezra or his brethren, it must have been produced in Babylon, for he is represented (Ezra vii. 14) as having the law of his God in his hand before he left Babylon. This law, which he had in his hand before he left Babylon, is the law he came to Jerusalem to establish—the law in which he read from day to day in the hearing of the people, and the law according to which he carried forward, in conjunction with Nehemiah, the reformation in Judah. To say that this law was hitherto unknown to the people, to their princes or priests, is not only to assert without proof, but it is to affirm what the narratives of Ezra and Nehemiah disprove. For example, when Ezra and his company came to Jerusalem, we find that the princes were not ignorant of some enactments of this Torah before he had read a word of it in their hearing; for they approached him saying, "The people of Israel, and the priests, and [the '*and*' is in the LXX. as well as in the Hebrew] the Levites" (showing that they were aware of the distinction between priests and Levites), "have not separated themselves from the peoples of the lands, ... for they have taken (contrary to the law of Moses, Ex. xxxiv. 16; Deut. vii. 4) of their daughters for themselves and for their sons," etc. etc. (Ezra ix. 1, 2). And long before Ezra had left Babylon or come to Jerusalem, in the sixth year of the reign of Darius, it would seem from Ezra's narrative that the children of the captivity were not unacquainted with this Esdrine Torah, for at the dedication of their new temple they "stationed the priests in their orders, *and* the Levites in their divisions for the service of God, which is in Jerusalem, as it is written in the Book of Moses" (Ezra vi. 18; Num. iii., iv., and viii.).

A reference to these passages and their contexts will show that the men who came out of Babylon "who were minded" (as the decree of Artaxerxes puts it) "of their own free will to go up to Jerusalem," or (as it is put by Ezra, chap. i. 5) "whose spirit God had raised to go up to build the house of the Lord which is in Jerusalem," were fully aware of the Levitical system before they left Babylon. They had sufficient knowledge of the use and wont of the pre-exilic period to enable them to build the house of the Lord, to arrange the service of the house according to the Book of Moses, making the distinction between the priests and the Levites, and to observe the feast of the Passover. Knowledge of these things did not grow up in an hour. These God-fearing men, who, for the faith of their fathers and the love of the God of Israel, exposed themselves to the peril and privation necessarily attendant upon the execution of their high commission, were surely not the dupes of a sacerdotal conspiracy. The men who laid the foundations of the house were no novices. There were old men among them; "many of the priests *and* Levites, and chief of the fathers who were ancient men, had seen the first house" (Ezra iii. 12). These men, who wept because of the memories of the former house, were not the men to give countenance to a newly devised ritual. Every act of the restoration programme shows that these pioneers were moved out of regard to the ancient Mosaic Torah, and that they were thoroughly conversant with its most minute provisions. "Jēshua, the son of Jozadak, and his brethren the priests, Zerubbabel the son of Shealtiel and his brethren," knew how to build "the altar of the God of Israel, and to offer burnt-offerings thereon, as it is written in the law of

Moses, the man of God." They knew how "to set the altar upon his basis," and "to offer burnt-offerings morning and evening;" and they knew how to "keep the feast of Tabernacles, as it is written," and to offer "the daily burnt-offerings by number according to the custom as the duty of every day required," and to offer "the continual burnt-offering, both of the new moons and of all the set feasts of the Lord that were consecrated, and of every one that willingly offered a free-will offering unto the Lord." "But," it is added, "the foundation of the temple of the Lord was not yet laid" (Ezra iii.).

Any one who will weigh these historic statements (and they are but specimens of the Esdrine narrative), will read these lectures with feelings of surprise if not of astonishment. He will naturally ask the question, How could any critic, who believed the narrative of these things as given by Ezra, represent Ezra as establishing, ninety years afterwards, "the Pentateuch as the canonical and authoritative book of the Jews," and giving it "the position which it holds ever afterwards"! P. 158. This is simply saying, that ninety years after "the children of the captivity" had re-instituted the Mosaic economy in the minutiæ of its details, and had done this by the counsel and in the presence of "ancient men who had seen the first house," and had mingled in its services, Ezra came, fresh from Babylon, and "led them to accept a written and sacred code," hitherto unheard of, "as the absolute rule of faith and life," and "this Canon of Ezra was the Pentateuch!"

He will likely ask still further, How can the Levitical legislation, which our author restricts to the second temple, have found its way to these fathers or ever a stone was laid in its foundations?

Author's Counsel accepted.

The author cannot object to the principle of this argument from the narratives of Ezra and Nehemiah, for he blames the traditionists (p. 158) for not opening their eyes, and for not simply looking at the Bible itself for a plain and categorical account of what Ezra and Nehemiah actually did for the Canon of Scripture. Now, when we accept this counsel and open our eyes, and "simply look at the Bible itself," and not at Kuenen, or Wellhausen, or other representatives of this "newer criticism," we find, if we are to give credit to Ezra and Nehemiah, as we are advised to do, that the children of the captivity knew the very portions of this Pentateuchal Torah, which "the newer criticism" alleges were brought in and established by Ezra, full ninety years before Ezra came to Jerusalem. Nor had the lapse of these ninety years extinguished the knowledge of this Torah, for before Ezra had read a single line of it the princes informed him that the people of Israel, and the priests, *and* the Levites, had not been observing it in one of its most imperative injunctions. They do not await the action of Ezra, but come to him beforehand, complaining of the transgression of the law by the people, the priests, and the Levites. This transgression is recognised both by the people and Ezra as a transgression of the commandments of God, and is acknowledged as a part of that course of sin which had brought down the judgments of God upon them and their fathers,—a confession which assumes that the Torah was known to their fathers.

Confirmatory of the position that the law read by Ezra, in the hearing of the people, was not unknown, is the account given of their assembling together at Jerusalem on the occasion on which he read it. They came together in the seventh month, a notable month in Israel's year, and came together manifestly in accordance with an established custom, for there is no mention made of any command to that effect having been issued by Ezra or Nehemiah. This fact seems to warrant the inference that these children of the captivity were aware of the law of Leviticus regarding the feasts of the Lord (Lev. xxiii.–xxv.). And further, it would seem that they were aware of the special command of Moses regarding the reading of the law in the hearing of all Israel, at the end of every seven years, at the feast of Tabernacles, for it was at their request that Ezra brought "the book of the law of Moses, which the Lord had commanded to Israel" (Neh. viii. 1), before the congregation, and read it in their hearing. Surely it is not unwarrantable to conclude from their coming together at the time prescribed in this Mosaic Torah, and their asking Ezra to bring it forth, that they knew of its existence and its laws. Even ninety years before this memorable event, "the people gathered themselves together as one man to Jerusalem, when the seventh month was come." "From the first day of the seventh month began they to offer burnt-offerings unto the Lord" (Ezra iii. 1, 6). Comp. Lev. xxiii. 23-44; Num. xxix.

When, therefore, Ezra and his associates read from this book, they proclaimed to Israel no new law for their endorsement. Ezra did not read it to establish or authenticate it, but read it as the recognised and authentic law of God.

We are thus carried back behind the days of the restoration to the days of the exile; for the men of the restoration, at all its stages, prove themselves well acquainted with the Mosaic Torah in all its essential features. This, of course, is all one with saying that the so-called Esdrine Canon was known before Ezra was born, and was the recognised law of Israel in the days of their sojourn in Babylon. In view of this result, we may recommend the lecturer's aforesaid counsel to the traditionists, to himself, and the school he represents, viz., "Scholars have sometimes been so busy trying to gather a grain of truth out of these fabulous traditions" (of critics from Maimonides and Spinoza to Kuenen and Wellhausen), "that they have forgotten to open their eyes, and simply look at the Bible itself for a plain and categorical account of what Ezra and Nehemiah actually did for the Canon of Scripture," p. 158. Their own action and the attitude and action of the people, as described by them, prove that whatever else Ezra and Nehemiah did for Israel, they did not compose or compile for them a new Torah, unknown to them or their fathers.

The Ezekielian Hypothesis of the Origin of the Levitical Torah.

But here we are brought face to face with the hypothesis that "a written priestly Torah" originated with Ezekiel. Our author finds no difficulty, such as other writers have found, in dealing with the marvellous imagery of this most figurative of all the prophets. To him the last nine chapters, taken literally, exhibit, at least in germ and principle, the essence and outline of the Levitical legislation. "Its distinctive features," we are told, "are all found in Ezekiel's Torah," p. 382. The proof of this assertion is to be found in "the care with which the Temple and its vicinity are preserved from the approach of unclean things and persons, the corresponding institution of a class of holy ministers in the person of the Levites, the greater distance thus interposed between the people and the altar, the concentration of sacrifice in the two forms of stated representative offerings (the tamîd) and atoning sacrifices." "In all these points," it is alleged, "the usage of the law is in distinct contrast to that of the first Temple, where the temple plateau was polluted by the royal sepulchres, where the servants of the sanctuary were uncircumcised foreigners, the stated service the affair of the king, regulated at will by him (2 Kings xvi.), and the atoning offerings essentially fines paid to the priests of the sanctuary (2 Kings xii. 16). That Ezekiel in these matters speaks not merely as a priest recording old usage, but as a prophet ordaining new Torah with divine authority," the author affirms, "is his own express claim, and appears in the clearest way in the degradation of the non-Zadokite priests, which is actually carried out in the Levitical legislation, with the natural consequence that, on the return from the captivity, very few Levites in comparison with the full priests cared to attach themselves to the Temple" (Neh. vii. 39 seq.), pp. 382, 383.

It would be difficult to crowd into the same space a larger number of historical inaccuracies, reckless conjectures, and doctrinal errors than have been put on record in these few sentences. The principle underlying the author's argument is, that the religious practice of a people is always in harmony with their doctrinal system as exhibited in their sacred books. As he does not find the religious practice under the first Temple conformable to the Levitical system sketched in the prophecies of Ezekiel, he concludes that the Torah of Ezekiel " was in distinct contrast to that of the first Temple." To such fallacious reasoning it would be sufficient to reply, that his premises simply warrant the conclusion that the Torah of Ezekiel was in distinct contrast, not to the Torah, but to the practice under the first Temple. This is the only conclusion warranted by the author's premises, and it is difficult to see how it helps his argument. His object is to prove that the distinctions above specified were not recognised (or recognised with such care) in the Torah of the first Temple as the Torah of Ezekiel demands; and his proof is, that there is not so much care displayed in the religious practice of that period! In a word, the fundamental canon of the author and the school he represents, the canon of criticism whereby they would disprove the existence of the Levitical system, as a perfected scheme, prior to the days of the exile, when its leading principles were sketched by Ezekiel, and wrought out by Ezra or somebody else, is the palpably false principle, that men do not "resist the truth in unrighteousness," but, despite the testimony of all history, sacred or profane, live up to the full measure of the light they possess! It is sometimes said that a man is better than his creed, but history proves that men are oftener worse than their creeds; and this is specially true of Israel. It was certainly Christ's view of the Jewish practice in His time. "Did not Moses give you the law, and yet none of you doeth the law?" John vii. 19. On this principle of "the newer criticism," there was no ground for such rebuke.

But the unfairness of our author's line of argumentation, and of the critical principles and methods he represents, is still further manifest from the section of Israel's history to which he appeals as an index to the character of the pre-exilic Torah. His appeal is to the history of the first Temple as given in the Books of the Kings, and indeed, practically, as given in

2 Kings, chapters xii. and xvi. Is this fair? Is it scientific criticism? It is surely neither fair nor scientific to adduce, as evidence of the laws of Jehovah made known to Israel, the conduct of Israel and Israel's kings at any period of Israel's history; but it confounds all reason, and sets all criticism at defiance, to select for this purpose, those sections of Israel's history in which the laws of Jehovah were set at naught, His sanctuary profaned, and idolatry made an institution of state. This, however, is what our author, in the name of criticism, has done. A reference to the principal passage cited, will show that this is no misrepresentation of his critical method. His proof that the stated service of the sanctuary "was the affair of the king, regulated at will by him," is taken from the 16th chapter of 2 Kings, which gives an account, not of the Torah of the time, but of the violation of the Torah by Ahaz, who, enamoured by a Damascene altar, had one made " according to all the workmanship thereof," which he set up in the forefront of the house of the Lord, displacing the great brazen altar of Solomon. There is no doubt that the service of the house, as thus arranged, was " the affair of the king." He commanded Urijah the priest to build the altar, to transfer the brazen altar from between the new altar and the house to the north side of the new altar, and to substitute this new altar for the altar of Jehovah in all the stated services of the house of the Lord for the king and all the people. So did the king command, and so did the pliant Urijah,

who, however faithful to record a transaction for Isaiah, was recreant to the trust reposed in him as the high priest of Jehovah. And this is one of the proofs that the Torah of Ezekiel is in distinct contrast to that of the first Temple! This is simply saying, that the idolatrous innovations of Ahaz, copied after the heathen rites of Damascus, are the standard whereby we are to judge the Torah by which the service of the first Temple, from Solomon to Ahaz, was regulated; and that the sinful compliance of Urijah with the king's command, is proof, not of Urijah's sin, but of the rights of the king under the pre-exilic Torah! This may be the science of "the newer criticism," but it were an abuse of language to call it scientific criticism.

Turning to the other passage submitted in proof of the contrast between the Torah of Ezekiel and the Torah of the first Temple, 2 Kings xii. 16 (Heb. 17), we find another illustration of the scientific methods of this critical school. Our author alleges that "the atoning offerings were essentially fines paid to the priests of the sanctuary," and the proof given is, that "the trespass money and sin money was not brought into the house of the LORD: it was the priests'." Here is certainly a sweeping generalization from very slender premises. Indeed, it is not saying all to speak of the premises as slender; the fact is, they are, to say the least, exceedingly questionable. The Hebrew warrants the following rendering: "The money of the trespass-offering (*asham*), and the money of the sin-offerings (*chataoth*), was not brought into the house of the Lord; they were the priests'." Such a translation is perfectly grammatical, and, so far as the principal terms are concerned, is confirmed by the Septuagint. That version substitutes for the phrase *keseph asham*, money of the sin-offering, and for the phrase *keseph chataoth*, money of the trespass-offering, differing from the translation here given in the order of these expressions. Although the order is changed, the version gives the correct idea of the object aimed at in giving the money to the priest. This is manifest from the law of the trespass-offering, as given Lev. v. 15, 16: "If a soul commit a trespass, and sin through ignorance, in the holy things of the LORD; then he shall bring for his trespass unto the LORD a ram without blemish out of the flocks, with thy estimation by shekels of silver, after the shekel of the sanctuary, for a trespass-offering (*asham*): and he shall make amends for the harm that he hath done in the holy thing, and shall add the fifth part thereto, and give it unto the priest: and the priest shall make atonement for him" (not with the money, but) "with the ram of the trespass-offering (*asham*), and it shall be forgiven him." The money, therefore, was not given as the sole atonement. It was one of the conditions of reconciliation, that restitution, or, as the Hebrew has it, *recompense* for the wrong done in the case, should be made; but there was needed, besides, a veritable atoning sacrifice.

In Num. v. 8 we have a similar instance of money

paid to the priest, in addition to the ram of atonement: "But if the man have no kinsman to recompense the trespass unto, let the trespass be recompensed unto the Lord, even to the priest, besides the ram of the atonement whereby the atonement shall be made for him." This is the law of the *asham*, the trespass-offering, as is shown both by the Hebrew text and the Septuagint version, and its provisions are obviously implied in the very passage (2 Kings xii. 16) relied on by our author to prove that, under the first Temple, "the atoning offerings were essentially fines paid to the priests!" The money paid to the priest was regarded as a recompense for the harm done, and the ram was offered as the atonement for the trespass. In passing, it may not be out of place to note the singular fact, that a critic who would have us correct the Hebrew text by the Septuagint, and who is so ready to quote its arrangement, or its renderings, wherever it seems to aid him in his strictures on the sacred text, did not think of looking into its rendering of this 16th verse before making it the basis of so comprehensive a generalization.

But while this passage, fairly rendered and interpreted, does not serve the cause in whose interests it has been appealed to, it renders eminent service to the other side. It proves that the law of the trespass-offering, one of the characteristic laws of the Levitical system (Lev. v. 15, 16), was known as an old law in the days of Jehoash the king, and Jehoiada the priest, at least 280 years before the prophecy of

Ezekiel, in which, if we are to credit "the newer criticism," the principles of the Levitical system were first made known to Israel.

Acting, then, on our author's recommendation to open our eyes and ascertain from Ezra and Nehemiah themselves, and not from any outside source, such as tradition, whether ecclesiastical or rationalistic, what they have done for the Canon of Scripture, and accepting the proof texts he has brought forward in support of the exilic or post-exilic origin of the Levitical Torah, we are compelled to reject his conclusion, and must hold that the priestly Torah was known, and departures from its enactments treated as sins, under the first Temple.

Arguments from the History of the First Temple.

This conclusion is confirmed by the entire history of the Temple from its erection by Solomon. The fact is, it were just as reasonable to challenge the existence of the Temple itself, as to challenge the existence of a law for the regulation of its service, to all intents and purposes the same as the Levitical Torah. The dedication service implies a very minute Levitical Torah. The month chosen, the seventh month, was the chief month in the priestly Torah. It is the priests who bring up the ark from the city of David. "They brought up the ark of the Lord, and the tabernacle of the congregation, and all the holy vessels that were in the tabernacle, even those did the priests and the Levites bring up. And King Solomon, and all the congregation of Israel that were assembled unto him, were with him before the ark, sacrificing sheep and oxen, that could not be told nor numbered for multitude. And the priests brought in the ark of the covenant of the LORD unto his place, into the oracle of the house, to the most holy place, even under the wings of the cherubims. . . . There was nothing in the ark save the two tables of stone, which Moses put there at Horeb, when the LORD made a covenant with the children of Israel, when they came out of the land of Egypt. And it came to pass, when the priests were come out of the holy place, that the cloud filled the house of the LORD, so that the priests could not stand to minister because of the cloud: for the glory of the LORD had filled the house of the LORD. . . . And the king, and all Israel with him, offered sacrifice before the LORD. And Solomon offered a sacrifice of peace-offerings, which he offered unto the LORD, two and twenty thousand oxen, and an hundred and twenty thousand sheep. So the king and all the children of Israel dedicated the house of the LORD. The same day did the king hallow the middle of the court that was before the house of the LORD: for there he offered burnt-offerings, and meat-offerings, and the fat of the peace-offerings, because the brazen altar that was before the LORD was too little to receive the burnt-offerings, and meat-offerings, and the fat of the peace-offerings," 1 Kings viii.

Here, then, at the very outset, we have a service in which the priests are distinguished not only from their brethren of the children of Israel, but also, ver. 4, from their kinsmen of the tribe of Levi. "The newer criticism," it is true, is puzzled to find this alleged post-exilic distinction occurring more than 430 years before the vision of the house vouchsafed to Ezekiel, and resorts even to the Chronicles for a correction. It is, however, difficult to see how the phrase: "priests and Levites," of 1 Kings viii. 4, is in conflict with the phrase: "the priests, the Levites," of 2 Chron. v. 5. If the chronicler, whose credibility is impugned by Graf, and Kuenen, and Colenso, etc., for making the distinction between priests and Levites, can use this phrase, surely it cannot be argued that the use of it is inconsistent with the distinction. It is remarkable that whilst the Septuagint, on which the lecturer places such reliance, omits all reference to the Levites in the passage in Kings, it not only mentions them in Chronicles, but distinguishes them from the priests, as the Hebrew does in 1 Kings viii. 4.

But in addition to its recognition of the distinction between the priests and other Levites, this passage proves the existence of an extensive Torah, embracing all the essential features of the Levitical system. The things done were very numerous. They embraced the transfer of the ark and the sacred vessels from the Tabernacle which David had pitched for it in Zion, to the new edifice erected for it by Solomon; the setting of the ark in the prescribed place, and after the manner described, which was manifestly a matter of divine appointment;

the offering of burnt-offerings, and meat-offerings, and the fat of the peace-offerings; and the hallowing of the middle of the court that was before the Lord. These are the great outstanding features of that great dedication service, and any one who will carefully weigh the facts as given in this graphic sketch, will wonder how any one who regards it as veritable history can accept the theory of "the newer criticism," which denies that the Levitical system was known or sanctioned before the days of Ezekiel or Ezra, and teaches that "the usage of the law was in distinct contrast to that of the second Temple." Almost every point of the alleged contrast specified as known to the Torah of Ezekiel, and unknown under the first Temple, comes out in this dedication service. 1. "The care with which the Temple and its vicinity are preserved from the approach of unclean things and persons," is manifest in the hallowing of the middle court, a ceremonial action by which it was rendered as sacred as the brazen altar itself, which none but the priests dare approach. 2. We have "the corresponding institution" (not then made, but actually existing) "of a class of holy ministers," who approach unto, and take charge of the holy things which others might not touch. 3. We find also the chief "forms of stated representative offerings and atoning sacrifices" in the *'olah*, or burnt-offering; the *minchah*, or meat-offering; and the *shelamim*, or peace-offerings. The Torah of these offerings is given, Lev. i.–iii., and, whatever exception may be taken to the *minchah*, there can be no doubt regarding the atoning character of the ʻolah and the *shelamim*. All the elements which enter into and characterize a ritual of atonement are found connected with the latter. 1. There is the laying on of hands, by which the sins of the offerer are imputed to the victim, and the victim constituted his substitute. 2. There are the expiatory actions of blood-shedding, and of blood-sprinkling upon the altar round about. 3. There is the burning of the victim upon the altar. These actions are common to both the ʻolah and the *shelamim*, and where these are, there is atonement. Indeed, it is because of its atoning character that the ʻolah is chosen as the designation for the morning and evening sacrifice, which was certainly both a stated representative offering, representing all Israel, and a perpetual atonement for their sins—an ʻolah *tamîd*—ever burning on the altar before the Lord. However these offerings may have differed in other respects, they agreed in all that is essential to the idea of mediatorial expiation.

Now that which in this narrative is fatal to the theory that the Levitical Torah was unknown under the first Temple, is the manifest fact, that priestly functions are executed in connection with a round of sacrificial and other acts of a most extensive range, without the slightest hint of the existence of a sacrificial or other Torah. It is this absence of all reference to rule or ritual that bespeaks the knowledge of their work as possessed by the priests and Levites of the day. They set to their sacred work as men who are accustomed to it. They know that it is they alone who may take charge of the Tabernacle or its furniture, or transfer the ark and the holy vessels to their place in the newly-erected house of the LORD. They know that if the middle of the court is to be used for sacrifice, it must be hallowed, as by implication the brazen altar was—a hallowing which afterwards precluded the approach of any one save the priests, and their assistants the Levites. They know how to prepare and offer the ʻolah, and the *shelamim*, and the *minchah*. None of these offerings, each of which, we know, had and must have had its own distinctive ritual, both of preparation and presentation, appears the least strange to Solomon, or the priests, or the Levites, or the people. It is sciolists, and not the masters of an art, who are wont to be ever referring to its rules.

Argument from the Sin of Jeroboam.

But while there is no account of a full ritualistic programme given under the first Temple, there are incidental references which prove that the Levitical system was not unknown. We find among the other sins which are laid to the account of Jeroboam, that he " ordained a feast on the eighth month, on the fifteenth day of the month, like unto the feast that is in Judah; and he offered upon the altar . . . on the fifteenth day of the *eighth* month, *even in the month which he had devised of his own heart*" (1 Kings xii. 32, 33). Here there is manifestly allusion to Jeroboam's departure from the Levitical calendar, Lev. xxiii., in which the fifteenth day of the *seventh* month (not the *eighth* month) was appointed by divine authority as a day of holy convocation, ushering in the seven days of the Feast of Tabernacles. He is also charged with a breach of the law of the priesthood, in making priests of the lowest of the people which were not of the sons of Levi.

Argument from Elijah's Sacrifice on Carmel.

In like manner there is revealed, even in the brief account of Elijah's sacrifice on Carmel (1 Kings xviii.), a knowledge of the Levitical ritual; for there are two references in it to the Levitical institute (Ex. xxix.) of " the evening sacrifice." The priests of Baal cried and prophesied from *morning* till noon, and from noon till " *the time of the offering of the evening sacrifice* " (vv. 26-29). "And it came to pass, *at the time of the offering of the evening sacrifice,* that Elijah the prophet came near," etc., ver. 36. Notwithstanding the brevity of this wondrously graphic narrative, it shows plainly that Elijah at least, and the narrator as well, were acquainted with one of the chief of the institutions of the Levitical Torah—the evening sacrifice. Without delaying to enter upon the details of the evidence, suffice it to say, what a candid examination of the facts will confirm, that the history given in the two books of the Kings implies the existence of a Torah which must have contained all the characteristic provisions and ordinances of the priestly Torah. The sins of the two kingdoms of Israel and Judah, for which they are rebuked by prophets and chastised by God, and the temporary and the partial reformations wrought by good kings, alike imply the existence of a central sanctuary and a divinely ordained priesthood, with an authoritative ritual and calendar, from whose instructions neither kings nor priests might deviate without incurring the displeasure of Jehovah.

CHAPTER II.

THE NEWER CRITICISM AND THE HISTORY—*continued.*

A REFORMATION in its very conception implies a Torah whose commandments have been violated. If a reforming king took away the high places, and was approved of God for doing so; or if he carried on his reformation but in part, as Jehoash did (2 Kings xii.), or as Amaziah did (2 Kings xiv.), or as Azariah (2 Kings xv.), stopping short of their abolition, and was condemned for doing so, there must have been an existing law against such local sanctuaries. To this latter class of reformations there is always a *"but"* appended,—" but the high places were not taken away," manifestly implying that they were allowed to remain, contrary to the divine law. The history of the last-named king, who was smitten with leprosy (2 Kings xv. 5; 2 Chron. xxvi. 19) for invading the office of the priesthood, and attempting to burn incense upon the altar of incense in the Temple of the LORD, is peculiarly instructive, proving, as it does, the existence of a Levitical Torah, recognised and enforced by God Himself, according to which none save the priests, "the sons of Aaron, who were consecrated to burn incense," might arrogate to themselves the right to execute that sacred function. Azariah, doubtless, had views of the king's relations to the Temple very much akin to those held by our author, and very likely regarded the house as his own private chapel, and its "stated service as his own affair;" but the leprosy wherewith Jehovah rebuked his arrogance proclaims the folly and the profanity of those whose critical principles would justify his irreverent usurpation of the priestly office. It is because the Chronicles abound in testimonies of this kind to the existence of the priestly Torah, that these books are placed under ban by "the newer criticism."

Argument from the Reformation of Josiah.

The principle that a reformation implies an existing Torah, is very clearly brought out in the reformation effected by Josiah (2 Kings xxii., xxiii.). Josiah's reformation owes its inauguration to the discovery of the book of the law by Hilkiah the priest. It is when the king hears "the words of the book of the law" [rendered "law-book" most unwarrantably in the article "Bible"] that he rends his clothes, sends to consult the prophetess Huldah, and enters upon the work of reforming abuses. That book was called "the book of the covenant" (2 Kings xxiii. 2), and contained an account of the original covenanting of Israel under Moses (Ex. xxiv.); and in conformity with that ancient august transaction at the foot of Sinai, the king, and the priests, and the prophets, and all the people, renewed the covenant before the Lord. In pursuance of this covenant engagement, the work of reformation is entered upon and carried forward. "The king commanded Hilkiah the high priest, *and the priests of the second order*, and *the keepers of the door* (undoubtedly the Levites), to bring forth out of the temple of the Lord all the vessels that were made for Baal, and for the grove, and for all the host of heaven: and he burned them without Jerusalem. . . . And he put down the idolatrous priests whom the kings of Judah had ordained to burn incense in the high places in the cities of Judah, and in the places round about Jerusalem. . . . Moreover, the altar that was at Bethel, and the high place which Jeroboam the son of Nebat, who made Israel to sin, had made, both that altar and the high place he brake down, and burned the high place, and stamped it small to powder, and burned the grove. . . . And all the houses also of the high places that were in the cities of Samaria, which the kings of Israel had made to provoke the LORD to anger, Josiah took away, and did to them according to all the acts that he had done in Bethel. And he slew all the priests of the high places that were there upon the altars, and burned men's bones upon them, and returned to Jerusalem."

The Bearing of these Facts on the Author's Theory.

This reformation is itself a sufficient reply to all that part of this singular book in which the author endeavours to prove that it was not on the basis of the Pentateuchal theory of worship that God's grace ruled in the kingdoms of Israel and Judah, and that it was not on that basis the prophets taught prior to the exile. The portion of his book formally occupied with this endeavour extends over a large number of pages; but the fact is, his mind is so set upon the establishment of this most erroneous and unhistorical theory of the pre-exilic administration of the covenant of grace, that he is ever referring to it, and shaping his treatment of the sacred record so as to give to it countenance and support. It rules his conception of the history of Israel under judges, kings, and prophets, and all that is adverse to this theory is to be regarded as the work of some blundering editor, or of a self-interested priestly guild.

Now all these speculations of "the newer criticism" are proved utterly baseless by this reformation of King Josiah. It extends over the whole area covered by the kingdoms of Israel and Judah, and deals with and abolishes all the forms of worship practised in both which were inconsistent with the book of the law, overthrowing, and that on "the basis of the Pentateuchal theory of worship," those very institutions which our author has adduced as evidence that the Levitical Torah was not in existence, or its observances obligatory, during the pre-exilic period of the history of Israel and Judah. It assumes that the covenant read out of that book of the covenant, then renewed by the reforming king, and priests, and prophets, and people, was a covenant whose laws not only they but their fathers had violated, and for the violation of which the great wrath of Jehovah was kindled against them. It assumes, therefore, that the laws of that book of the covenant had been in existence in the days of their fathers, for where there is no law there is no transgression. This rule is especially applicable to *positive* laws which have their reason simply in the divine will, and have not their foundation in the constitution of man. The *moral* law, whose works are written in the hearts of men, is binding upon men who have never read or heard the precepts of the Decalogue as delivered to Israel, and the ground of the obligation is the self-evident, constitutionally revealed character of its moral principles. Very different, however, is it in the case of a *positive* law such as that on which our author chiefly relies— the law of the single central sanctuary. From its very nature, resting, as it does, upon the divine will alone, it can bind none save those to whom it is made known. There could therefore be no wrath of the LORD entertained toward the king, or his people, or their fathers, for the violation of a *positive* law of whose commandments and ordinances the LORD had kept them in ignorance.

This reformation did not abolish the distinction between the high priest and "the priests of the second order," or the distinction between these latter and "the keepers of the door." These distinctions are recognised as of divine appointment, and are not looked upon as among the causes which have kindled the wrath of the LORD against Judah. Whatever else might be wrong in connection with the arrangements and services of the first Temple, the distinction in question was not regarded as among the procuring causes of the divine displeasure, and must have been regarded by the king as a distinction authorized by the very book which had so moved him by the revelation it made of Israel's sins.

There is manifest recognition of the law of the central sanctuary in the destruction of the high places throughout the bounds of the entire kingdom, while the Temple at Jerusalem is spared. These places were not abolished, as "the newer criticism" alleges, simply because "they were a constant temptation to practical heathenism," p. 265, or simply because "the worship there was in later times of a heathenish character," p. 267. This had been a reason for abolishing not only the worship of the high places, but the worship of the Temple as well, for the state of the Temple worship in this respect was as bad as anything known in the high places. The worship of Baal, and of Ashtaroth, and of all the host of heaven, was practised in the sanctuary itself, as well as in the high places; and if Josiah had proceeded in his reformation-work on the principle suggested in this book, he should certainly have begun with the Temple and its idolatrous environments, and have done with the central seat of the abounding corruption, "according to all the acts that he had done at Bethel." The fact that he did not abolish the Temple as a seat of divine worship, while he abolished other seats of worship which were no worse than it was, proves that his action must have been regulated by other considerations besides the heathenish character of the worship practised in those local centres. As the alleged ground of their destruction was common to both them and the Temple, there must have been a special reason for their destruction while the Temple was spared. The simple and all-sufficient reason for the discrimination in their doom was the law of the central sanctuary, which, from the time of its dedication, rendered all other seats of worship illegal save those places which God had sanctioned by His manifested presence, or by the mouth of His prophets.

Author's Method of meeting the Argument from Josiah's Reformation Unhistorical.

All that "the newer criticism" has to say in reply to this argument from Josiah's reformation is, that the law by which it was regulated is found in Deuteronomy. "In truth," it is alleged, "when we compare the reformation of Josiah, as set forth in 2 Kings, with what is written in the Pentateuch, we observe that everything that Josiah acted upon is found written in one or other part of Deuteronomy" (p. 246). In confirmation of this statement our author gives a list of references to 2 Kings xxiii., specifying some of Josiah's acts, with parallel references to Deuteronomy, in which *alone*, we are to understand, the law authorizing such acts is to be found. The chief acts mentioned in 2 Kings xxiii. are the overthrow of the worship of Baal, and of the sun and moon and planets, and all the host of heaven; the destruction of the grove that was in the house of the Lord; the breaking down of the high places; the defiling of Tophet, and the abolition of the worship of Molech; the restoration of the feast of the Passover; and the putting away of the Sodomites, and of the workers with familiar spirits, and the wizards. Because there is a Torah against all these abominations "found in one or other part of Deuteronomy," and because Josiah acted in accordance with it, we are asked to believe that no such Torah was previously known, or obligatory upon Israel! Now, even though there were not a syllable of a Torah in existence, as a thing of record, is it possible to believe that the idolatrous practices, barbarous rites, divinations, orgies, and abominable pollutions enumerated above, were not violations of the law of God, and breaches of His covenant with Israel? Are we to give heed to a system of criticism which requires for its support the assumption, that up to the time of Josiah there was no Torah of God or man against these abominations? How can such a system adjust itself to the teaching of the Apostle Paul (Rom. i. 23–32), in which he speaks of the chief sins here enumerated as dealt with by Josiah, as sins against the light of nature? Is it within the possibilities even of the unscientific imagination of this critical school, to conceive of the God of Israel giving no Torah against such sins until the days of Josiah, and that even then He sent His Torah to His people by methods which the subtlest casuistry cannot defend? That such reticence on the part of Israel's God regarding such sins is not possible, all men having right conceptions of His holiness and truth will agree; and that it was not actual, is proved by this same book of Kings. A reference to chapter seventeenth will satisfy any candid mind that the sins for which God banished the kingdom of the ten tribes from their land for ever, were the very same sins for which He was about to visit Judah, and for which He would have also carried her into captivity, had it not been for the reformation effected by King Josiah, which for a time stayed execution of sentence. It is charged against the kingdom of Israel as the reason of their banishment, "that the children of Israel did secretly those things that were not right against the LORD their God, and they built them high places in all their cities, from the tower of the watchmen to the fenced city. And they set them up images and groves in every high hill, and under every green tree. And there they burnt incense in all the high places, as did the heathen whom the Lord carried away before them; and wrought wicked things to provoke the Lord to anger;" that "they went after the heathen that were round about them, concerning whom the LORD had charged them, that they should not do like them." (Was not this very comprehensive charge a Torah?) "And they left all the commandments of the LORD their God, and made them molten images, even two calves, and made a grove, and worshipped all the host of heaven, and served Baal. And they caused their sons and their daughters to pass through the fire, and used divination and enchantments, and sold themselves to do evil in the sight of the Lord, to provoke Him to anger. Therefore the Lord was very angry with Israel" (although, according to "the newer criticism," He had given them no Torah condemnatory of these sins, as He had not as yet given the Book of Deuteronomy either to Israel or Judah!), "and removed them out of His sight: there was none left but the tribe of Judah."

The reader is requested to compare these two chapters of 2 Kings (xvii. and xxiii.) for himself, and then judge of the science of the criticism which concludes from the latter that the sins there enumerated prove that the Torah condemning them had just then come into existence, or was just then published, while it declines to draw a similar inference from the fact that the same sins are enumerated in the former chapter, or to conclude from the identity of the transgressions that Deuteronomy must have been known to the kingdom of the ten tribes almost one hundred years before the reformation of Josiah. If the sins of Judah dealt with by Josiah find their condemning Torah in Deuteronomy, surely the same sins charged against Israel and dealt with by Jehovah Himself, must also find their condemnation written in the same book. In a word, if the Torah whereby Josiah wrought reformation in Judah was the Book of Deuteronomy, the Torah whereby Jehovah condemned Israel, and for the violation of whose laws He carried her into captivity, must have been this same Deuteronomic code. Where there is no law there is no transgression; and identity of sin proves identity of Torah.

And at a still earlier date, even in the days of the Judges, we find evidence of the existence of the leading points of this reformatory Deuteronomic Torah. As soon as Joshua and the elders who overlived him passed away, the children of Israel forsook the LORD God of their fathers, and served Baalim, provoking the LORD to anger by worshipping Baal and Ashtaroth. An attentive reader will find, on a comparison of Judges ii., iii., vi., x., with the chapters of 2 Kings already cited, that while there is more minuteness of detail in the latter than in the former, the sins enumerated, for which Jehovah was ever delivering Israel into the hands of their enemies round about, were substantially the same sins as those taken cognizance of in the days of Hoshea, king of Israel, and in the days of Josiah, king of Judah. The parallel is sufficiently close to justify the conclusion that the Torah of the Judges must have contained the essential elements of the Torah carried into execution against the kingdom of the ten tribes, and applied by Josiah in the reformation of Judah.

Our author, therefore, cannot assign as a reason for

the sparing of the Temple, while the local centres of worship and the high places were abolished, that the Deuteronomic law respecting the single central sanctuary had just then been published. He has enumerated too many points of relation between the reformation and the Deuteronomic Torah to have recourse to this argument. He has made the identification of the law regulating the reform effected by Josiah with the Deuteronomic Torah to depend upon a long catalogue of sins which, by reference [see author's list of passages, p. 425], he has specified, and therefore cannot now argue as if he had based the whole issue upon this one point regarding the central sanctuary,— a point, by the way, which is not one whit more prominently presented in the reformation services of Josiah than it is in the dedication services of Solomon, as may be seen on a comparison of 1 Kings viii. 16, 29, ix. 3 (and, indeed, the whole dedication prayer offered by Solomon), with 2 Kings xxiii. 27. The fact is, that this point is much more prominent in Solomon's prayer than it is in Josiah's reformation. The law of the one single central sanctuary underlies every utterance of it from beginning to end; and the reader is requested to ask himself the question, as he reads that greatest of all Old Testament prayers, whether the royal suppliant could have been ignorant of the existence of the Deuteronomic Torah of the single central sanctuary.

To conclude then, if the Torah of Josiah's book embraced the sins specified by our author, it must have been in existence before the captivity of the ten tribes; and if its characteristic was the law of the single central sanctuary, it must have been known to Solomon when he dedicated the Temple.

Such, then, is the conclusion to which we are conducted by the history of the first Temple from its inauguration to its close. That history assumes the existence of a Torah which, in all its essential elements and features, coincides with the Pentateuchal system. That such a coincidence does exist, our author is constrained partially to confess. "Although many individual points of ritual resembled the ordinances of the law," he says, "the Levitical tradition as a whole had as little force in the central sanctuary as with the mass of the people," p. 266. To this it is very easy to reply, that it is just as true of *positive* laws as of moral, that the non-observance of them does not prove their non-existence. In Josiah's estimation, the sin of Judah consisted in the non-observance of a law which should have had force in the central sanctuary. In the estimation of "the newer criticism," the fact that it had no force in the central sanctuary proves that no such law was in existence!

The position now established is, *that there is no ground for the allegation that, in its leading features, the Torah of Ezekiel " is in distinct contrast to that of the first Temple."* So far is it from being true that there is such a contrast, the fact is, that in all its essential features the worship as inaugurated by Solomon, and restored in whole or in part by his successors, is in perfect accord with that Torah. Whether the kings and priests are praised or blamed, there is assumed the existence of a Torah which in all its essential elements coincides with the Torah of Ezekiel. This, of course, is simply saying that there is no scriptural warrant for the dogma of "the newer criticism," that "the law in its finished system and fundamental theories was never the rule of Israel's worship, and (that) its observance was never the condition of the experience of Jehovah's grace" (p. 266) prior to the days of Ezekiel or Ezra.

The force of this historical fact will be all the more manifest, when it is considered that the design of the historical books, after the Mosaic legislation, is not to give details of existing Torahs, but to narrate God's dealings with Israel as a people whose chief advantage consisted in their possessing these divine oracles. Assume that Israel possessed the Pentateuchal system, and the history of God's dealings with them, not only under the first Temple, but throughout their residence in Canaan, is explained; assume that they came to the knowledge of that system after the exile, and that history becomes an unsolvable riddle.

Ethical Difficulties in the way of this Deuteronomic Theory.

Nor is the mystery of the divine administration cleared up by the device of an intermediate Torah, discovered in the days of Josiah; for, prior to the alleged discovery, its leading enactments (as, for example, the law of the central sanctuary, Deut. xii. 10) are the rule according to which the kings, and priests, and people are judged, while some of its special ordinances are meaningless after the inauguration of the kingdom in the days of Saul or David. Why blame kings prior to the days of Josiah for not taking away the high places, when the law of the central sanctuary, rendering them illegal, was not, according to "the newer criticism," made known before the eighteenth year of that good king's reign? And how reconcile with the wisdom of the divine Lawgiver the law of Deut. xvii. respecting the appointment of a king—the first Israelitish king— 470 years after the king had been chosen and crowned, and 100 years after the kingdom of the ten tribes had been carried into captivity? The difficulties which this device has been devised to obviate are as mole-hills before this impassable mountain of "the newer criticism." If the Lawgiver of Israel be, as our author admits, "all-wise," p. 39, He can no more issue laws for the guidance of men hundreds of years after the men for whose guidance they were written are dead, than He can "contradict Himself." Folly is just as impossible to an all-wise Being as contradiction is; and it is just as irreverent to impute to the omniscient Jehovah the former, as it is to impute the latter. This "the newer criticism" does by its intermediate Deuteronomic Code, and in doing so writes its own condemnation. The *ex post facto* legislation it assumes, in the case of Deuteronomy, is impossible in a divine legislator, and, consistently, its rationalistic authors and advocates openly and avowedly pronounce it a premeditated fraud. "The newer criticism" in Scotland is on the search for an ethical principle which will enable them to hold the rationalistic theory regarding this literary imposture, and the author of the article "Bible" in the *Encyclopædia Britannica* thinks he has found it in the peculiar notions which prevailed among ancient writers regarding copyright—a solution repeated in these lectures, pp. 106, 107. But Kuenen has anticipated him in this, for, by way of apology for the manifest fraud which the author of Deuteronomy must, on his theory, have perpetrated, he says: "At a time when notions about literary property were yet in their infancy, an action of this kind was not regarded as unlawful. Men used to perpetrate such fictions as these without any qualms of conscience" (*Religion of Israel*, vol. ii. pp. 18, 19). It does not occasion surprise that a German rationalist could frame such an apology, but it certainly does seem strange that there should be found in the bosom of the Free Church of Scotland, a professor or a minister who could "without any qualms of conscience" accept it, and, notwithstanding the acceptance of it, still profess to regard the book in which the alleged fiction was perpetrated as part and parcel of the word of God, thus making God Himself a *particeps criminis* in the perpetration.

Our author's argument, then, against the existence

of the Pentateuchal Torah before the days of Ezekiel, drawn from the history of the first Temple, proves to be a failure. He has adduced nothing from that history save transactions condemned by the Pentateuch, this very condemnation itself proceeding upon the assumption of the existence of the law whose non-existence it is adduced to prove. The principle underlying this argument is the palpably false one, that the non-observance of a law implies its non-existence,—a principle which may hold good among the unfallen angels or the spirits of the just made perfect, but which, among the fallen sons of men, and especially among a race who could be fairly charged with always resisting the Holy Ghost, cannot be recognised.

Argument from Ezekiel against a Pre-exilic Priestly Torah.

But apart from the history of the first Temple, our author thinks he can find in the Book of Ezekiel evidence of the non-existence of the Levitical law prior to his day. His first proof is, that Ezekiel places his new ordinances in contrast with the actual corrupt usage of the first Temple. One of the passages adduced in illustration of this contrast is as follows: "Thou shalt say to the rebellious house of Israel, Thus saith the Lord GOD; O ye house of Israel, let it suffice you of all your abominations, in that ye have brought into my sanctuary strangers, uncircumcised in heart, and uncircumcised in flesh, to be in my sanctuary, to pollute it, even my house, when ye offer my bread, the fat and the blood, and they have broken my covenant because of all your abominations. And ye have not kept the charge of my holy things: but ye have set keepers of my charge in my sanctuary for yourselves" (chap. xliv. 6–8). Such was their conduct in the past for which they are rebuked: now let us hear Ezekiel's "new ordinances," which he "places in contrast with this corrupt usage of the first Temple." "Thus saith the Lord God; No stranger, uncircumcised in heart, nor uncircumcised in flesh, shall enter into my sanctuary, of any stranger that is among the children of Israel. And the Levites that are gone away far from me, when Israel went astray, which went astray away from me after their idols; they shall even bear their iniquity. Yet they shall be ministers in my sanctuary, having charge at the gates of the house, and ministering to the house: they shall slay the burnt-offering and the sacrifice for the people, and they shall stand before them to minister unto them. Because they ministered unto them before their idols, and caused the house of Israel to fall into iniquity; therefore have I lifted up my hand against them, saith the Lord God, and they shall bear their iniquity. . . . But the priests the Levites, the sons of Zadok, that kept the charge of my sanctuary when the children of Israel went astray from me, they shall come near to me to minister unto me, and they shall stand before me to offer unto me the fat and the blood, saith the Lord God" (vv. 9–15). The passage is given with sufficient fulness to enable the reader, without the trouble of reference, and at a glance, to judge of the alleged contrast between the *usage* of the first Temple (as our author puts it) and the " new ordinances " of Ezekiel. Ezekiel is instructed to rebuke the house of Israel for what our author styles " the *usage*" of the first Temple ; a usage by which, as we are told in ver. 7, they had broken Jehovah's covenant. Is there any room for a second opinion here, as to whether that usage was in accordance with the ordinances of the first Temple ? Could the house of Israel have been condemned for a usage by which they had broken the Lord's covenant, if there had been no covenant with laws annexed which had been violated by that usage ? No logic, save the logic of " the newer criticism," could infer from a usage rebuked by the Lord's prophet as a violation of the covenant, the non-existence of a Torah condemning such usage.

Ezekiel's New Ordinances.

But let us look at Ezekiel's " new ordinances " " for the period of the restoration," which, we are informed, he so often " places in contrast with the actual corrupt usage of the first Temple." In the first place, the chief of these ordinances are not " new ordinances " at all. They are simply old ordinances of which the condemned usage was a violation, as has been already shown by the fact that, before the prophet proclaims them, Israel is rebuked for the usage they condemn.

A comparison of the seventh verse with the eighth and ninth will put this point out of the pale of dispute. Nor is the ordinance against the "non-Zadokite priests" an exception. It is true their status subsequent to its enactment became different from what it was before, but this proves that they had a status under the first Temple established by a Torah whose laws they had violated. For the sons of Zadok the old Torah remains; for the non-Zadokite priests the new ordinance is simply a penal enactment, which is designed not to abolish, but to fortify the pre-exilic priestly Torah. How any one, with these facts before him, could say, as our author does, p. 374, that Ezekiel "makes no appeal to a previous ritual," or that "the whole scheme of the house is new," is hard to be understood. Surely, if Israel was rebuked by this prophet for allowing "strangers uncircumcised in heart and flesh" to come into the house of the Lord, he must have assumed that there was a "previous law of ritual" forbidding such intrusion; and surely, if the non-Zadokite priests were degraded from the special functions of the priesthood for not keeping the charge of the house, as the sons of Zadok did, and for ministering before idols, there must have been a law requiring them to do the one and to abstain from the other. The first conclusion which the author draws from this degradation of the non-Zadokite priests is, that the ministers of the old temple were uncircumcised foreigners! He alleges that Ezekiel tells us this! Ezekiel, however, tells us no such thing. He tells us that there was such a usage, but he does not tell us that such men were the recognised ministers of the first Temple. They did come into the sanctuary; but in allowing them to come in, and in setting them as keepers of the charge, the house of Israel broke the covenant of the Lord. So far is Ezekiel from representing these uncircumcised strangers as *the* ministers of the sanctuary, that he speaks of their admission to the charge of the house as a violation of the Torah, degrades the non-Zadokite priests for abandoning the charge of the holy things of the house for the shrines of the idols of Israel, and commends and rewards the sons of Zadok for their loyalty to the temple Torah. So far as the status of the non-Zadokite priests is concerned, they were dealt with as their sinning brethren had been in the reformation of Josiah.

Our author sees this, and tries to parry its force, and actually affirms that the treatment of these erring priests, prescribed in the ordinance of Ezekiel, differs from that dealt out to their brethren of Josiah's time. A reference to 2 Kings xxiii. 9 will show that the treatment is precisely similar in the two instances. The penalty inflicted under Josiah was, that "the priests of the high places came not up to the altar of the LORD in Jerusalem, but they did eat of the unleavened bread among their brethren." It is difficult to see how the penalty inflicted under the Torah of Ezekiel differs from this. The priests of the high places are prohibited by his Torah, as well as by the Torah of Josiah, from coming up to the altar of the Lord at Jerusalem, and are permitted simply to be ministers in the house, having charge at the gates of the house, slaying the burnt-offering and the sacrifice for the people, and standing before the people and ministering unto them, but not taking the place of priests before the Lord at His altar. The two reformations agree in the reduction of men who were once priests from the strictly priestly status, the offering of burnt-offerings, etc., at the altar of the Lord, and they agree in making a provision for the support of those who were thus degraded. Ezekiel's sketch tells us what service the degraded priests rendered for their living; while the narrative of Josiah's reformation simply informs us that provision was made for their support, without mentioning what service they rendered in return. How it is that our author, in view of these coincidences of the two reformations, can say that " under Josiah's reformation the Levite priests of the high places received a modified priestly status at Jerusalem," while he affirms that " Ezekiel knows this, but declares that it shall be otherwise in the future, as a punishment for the offence of ministering at the idolatrous altars" (p. 375), is hard to be conceived. There is no ground for the " otherwise " of this statement. Ezekiel's reformation, so far as the degradation and punishment of the idolatrous priests are concerned, is precisely similar to that of Josiah. Our author admits that the prophet knew how Josiah had dealt with the erring priests; and well he may,

EZEKIEL'S NEW ORDINANCES. 51

for he deals with their erring brethren exactly as Josiah did. The only reason for this denial of the coincidence of Josiah's reformation with that of Ezekiel, is that it upsets the theory that Ezekiel's Torah "is in distinct contrast to that of the first Temple."

CHAPTER III.

THE NEWER CRITICISM AND THE INTERPRETATION OF THE PROPHETS.

TO help out the above argument, our author alleges that "Ezekiel only confirms Jeremiah, who knew no divine law of sacrifice under the first Temple," p. 374. This statement is made again and again with all the confidence of an unchallengeable fact (see pp. 117, 263, 288, 297, 304, 311, 370). Thus, on p. 372, it is affirmed that "Jeremiah denies in express terms that a law of sacrifice forms any part of the divine commands to Israel. The priestly and prophetic Torahs are not yet" (in Jeremiah's day) "absorbed into one divine system." Or, to put this latter statement more plainly, God had not yet ceased rebuking Israel for observing the unauthorized Torah of the priests, which, through Jeremiah's contemporary, Ezekiel, he was already sanctioning and absorbing. Jeremiah, in the meantime (p. 307), recognises no "necessity for such a scheme of ritual as Ezekiel maps out!" In fact, "the difference between Jehovah and the gods of the nations is, that He does not require sacrifice, but only to do justly, and love mercy, and walk humbly with God" (p. 298). This difference was, it is true, in process of being bridged over in the land of the captivity, or on a mountain in Israel, through communications made to Ezekiel; but of this change in the methods of God's grace Jeremiah knew nothing. The chief passage cited from Jeremiah in support of this marvellous doctrine of the pre-exilic way of salvation is Jer. vii. 21-23: "Put your burnt-offerings unto your sacrifices, and eat flesh. For I spake not to your fathers, nor commanded them in the day that I brought them out of the land of Egypt, concerning burnt-offerings or sacrifices: but this thing commanded I them, saying, Obey my voice, and I will be your God, and ye shall be my people," etc. One reads such a reference made for such a purpose with feelings of astonishment. Such feelings are not unnatural when the context of this passage is examined, and the institution of the Passover is brought to remembrance. In the context the prophet is commanded to rebuke Judah for their sins, among which there are specified their idolatrous worship and their fatalistic imputation of it to God's foreordination of their sin, in the house of the LORD, which was called by His name, but which had become a den of robbers in their eyes. While their sins are rebuked, the house is recognised as the LORD's house; and this one fact ought to have prevented the citation of the passage in question as a proof that God had not, in Jeremiah's day, or under the first Temple, sanctioned sacrifice. In this divine recognition of the Temple there is implied, beyond all reasonable challenge, the recognition of its historically established contents — the altar of burnt-offerings, and the altar of incense, and the table of shewbread, and the candlestick, and the mercy-seat over the ark of the covenant. What was the Temple, or its predecessor, the Tabernacle, without these? And what were these without the priesthood and their attendants — without the high priest to enter within the vail (which he did even in the days of the Tabernacle, and prior to the Temple, if we are to credit the author of the Epistle to the Hebrews), and without the priests of the second order, and their attendants, the Levites, needed for the heavy task of such a ritual as such a house for the whole nation implies? Take away the furniture of that house, which Jeremiah proclaims to be the house of Jehovah, and the history of the first Temple, including its solemn dedication, becomes a historical puzzle; but he who recognises the furniture of that house and its court, must recognise the entire Levitical system, with its priesthood and its sacrifices.

Consequences of denying a Levitical Torah under the First Temple.

Let us pause here, and consider for a moment what the denial of the divine authentication of the Levitical system under the first Temple carries with it. There can be no doubt that it carries with it, of necessity, the denial of all that we are told, not only of the Tabernacle, which "the newer criticism" regards as a device to give a Mosaic cast to the priestly legislation, but of all we read of the revelation of the plan of the house to David, and of the provision he made for the execution of the work, and of all we find recorded respecting the actual carrying out of the work under Solomon, and the dedication of the house when the cloud of the divine glory filled it, and the Most High God sanctioned by His manifested presence the entire work, and set His seal to the whole ceremonial of burnt-offerings, and meat-offerings, and the fat of the peace-offerings, which were presented before Him, not only on the brazen altar, but also in the middle of the court, hallowed especially for the occasion. He who says that "the theology of the prophets before Ezekiel has no place for the system of priestly sacrifice and ritual," as our author does, p. 288, is pledged to the denial of all this, and much more. He must, in fact, eliminate from his Bible all pre-exilic passages which prescribe or sanction sacrifice as a method of worship or a condition of pardon. His *index expurgatorius* must begin with the protevangelion, Gen. iii. 15, which foreshadows a sacrificial economy of redemption, and delete from the record every sacrificial incident from the offering of Abel to the first post-exilic victim. A theory demanding such a reduction of the extant Old Testament revelation bears its condemnation upon its own forehead.

The Theory in Conflict with the Institution of the Passover.

But the passage cited from Jer. vii. suggests another context, for it speaks of the attitude of God toward burnt-offerings and sacrifices on the day in which He brought Israel out of the land of Egypt, ver. 22. The language taken by itself, as will be seen by referring to this verse, seems to teach that the Lord at least did not command such modes of worship. But it is only by taking the passage by itself, and leaving out of view the institution of the Passover, that such an interpretation can be given to the language of Jeremiah. The paschal lamb was sacrificially slain, and was, 1 Cor. v. 7, a type of Christ as sacrificed for us. As this sacrifice was slain on the very day in which the Lord brought His people out of the land of Egypt, it cannot be true that God was then averse to sacrifice as a mode of worship. He had commanded that paschal service, and fixed its observance with a most minute ritual, the violation of which was to incur death, for that very night on which Israel's bondage in Egypt was to be broken for ever. However the passage in Jeremiah is to be interpreted, it must not be represented as teaching an absolute abnegation of sacrifice on the part of Him who ordained the Passover. The only reasonable view of the passage, when considered in the light of the history of the Exodus and the giving of the Law from Sinai, is, that God, at that stage of Israel's history, had not introduced the Mosaic economy with its elaborate sacrificial system and its tribal priesthood. This is simply stating a historical fact, and the fact stated is a sufficient justification of the language of Jeremiah. It is a historical fact, that for three months after the slaying of the Passover, there is no mention of burnt-offering or sacrifice, but simply a command to obey the voice of the Lord, and to walk in all the ways that He had commanded, Ex. xv. 26 and xix. 5, 6. The reference to this silence about sacrifice by Jeremiah was not intended to teach the Israel of his day that God disapproved of sacrifice, or stood toward it in a negative attitude; but to remind them, by one of the most remarkable incidents in their history, that He attached more importance to obedience than to their round of burnt-offerings and sacrifices, which they were evidently substituting for that obedience without which all sacrifice is vain. Could any argument be of more point or pertinence to such a generation as Jeremiah was addressing, than to refer to the historical fact, that at the time when God was manifesting His favour towards their fathers, by signs and wonders in the land of Egypt and on their march to Sinai, the great theme on which He dwelt was not burnt-offerings or sacrifice, but obedience? Such an explanation is natural and historical, while the inference drawn from the language of Jeremiah by "the newer criticism," is irreconcilable with the divinely-ordained institution of the Passover.

Its Exegesis of Jeremiah places him in Conflict with the Institution of the Passover.

Here, then, is a grave dilemma for "the newer criticism." By citing the testimony of Jeremiah to prove that sacrifice was not sanctioned prior to the restoration from the Babylonish captivity, it brings Jeremiah into conflict with the institution of the Passover, an institution whose historic verity it were nothing short of critical wantonness to challenge. If the observance of an institution by a whole nation throughout its entire history, in commemoration of an event which, from its very nature, must have been attested by all its families at the time of its occurrence, do not place the event beyond the pale of historical doubt, there can be no reliance placed upon any history whether sacred or profane. Assuming, then, that the event commemorated in the Passover occurred, " the newer criticism" has placed itself in this dilemma, that either their interpretation of Jeremiah is erroneous, or Jeremiah's prophecy contradicts the history of the Exodus from Egypt. If the Passover occurred (and it is impossible otherwise to account for the sudden and hasty release of Israel from bondage, or for the commemoration of the event in the mode in which it has ever been observed),—if the Passover occurred, sacrifice was sanctioned and ordained of God, and that, too, with a minute ritual, nearly 900 years before the utterance of Jeremiah in question, and more than 1000 years before the day in which our author alleges

Ezra, in presence of the congregation, established the Pentateuch as the law of Israel. It is true, a dilemma of this kind may not severely tax either the ingenuity or the reverence of "the newer criticism," as one of its favourite methods is to bring the sacred writers into conflict with one another; but those who respect the Scriptures as the word of God will regard all interpretations originating such dilemmas as *ipso facto* condemned, and will have no hesitation in accepting that horn which attributes misinterpretation to the anti-sacrificial critics.

But it is not by denying the historical fact that there was such an institution as the Passover ordained of God for Israel, that "the newer criticism" tries to work its way out of this dilemma. Instead of denying the historical fact, it tries to neutralize it by denying its strictly sacrificial character. The proof that "the paschal victim" was not a sacrifice for sin is, "that it might be chosen indifferently from the flock or the herd, and is presumed to be boiled, not roasted as is the case in all old sacrifices of which the history speaks," p. 371. As to the former point, it is manifestly pointless. The *'olah* of the morning and evening sacrifice was a lamb, and the sin-offering on the great day of atonement was a goat, and Aaron's sin-offering, which was to make an atonement for himself on that day, was a bullock. As to the latter, while it is true that, according to one meaning of the Hebrew word *bashal* in Deut. xvi. 7, "(the paschal victim) might be presumed to be boiled," it is also true that, according to the Hebrew of Ex. xii. 8 and 2 Chron. xxxv. 13, the lamb was roasted with fire, and that it was not to be eaten raw, or sodden at all with water. In view of this apparent contradiction, a friendly critic would seek a solution, rather than fasten on the former passage a meaning which our translators have avoided to prevent the appearance of contradiction. As the Hebrew *bashal* may mean to *cook*, without reference to the mode, it is certainly allowable to regard it as used in Deuteronomy in this general sense, and to regard the other passages, which affirm that the paschal victim was roasted and not boiled, or sodden at all with water, as specifying the mode in which it was cooked. That *bashal* is used in this general sense, the latter passage, 2 Chron. xxxv. 13, puts beyond all doubt: "And they roasted (*yebashshaloo*) the Passover with fire, according to the ordinance: but the other holy offerings sod they (*bishshcloo*) in pots, and in caldrons, and in pans," etc. This passage certainly proves, to say the least, that *bashal* does not necessarily mean to *boil*. The paschal victim was *cooked* with fire, that is, by naked exposure to the flame; the other holy offerings were *cooked* in pots, and caldrons, and pans. There were vessels used in the latter instances, there were none used in the former instance. It is therefore only in the general sense of *cooking* that the term *bashal* can be used to designate the two distinct and diverse processes or modes of preparation.

Boiling not inconsistent with Sacrifice.

Our author, however, gains nothing by his new translation. He has by his rendering, through which he has made Deuteronomy contradict Exodus and Chronicles, rendered a seeming service to "the newer criticism," which delights in arraying Scripture against Scripture; but he has gained nothing that will help his argument against sacrifice by translating *bashal* to *boil*. Even though the paschal victim were boiled and not roasted (or cooked) with fire, it would not follow that it was not a veritable sacrificial victim. The character of the victim, as sacrificial or otherwise, does not depend upon such sacrificial accessories as roasting or boiling. The primary, essential, fundamental sacrificial actions were the shedding and sprinkling of the victim's blood. Other important and necessary actions there were, but these proclaimed the transaction sacrificial. Whether the victim were ox, or sheep, or goat, or fowl, its blood was shed and sprinkled, for "without shedding of blood there is no remission." This is the New Testament account of the method of God's grace under the Tabernacle (which certainly antedates the first Temple), whether Jeremiah knew of it or not, or whether "the newer criticism" will allow it or not; and in the Passover these fundamental elements of a sacrifice are found. The blood of the paschal victim was shed, and, when shed, was sprinkled upon the lintel and door-posts of the houses of the Israelites. These actions proclaimed the paschal lamb a sacrifice.

They showed that its blood was shed on behalf of the household, that it was slain as their substitute, and that the design of the shedding and sprinkling was to avert from them the divine wrath, due to them as well as to the Egyptians. Reduce the Passover to the rank of a farewell feast, and what would be the import of that sprinkling? Such reduction is rendered impossible, not only by the use made of the blood, but by the very ordinance by which it was instituted, and by Jehovah's own explanation. It was the Lord's Passover, and it was so called because He "passed over the houses of the children of Israel in Egypt when He smote the Egyptians."

That such was the view of the nature and the category of the "paschal victim" entertained by Josiah, and his princes, and the priests, at the great Passover connected with his reformation, is manifest from the account given of the service, 2 Chron. xxxv., "They killed the Passover, and the priests sprinkled *the blood* from their hands, and the Levites flayed *them*" (ver. 11). If this action of sprinkling the blood by the priests does not bespeak the sacrificial character of the victim, then it is impossible to prove that any truly sacrificial victim was ever slain either under the first Temple or the second. The action implies an expiatory death, the acceptance of that death in the room of the death to which the offerer was justly exposed (as is shown by the sprinkling of the blood upon and before the mercy-seat on the great day of the atonement), and the consequent propitiation of God toward those in whose stead the victim died.

But is the principle assumed by our author in his argument against the sacrificial character of the feast of the Passover one that can be accepted? Is it true, is it a Biblical doctrine of the law of sacrifice, that the flesh of the victim is not, at any stage of the ceremony, to be boiled? The ram of the consecration was sacrificial, and by shedding of its blood atonement was made for Aaron and his sons, and yet the Torah of the consecration embraces seething, and the seething is expressed by this same verb "*bashal*," which our author alleges means to boil: "And thou shalt take the ram of the consecration, and seethe his flesh in the holy place," etc. etc. (Ex. xxix. 31). In Lev. viii. there is a detailed account of the actual execution of this consecration Torah by Moses, and in the 31st verse we read: "And Moses said unto Aaron and to his sons, Boil (*bashshcloo*) the flesh at the door of the tabernacle of the congregation, and there eat it with the bread that is in the basket of consecration," etc. Still more conclusive, if possible, is the Torah of the sin-offering (*chattath*), as given in Lev. vi. This Torah also gives instructions regarding the boiling of the flesh of the sacrifice: "But the earthen vessel wherein it is sodden (*tebŭshshăl*) shall be broken; and if it be sodden (*bŭshshalah*) in a brazen pot, it shall be both scoured and rinsed in water."

It were not much of a compliment to the reader's intelligence, to proceed by formal argument to prove that these Torahs forbid the acceptance of the principle of the author's argument against the sacrificial character of the Passover from the Hebrew term *bashal*, even though it always meant to boil, which we have seen it does not.

No ingenuity, therefore, can deliver "the newer criticism" out of this dilemma. Either Jeremiah's language has been misinterpreted by it, or Jeremiah was ignorant of the original institution of the Passover, of its existence under the first Temple, and of its memorable celebration by the good King Josiah, which had taken place, as his own note of time, chap. i. 2, informs us, in his own day! As this prophet may be presumed to have known something of the history of the Exodus, and something of the history of his own times, it would seem to be safer, as it is certainly more reverent, to conclude that his interpreters have mistaken his meaning, than to charge him with ignorance.

But the erroneousness of such an interpretation of this prophecy is manifest from the language of this same prophet Jeremiah, in chap. xvii. 25, 26, where he predicts the restoration of the regal, and civic, and priestly glory of Jerusalem. After enjoining a strict observance of the Sabbath in all its sanctity, the prophet proceeds: "Then shall there enter into the gates of this city kings and princes sitting upon the throne of David, riding in chariots and on horses, they and their princes, the men of Judah, and the inhabitants of Jerusalem : and this city shall remain for ever. And they shall come from the cities of Judah, and from the places round about Jerusalem, and from the land of Benjamin, and from the plain, and from the mountains, and from the south, bringing burnt-offerings and sacrifices, and meat-offerings, and incense, and bringing sacrifices of praise, unto the house of the Lord."

"The newer criticism" may say of Jeremiah here, as it says of Ezekiel, p. 383, that he is "not speaking as a priest recording old usage, but as a prophet ordaining new Torah with divine authority." It is true that he is speaking as a prophet, and is speaking of what shall be when Judah shall be restored. But his prophecy speaks of the restoration of institutions already known to those he is addressing. Accepting the critical canon, that a prophet always speaks to his own time, it must be conceded, by those who insist upon this canon, that the men to whom Jeremiah spoke knew what he referred to when he enumerated the blessings of the coming restoration. They must therefore have known what he meant when he spoke of the burnt-offerings, and sacrifices, and meat-offerings, and incense, and sacrifices of praise, and of the gathering of the people to Jerusalem to offer them, as well as what he meant when he spoke of the kings and princes sitting on the throne of David; and there is no more reason for thinking that in the latter case the prophet meant a restoration of an ancient well-known institution, viz. the kingdom of David, than there is for believing that in the former he meant the restoration of services with which the people were perfectly familiar, whose loss he regarded as proof of God's displeasure, and whose restoration he proclaimed as a token of His returning favour. It is true there is no mention made in this passage of a priesthood as among the blessings of the promised restoration; but no counter argument can be based on this omission, as a priesthood is obviously implied in the reference to burnt-offerings, and thank-offerings, and incense.

Our Author cannot exorcise the Priesthood out of Jeremiah.

We are, however, not left to inference or conjecture in this case; for, referring to this same prophecy, and renewing the promise, this same prophet, chap. xxxiii. 18, says: "And unto the priests, the Levites, there shall not be wanting a man before me to offer burnt-offerings, and to burn meat-offerings, and to do (or to prepare) sacrifices at all times." If it be objected, as it is by "the newer criticism," that the passage is omitted by the LXX., and that it should not, therefore, be adduced as proof in this controversy, the answer is obvious. "The newer criticism" cannot exorcise the priesthood, *and that, too, as an ancient pre-exilic institution,* or sacrifice, from the writings of this prophet by the excision of this passage; for this prophet was himself a priest, "of the priests which were in Anathoth in the land of Benjamin," a city which, with her suburbs, as we find from Josh. xxi. 18, belonged to "the children of Aaron the priest." He is commissioned to rebuke the priests, but he is not commissioned to rebuke them for the exercise of priestly functions. His rebukes are so administered as to show that it is not for their holding or executing priestly functions they are condemned, but for their impiety and immorality. This is manifest—1. Because he connects his rebukes of them with his rebukes of kings and prophets. Now it must be conceded that the kingly and prophetic offices were divinely sanctioned. The argument which would conclude from the rebuke of the priests that the priesthood and the sacrifices were destitute of divine sanction, must warrant the conclusion that the prophetic and kingly offices were also displeasing to God, for kings and prophets, as well as priests, were subjected to Jeremiah's rebukes. 2. Because, as the former of the two passages just cited proves, the blessings promised under the restoration embrace burnt-offerings, and sacrifices, and meat-offerings, and incense, brought from all quarters of the land to the house of the Lord, the one central sanctuary at Jerusalem. This fact implies two things. It implies that the men of Judah addressed by Jeremiah (for a prophet, we are told, always speaks to his own times) were familiar with burnt-offerings, and sacrifices, and incense, and with the concentration of the people at Jerusalem to offer them; and it also implies that, in the divine estimation, the restoration of these at the central seat of worship would be among the chief of the blessings in store for the children of the captivity. Language of this kind would certainly be strangely out of place if priesthood, and sacrifice, and a central seat of worship, were disowned by the God of Jeremiah in pre-exilic times.

And this style of representation is not exceptional. It is, in fact, the use and wont of Jeremiah when speaking of the returning favour of God in store for the restored Israel. Thus in chap. xxxi., in the midst of a most glowing and eloquent description of the blessings wherewith the heart of the children of the captivity would be gladdened, the prophet does not lose sight of the priesthood. There are blessings of wheat, and wine, and oil, and flocks and herds for the people, which shall make "their soul as a watered garden," and fill their mouths with songs of rejoicing; but there are also blessings for the priests, and blessings which are appropriate to, and inseparable from, their exercise of priestly functions: "I will satiate the soul of the priests with fatness, and my people shall be satisfied with my goodness, saith the LORD." Such language were impossible if the things promised had been unknown to Israel, or unapproved by Israel's God. In a word, the prophecies of Jeremiah, fairly interpreted, prove that there is no warrant for the assumption of our author (p. 370), that this prophet declares "that a law of sacrifice is no part of the original covenant with Israel."

Recognition of Deuteronomic Code in Josiah's day creates a Difficulty.

It is interesting to note the difficulties wherewith "the newer criticism" encompasses its path as it tries to thread its way among the prophets. Having taken up the position (p. 374) that Jeremiah "knew no divine law of sacrifice under the first Temple," the question has to be met, "How reconcile that theory with the alleged discovery of the Deuteronomic Code in the days of Josiah?" This Code, "the newer criticism" itself admits, was authoritative, and divinely authoritative, from the time of its discovery, 624 B.C., till the overthrow of the kingdom of Judah and the destruction of the Temple. But in this authoritative Code, which was the rule under the first Temple for about forty years, we find the following law respecting Israel's sacrifices and central sanctuary: "Unto the place which the Lord your God shall choose out of all your tribes to put His name there, even unto His habitation shall ye seek, and thither shalt thou come: and thither ye shall bring your burnt-offerings, and your sacrifices, and your tithes, and heave-offerings of your hand, and your vows, and your freewill-offerings, and the firstlings of your herds and of your flocks," Deut. xii. 5, 6. We have already seen how "the newer criticism" has brought Jeremiah into conflict with the historic national institute of the Passover, and we see here how it has brought this same prophet into collision with the Deuteronomic Code. That Code, according to the admission, and even the contention, of "the newer criticism," had sway throughout, and actually determined the whole enterprise of, Josiah's reformation, which certainly occurred under the first

Temple, and yet this same "newer criticism" tells us "that Jeremiah knew no divine law of sacrifice under the first Temple!"

Attempted Solution of this Difficulty.

But "the newer criticism" has a solution; let us see what it is. "Jeremiah," we are told, "in speaking thus, does not separate himself from the Deuteronomic law; for the moral precepts of that Code — as, for example, the Deuteronomic form of the law of manumission (Jer. xxxiv. 13-16) — he accepts as part of the covenant of the exodus. To Jeremiah, therefore, the Code of Deuteronomy does not appear in the light of a positive law of sacrifice; and this judgment" (*i.e.* Jeremiah's, it is presumed!) "is undoubtedly correct. The ritual details of Deuteronomy are directed against heathen worship; they are negative, not positive. In the matter of sacrifice and festal observances, the new Code simply directs the old homage of Israel from the local sanctuaries to the central shrine, and all material offerings are summed up under the principles of gladness before Jehovah at the great agricultural feasts, and of homage paid to Him in acknowledgment that the good things of the land of Canaan are His gift (xxvi. 10). The firstlings and the first-fruits and tithes remain on their old footing, as natural expressions of devotion, which did not begin with the exodus, and are not peculiar to Israel," etc. etc. And so the sweeping conclusion is reached, that "Deuteronomy knows nothing of a sacrificial priestly Torah, though it refers the people to the Torah of the priests on the subject of leprosy (xxiv. 8), and acknowledges their authority as judges in lawsuits," pp. 370, 371.

Examination of the foregoing Solution.

Now it would seem quite enough, as an exposure of the weakness and unprofitableness of this solution, to refer the reader to the two verses already quoted from Deut. xii. What "the newer criticism" affirms, these verses deny; and what they affirm, "the newer criticism" denies. They affirm, contrary to "the newer criticism," that sacrifices, etc., are to be brought to the central shrine by a divine ordinance. Deuteronomy therefore knows something of at least a sacrificial Torah. This sacrificial Torah, however, is priestly as well as sacrificial; for Israel is to bring the tithes as well as the sacrifices to the central shrine. For what purpose or for whom were these tithes? Were they not for the sons of Levi, who, if we are to credit the Epistle to the Hebrews (vii. 5), had a Torah giving them authority to receive tithes of their brethren, "though these have come out of the loins of Abraham." This point would seem to be put beyond doubt by the frequent reference made in this Deuteronomic Code to the duty of providing for the Levite, and to the priests the Levites, and all the tribe of Levi. and to the fact that "they have no part nor inheritance" with the other tribes (Deut. xii. 12, 19, xiv. 27, 29, xvi. 14, xviii. 1–8). The latter of these passages puts the priestly status of the sons of Levi beyond question: "For the Lord thy God hath chosen him (Levi) out of all thy tribes, to stand to minister in the name of the LORD, him and his sons for ever" (ver. 5).

Here, then, we have not only a sacrificial, but a "sacrificial priestly Torah," with all the conditions thereof, and with provision annexed for the support of the priests and their attendants. We have, in fact, a whole tribe set apart for doing, as their chief business, a work for the regulation of which, we are told by "the newer criticism," there was no Torah enacted !

CHAPTER IV.

THE NEWER CRITICISM AND THE INTERPRETATION OF THE PROPHETS—*continued.*

"THE newer criticism," as it denies the existence of any sacrificial priestly Torah in Deuteronomy, may be expected to find no place therein for sacrifice or offerings of an *expiatory* character for sin. A reference to the passage quoted above will show that such is the doctrine, so far as Deuteronomy is concerned, laid down in these lectures! "All material offerings are summed up under the principles of gladness before Jehovah at the great agricultural feasts, and of homage paid to Him in acknowledgment that the good things of the land of Canaan are His gifts," etc. etc. (pp. 370, 371). Such is the sum and substance of all that "the newer criticism" can find in this Deuteronomic Code about sacrifice, or burnt-offerings, or offerings for sin! In the same context the advocate of this monstrous summation, as we have already seen, tries to get rid of the sacrificial element in the paschal victim, and here the wide, sweeping generalization is reached, "that all the material offerings" described in this Deuteronomic Code are not hilastic or expiatory, but simply eucharistic, and designed to give no indication of Israel's sense of sin before Jehovah, or of the way of acceptance with Him, but simply to express Israel's recognition of His sovereignty, and their devotion to His rule!

Theory of Religion in Pre-exilic Times.

Such was the character of Israel's worship in the days of Josiah, even after that good king had inaugurated the newly-discovered Deuteronomic Code. As might be expected, it was, to say the least, no better in earlier times. The religion of Israel, as sketched on pp. 343, 344, is as follows: "Jehovah alone is Israel's God. It is a crime analogous to treason to depart from Him and sacrifice to other gods. As the Lord of Israel and Israel's land, the giver of all good gifts to His people, He has a manifest claim on Israel's homage, and receives at their hands such dues as their neighbours paid to their gods, such dues as a king receives from his people (comp. 1 Sam. viii. 15-17). The occasions of homage are those seasons of natural gladness which an agricultural life suggests. The joy of harvest and vintage is a rejoicing before Jehovah, when the worshipper brings a gift in his hand, as he would do in approaching an earthly sovereign, and presents the choicest first-fruits at the altar, just as his Canaanitish neighbour does in the house of Baal (Judg. ix. 27). The whole worship is spontaneous and natural. It has hardly the character of a positive legislation, and its distinction from heathen rites lies less in the outward form than in the different conception of Jehovah which the true worshipper should bear in his heart. To a people which 'knows Jehovah' this unambitious service, in which the expression of grateful homage to Him runs through all the simple joys of a placid agricultural life, was sufficient to form the basis of a pure and earnest piety. But its forms gave no protection against deflection into heathenism and immorality when Jehovah's spiritual nature and moral precepts were forgotten. The feasts and sacrifices might still run their accustomed round when Jehovah was practically confounded with the Baalim, and there was no more truth, or mercy, or knowledge of God in the land (Hos. iv. 1). Such, in fact, was the state of things in the eighth century, the age of the earliest prophetic books. The declensions of Israel had not checked the outward zeal with which Jehovah was worshipped. Never had the national sanctuaries been more sedulously frequented, never had the feasts been more splendid or the offerings more copious. But the foundations of the old life were breaking up. The external prosperity of the State covered an abyss of social disorder."

Essential Elements of Religion as known in Pre-exilic Times.

This section has been given at some length, as it gives us an instructive insight into the author's theory of the essential elements of religion. It will be seen at once that this theory of Israel's pre-exilic worship assumes an entirely sinless estate on the part of the worshipper. Israel stands out before us as a pious people rejoicing in a placid agricultural life, and giving expression to their rural joys before Jehovah with accompanying tokens of grateful homage. This unambitious service, consisting exclusively of gifts presented to Jehovah as their Lord and the Lord of their land, " was sufficient to form the basis of a pure and earnest piety." There can be no mistaking of this language. It means simply what our author says, p. 379, that " the sense of God's favour, not the sense of sin, is what rules at the sanctuary ;" and it means what he insists on, p. 288, that " worship by sacrifice, and all that belongs to it, is no part of the divine Torah to Israel;" and what he affirms with increasing emphasis on p. 303, that " according to the prophets this law of chastisement and forgiveness works directly, without the intervention of any ritual sacrament." During all the pre-exilic period under Moses, under the Judges, under Samuel, under the kings, there was nothing in the religion of Israel, nor in their forms of worship, to indicate the existence of sin. The last-mentioned passage gives intimation of sin, as it speaks of chastisement; but chastisement was an act of Jehovah, and not an act, or element, of Israel's worship. Its design was subjective, to work penitence. Our author gives his theory on this point, p. 302: " Jehovah's anger" (according to his account of the teaching of the prophets) "is not caprice, but a just indignation,—a necessary side of His *moral kingship* in Israel" (as Grotius would say). "He chastises to work *penitence*" (as Socinus would say); "and it is only to the penitent that He can extend forgiveness. By returning to obedience the people regain the marks of Jehovah's love, and again experience His goodness in deliverance from calamity and happy possession of a fruitful land."

It is true then, beyond doubt, that the doctrine taught by our author in the extract given above from pp. 343, 344, and in the confirmatory references, is, that Israel's worship was destitute of any rite by which they gave expression to their sense of sin, and, further, that God required no element in their forms of approach to Him beyond what a good king would require at the hands of his subjects. If they sinned against Him as their Lord paramount, His remedy was chastisement; but, so far as they were concerned, the only thing required in order to regain His favour was penitence and a return to obedience. As this theory of Israel's worship can consist only with most defective views of the relation of fallen, guilty moral agents to a holy and righteous God, it will be necessary to examine it more fully at a subsequent point in this review. At present let it suffice to call attention to the fact that this book teaches, that for more than three thousand years of the history of the covenant of redemption, God's own chosen people, whether they lived in antediluvian or patriarchal times, or in the pre-exilic times of Israel's history as a nation, were permitted, *in their acts of worship,* to proceed upon the assumption that there was no need of an atonement for sin! It is true they did, during all this vast period, practise sacrifice,—a practice which it is difficult not to associate with the idea of sin and the felt need of an atonement,—but this practice was destitute of any positive divine sanction, and was common to them with the heathen nations around them!

Israel's Ignorance of the Doctrine of Atonement in Pre-exilic Times.

In a word, up to the time of the return from Babylon, Israel had no idea that there was needed any such thing as an atonement for sin in the sense of an expiatory sacrifice, in which the life of ox, or sheep, or other atoning substitute, was given in the stead of the transgressor!

With the wider generalization we are not, however, dealing at present. The only point now before us is the dilemma arising out of the historical position which "the newer criticism" has assigned to Deuteronomy. By admitting it to a pre-exilic date at all, even though it should antedate the exile only by one generation, this critical school have involved themselves in inextricable confusion, and do not know what to do with its priesthood, and sacrifices, and Torahs. They would fondly rid themselves of the difficulties wherewith their own theory has beset them; but there is no help from new renderings or from new modifications of their ever changing theories; and even the LXX. but confirms the old-fashioned doctrine which their theory was designed to supplant. When all is done, it still remains true that Deuteronomy in the days of Josiah presents as veritable an obstacle to the post-exilic theory of a sacrificial priestly Torah, as Deuteronomy in the days of Moses can do. So patent is this fact, that our author, after all, has to acknowledge, p. 372, that "there was at this time (Jeremiah's) a ritual Torah in the hands of the priests containing elements which the prophets and the old codes pass by." Tracing the ritual backward, he finds that there was, even in the time of Ahaz, "a daily burnt-offering in the morning, a stated meat-offering in the evening" (2 Kings xvi. 15). But further, he actually discovers "an *atoning* ritual." In the time of Jehoash there were, he admits, atonements; but this admission is accompanied by the saving clause, that these "atonements were paid to the priests," and were simply "pecuniary,"—a common enough thing in ancient times. There were, however, he confesses, "also *atoning sacrifices*" in ancient times; for he observes that "the guilt of the house of Eli was not to be wiped away by sacrifice or oblation for ever." "The idea of atonement in the sacrificial blood," he is constrained to say, "must be very ancient; and a *trace* (!) of it is found even in the Book of Deuteronomy in the curious ordinance" (*curious*, indeed, such an ordinance must be to "the newer criticism") "which provides for the atonement (wiping out) of the blood of untraced homicide by the slaughter of a heifer." This is a pretty large confession to follow on an elaborate excursus whose chief object was to prove, that during the whole period covered by this confession no sacrificial priestly Torah had place or recognition, and designed, especially, to prove that such Torah was unknown under the first Temple. Such a confession required a word of explanation from the chief representative of "the newer criticism" in Scotland; and sensible of the necessity, he immediately subjoins the following: "Only, we have already seen that the details still preserved to us of the Temple ritual are not identical with the full Levitical system. They contained many germs of that system, but they also contained much that was radically different."

Such is our author's explanation, or *raison d'être*, of his elaborate excursus put forth as an argument against the existence of a priestly sacrificial Torah under the first Temple. Let us see the evidence he adduces as his warrant for such a statement. "In particular," he adds, "the Temple worship itself was not stringently differentiated from everything heathenish." His proof of this lack of differentiation of the divinely ordained, from the heathenish and profane, is taken from the state of the Temple service during the reign of the idolatrous King Ahaz and the priesthood of the pliant high priest Urijah (whose character as the alleged "friend of Isaiah" he would have us infer from the fact that Isaiah employed him *as a witness*), and from the patronage, in connection with the Temple, of prophets who were simply heathen diviners! (Pp. 372, 373.)

On this explanation it may be observed,—1. That it is not the design of the Books of the Kings and Chronicles, or of the prophets, to give the full details of the Levitical system. The knowledge of that system is assumed throughout. If Jeremiah, in whose time "the newer criticism" contends the Book of Deuteronomy first saw the light (for he lived in the reign of Josiah), rebukes Israel without giving a full detail of the miniature priestly Torah of that book, surely the other prophets may have rebuked the kings and priests of their day without giving full details of existing Torahs. 2. The argument from what was the use and wont of the Temple services under wicked kings and pliant priests, merits rebuke rather than serious argument in reply. One might as well cite the services of the Church of Rome as proof of the New Testament Torah of the present day, or the temporary prevalence of "the newer criticism" in some of the Theological Halls of Scotland as proof of the non-existence of the Torah of the Westminster Divines in the Free Church. 3. As to the points of identity and dissimilarity between the Temple ritual and the full Levitical system within the periods specified, the answer, if an answer were necessary, is obvious. The points of agreement bespeak a common Torah whose leading elements have survived all attempts of kings or priests to abolish them, and the points of disagreement are simply evidence of the measure of the success of the royal and priestly innovators. 4. Finally, it may be remarked that a theory of the structure of the Old Testament revelation and the relation of its several parts which has to resort to such critical methods—methods which are ever bringing their authors into conflict with manifest historical facts which they are constantly under the necessity of explaining away, or actually exscinding from the record—cannot long hold sway among an intelligent Christian people. When the Christian people of Scotland come to know how utterly unhistorical, illogical, and, to speak mildly, how unethical "the newer criticism" is, they will soon discard it and avenge themselves, and our common Christianity, of such irreverent speculations.

In view of the inconvenience, and of the critical, historical, and doctrinal difficulties of the theory, it is not to be wondered at that some of the ablest of its advocates in the earlier stages of its Scottish development have, since the publication of these lectures, publicly declared that they cannot endorse the Deuteronomic element of it. This is a hopeful sign; but it is just as well that these brethren should know, that they cannot hold with the author of these lectures in part without holding with him altogether. The critical methods which dismiss from the Pentateuch the extra-Deuteronomic Levitical Torah, are equally available for the dismissal of Deuteronomy itself.

The Theory arrays the Pre-exilic Prophets against the Post-exilic Prophets.

But this post-exilic theory not only brings the pre-exilic prophets into conflict with some of the most eminent of the divinely-appointed institutions of Israel, such as the Passover, and priesthood, and Tabernacle, and Temple, and, as in the case of Jeremiah, with Deuteronomy itself; it also arrays the prophets of the post-exilic period against the prophets of the pre-exilic. Our author actually institutes the comparison, and brings out the contrast himself: "Spiritual prophecy, in the hands of Amos, Isaiah, and their successors, has no such alliance with the sanctuary and its ritual" (as "that which co-operates with the priests"). This latter "is a kind of prophecy which the Old Testament calls divination, which traffics in dreams in place of Jehovah's word," etc. The former "develops and enforces its own doctrine of the intercourse of Jehovah with Israel, and the conditions of His grace, without assigning the slightest value to priests and sacrifices. The sum of religion, according to the prophets, is to know Jehovah, and obey His precepts." Such was the doctrine of the pre-exilic prophets; mark the contrast when the post-exilic prophets enter upon their office. "Under the system of the law enforced from the days of Ezra onwards, an important part of these precepts are ritual. Malachi, prophesying in or after the days of Ezra, accepts this position as the basis of his prophetic exhortations." In a word, the post-exilic prophets teach the doctrine of the pre-exilic diviners !! "The first proof of Israel's sin is to him neglect of the sacrificial ritual. The language of the older prophets up to Jeremiah is quite different." Then follows a passage from Isa. i. 11 seq., and another from Amos v. 21 seq., in support of this latter statement. Then, rejecting the ordinary explanation of the apparent discrepancy, viz. "that such passages mean only that Jehovah will not accept the sacrifice of the wicked," the unqualified dogma is enunciated, that the teaching of these and other texts is, that "sacrifice is not necessary to acceptable religion." This position is avowed and backed up with quotations from, or references to, Amos, Micah, Jeremiah, and Isaiah, pp. 286, 287.

Having taken this ground, our author immediately proceeds to distinguish it from that of an absolute prohibition of sacrifice and ritual. The prophets' condemnation "of the worship of their contemporaries," was pronounced "because it is associated with immorality, and because by it Israel hopes to gain God's favour without moral obedience. This does not prove that they have any objection to sacrifice and ritual in the abstract," p. 288.

The lecturer lays it down (p. 77) as the first rule of criticism, "that a good critic must be a good interpreter of the thoughts of another." This is a good rule, and judged by it "the newer criticism" must fare badly. Can he be regarded as a good interpreter of the thoughts of one whom he admits to be "an all-wise Author, and who cannot contradict Himself," p. 39, who thus sets the prophets of that all-wise Author in array against one another ? Wherein lies the difference between the doctrine that makes Ezekiel and Malachi contradict Amos and Isaiah, and the doctrine that makes the God of these men contradict Himself ?

The Author's Solution Suicidal and Inconsistent.

But the superfluity and critical wantonness of the procedure become utterly amazing, when one finds that the very principle by which good interpreters have sought to harmonize the language of condemnation in which these older prophets speak of the ceremonial observances of Israel with the historic fact of their divine institution, rejected by our author on p. 287, is quietly appropriated on p. 288, where it is made to do service to help to sustain the doctrine of will-worship as acceptable to God. On this latter page we are told that this condemnation of the worship of their contemporaries by the prophets, because of its being associated with immorality, etc., " does not prove that they have any objection to sacrifice and ritual in the abstract. But they deny that these things are of positive divine institution, or have any part in the scheme on which Jehovah's grace is administered in Israel. Jehovah, they say, has not enjoined sacrifice. This does not imply that He has never accepted sacrifice, or that ritual service is absolutely wrong" (p. 288).

Now, it is not unreasonable to ask, If the principle of this apology for an unauthorized sacrificial system be valid, why object to it when applied to a sacrificial system divinely sanctioned? If it can be said that the prophets, in rebuking Israel for an *unauthorized* service, " because it is associated with immorality, and because by it Israel hopes to gain God's favour without moral obedience," did not thereby wish Israel to understand that God had any objection to the sacrifice or the ritual of that unauthorized service, how is it that, in rebuking Israel for an *authorized* service, " because it is associated with immorality, and because by it Israel hopes to gain God's favour without moral obedience," the prophets are to be regarded as teaching that God had objection to the sacrifice and the ritual of that authorized service? If the explanation be valid in the case of the unauthorized, why should it not be valid in the case of the authorized? If "the newer criticism" can assume that the ground of the rebuke in the case of the uncommanded is the immorality, etc., of "them that drew nigh," why may we not assume that the ground of the rebuke in the case of the commanded was the immorality, etc., of the worshippers? Thrown into form, the explanation of the rebuke, as given by "the newer criticism" is as follows:—

> *Major.*—The rebuke of the worshipper because of his immorality, etc., does not imply the condemnation of the matter, or the form, of his worship.

Minor.—The rebuke of the worshippers, in the case of Israel, was administered by the prophets because of their immorality, etc.

Conclusion.—The rebuke of these worshippers does not imply the condemnation of the matter (sacrifice) or the form (ritual) of their worship.

Such, beyond challenge, is the syllogism lying behind the explanation by which "the newer criticism" would reconcile the prophetic rebuke of the worshippers with the non-condemnation of the matter or the form of the uncommanded worship; and it is our syllogism as well as theirs. Those who regard the worship as uncommanded, have no warrant for assuming that the ground of the rebuke was the immorality of the worshippers, and not the matter or the form of the service, which we have not for assuming the same ground of rebuke in the case of the worship, viewed as commanded. Why, then, it is asked again, reject this explanation of these prophetic rebukes in the latter case and accept it in the former? No reason can be assigned for adopting it in the former case which is not manifestly available in the latter.

Rule for the Interpretation of such Passages.

The right of applying the principle in question, in either case, must be determined by the prophetic record. The question is simply this: Does the prophetic record assign as a reason of the rebuke administered to Israel's worship, the immorality and spirit, etc., of Israel's worshippers? Isa. i. 13 settles this question: "Ye shall not add to bring a vain offering; incense is an abomination to me; new moon and sabbath, the calling of the convocation: I cannot bear iniquity and holy day." Is there any room for doubt here about the ground of the prophet's rebuke? It is not all offerings that God prohibits, but offerings of vanity—vain offerings, offerings presented in the same spirit as the prayers of the Pharisees, which Christ condemned as vain repetitions. It is not all holy days that the passage condemns; for surely the Sabbath at least was pre-exilic. What God cannot bear, is "iniquity and holy day." The latter combined with the former is intolerable to God.

In harmony with this exegesis of the 13th verse is the language of the next verse. Repeating for the sake of emphasis some of the institutions mentioned in the 13th, the prophet adds: "Your new moons and your convocations my soul hateth; they *have become* a burden upon me; I am weary of bearing" (or have wearied myself in bearing them). The idea here is manifest. Rites and institutions ordained of God Himself, and acceptable to Him, had, because of the impiety and hypocrisy of Israel, *become* hateful in His eyes. What the Lord hates, and loathes, and commands His prophets to condemn, is just what our author alleges when he is off his guard, viz. the immorality of the worshippers, and the vain hope that by such services they should gain acceptance with God.

Argument from such Passages proves too much.

The argument of "the newer criticism" from this condemnation of Israel's worship by Isaiah, in this passage, proves entirely too much; for Isaiah not only rebukes Israel for their approaching God by sacrifices and burnt-offerings, and for their observance of new moons and appointed feasts, etc., but he actually rebukes them for coming into the courts of the Temple at all. Now, on the principle on which this argument proceeds, the Temple and its courts must, in the days of Isaiah, which were certainly pre-exilic, have been regarded as at least unauthorized institutions. If the rebuke of Israel for bringing sacrifices, etc., implies the condemnation of sacrifices, or warrants the conclusion that God stood toward such worship in a negative attitude, surely it must follow from His rebuke of Israel for treading His courts, that these courts had not as yet received any positive divine sanction. This conclusion is inevitable if the principle of this critical argumentation be valid. But as soon as the principle is accepted, mark the difficulty it creates when applied. The conclusion to which it inevitably leads is simply a flat contradiction of the claim advanced by God Himself, who, in the administration of this rebuke, designates the courts as *His courts.* When ye come to appear before me, who hath required this at your hand, to tread *my courts?* ver. 12. Surely this claim, put forth on the very back of the rebuke, demonstrates the unwarrantableness of the inference of "the newer criticism," that the rebuke of the worshipper necessarily implies the non-recognition of the *matter* or the *form* of the worship. If God could rebuke Israel for treading the Temple courts, and yet claim the courts as *His*, thus giving both Temple and courts His sanction, it cannot be true that His rebuke of Israel for their sacrifices and feasts implies the non-recognition of these institutions. This conclusion is placed beyond challenge, as has been already shown, by the very structure and furniture of the Temple itself, which can have no meaning apart from priesthood, sacrifice, and ritual. To claim the courts was to claim both altar and sacrifice.

And what is true of this classic passage—classic in this controversy—is true of all the kindred passages cited by our author from the other pre-exilic prophets. They all admit of the same explanation. There is not a single passage adduced, or adducible, from Amos, or Hosea, or Micah, condemnatory of Israel's worship, in which stronger language is employed than that which occurs in this denunciation of it by Isaiah. All that is necessary to the solution of the problem presented by any one of these passages, or by all combined, is simply the application of the principle which our author has rejected on page 287, and adopted on page 288. If these denunciations do not imply the condemnation of the worship as not enjoined, it is clear that they cannot imply the condemnation of it viewed as a divinely authorized institution.

The Newer Criticism and the Fifty-first Psalm.

The fifty-first Psalm furnishes a striking confirmation of this view of passages which seem to be condemnatory of worship by sacrifice. No language could be more explicit, and there is no language in any of the passages cited from the prophets more explicit, on this point than the language of the psalmist. "Thou desirest not sacrifice, else would I give it Thee; Thou delightest not in burnt-offering (*'olah*). The sacrifices of God are a broken spirit: a broken and a contrite heart, O God, Thou wilt not despise." Here the psalmist describes both negatively and positively the sacrifices of God (*zivchê Elohim*). They are not burnt-offerings (the *'olah* being taken as a representative of all); they are immaterial and spiritual— a broken spirit, a broken and a contrite heart. But no sooner has he to all appearance excluded literal sacrifices, than he expresses his approval of them, and promises that God shall be pleased with the sacrifices of righteousness, with burnt-offerings and whole burnt-offerings; and that bullocks shall be offered upon God's altar.

Now, if such statements as these—one of them defining the sacrifices of God as purely spiritual and an affair of the heart, and the other specifying the material of them as embracing bullocks— can be placed side by side without any feeling of incongruity or inconsistency, it would seem that, to the Jewish mind at least, there was neither inconsistency nor contradiction in such forms of representation.

Argument not met by proving the Psalm Exilic.

Nor would it at all weaken the argument from this psalm, but, on the contrary, rather strengthen it, as against "the newer criticism," were it true, as our author argues (Lect. vii., note 10, p. 418), that the psalm is Exilic, and expresses the experience of a prophet of the Exile, who gives utterance to the experience of "the true Israel of the Exile." For, according to our author, the keynote of the Levitical system was struck by Ezekiel during the Exile. Certainly Ezekiel may be taken as a true representative of "the true Israel of the Exile;" and no less certainly must it be held that a true psalmist of "the true Israel of the Exile," speaking the experience of those he represented, would express himself in harmony with the Ezekielian Torah. This view is still further strengthened by the contention of "the newer criticism," that the Deuteronomic Torah (whose spirit is so thoroughly Levitical) was introduced before the Jews were carried into Babylon. Their own principles and arguments here again rise to confute themselves. Contending that this psalm is Exilic, they are simply proving that a psalmist who was in harmony with the spirit of the Levitical Torah, which they assign to the days of Ezekiel, could say, and that without any feeling of inconsistency, that God does not desire sacrifice, that His sacrifices are a broken spirit, and a broken and a contrite heart, and that nevertheless He was pleased with, and accepted burnt-offerings and bullocks upon *His* altar.

The Difficulty of "the Newer Criticism" is not met by omitting the last two verses of this Psalm.

Nor would "the newer criticism" get rid of the apparent incongruity by referring the last two verses of the fifty-first Psalm, as some do, to another period, and ascribing them to another psalmist than David. For David's language in the preceding verses has still to be harmonized with David's acts of public worship in connection with the bringing up of the ark to his own city, and with the propitiation of God on the threshing-place of Araunah the Jebusite. We are told (2 Sam. xxiv. 25) that "David built there an altar unto the LORD, and offered burnt-offerings and peace-offerings. So the LORD was entreated for the land, and the plague was stayed from Israel." If David believed that the *only* sacrifices of God were a broken spirit, and that a broken and a contrite heart was the *only* offering, which He would not despise, how is it that we find him passing beyond the limits of this spiritual Torah at the threshing-place of Araunah, and erecting an altar to Jehovah, and offering thereon burnt-offerings and peace-offerings? And if the purely spiritual are the only sacrifices of Jehovah, how is it that the Lord accepts these material offerings at the hands of the king, and is entreated for the land, and stays the plague from Israel?

Author's Views of the Status of God's People in Pre-exilic Times.

Before passing from the consideration of this fifty-first Psalm, notice must be taken of the teaching of our author upon a question vitally affecting the status of the people of God under the Old Testament. Commenting on ver. 11, "Take not Thy Holy Spirit from me," he makes the following statement as if it were the current doctrine of the Church of God: "Under the Old Testament the Holy Spirit is not given to every believer, but to Israel as a nation (Isa. lxiii. 10, 11), residing in chosen organs, especially in the prophets, who are *par excellence* ' men of the Spirit ' (Hos. ix. 7). But the Spirit of Jehovah was also given to David (1 Sam. xvi. 13; 2 Sam. xxiii. 2). The psalm, then, so far as this phrase goes, may be a psalm of Israel collectively, of a prophet, or of David" (p. 417). How Israel, in their collective capacity, could compose a psalm we are not informed.

His Doctrine Anti-confessional.

This is certainly singular doctrine to be avowed by any genuine Protestant, but its singularity is all the more surprising when it is remembered that the author of it, in the present instance, has subscribed the Westminster Confession of Faith. That Confession teaches (chap. vii. § v.) that the ordinances of the law " were for that time sufficient and efficacious, through the operation of the Spirit, to instruct and build up the elect in faith in the promised Messiah, by whom they had full remission of sins, and eternal salvation." There is manifestly diversity of doctrine here. If, as our Confession teaches, and as all Christians, save Romanists, Anabaptists, and Socinians, hold, the means of grace were efficacious under the Old Testament unto salvation, and efficacious only through the operation of the Spirit, it must follow that none, under that dispensation, were saved except those in whom the Spirit operated efficaciously, working faith and leading them to exercise it in the promised Messiah. Such is the common faith of the Church of God, with the exceptions mentioned; but such is not the faith avowed in our author's comment. The Old Testament, according to his teaching, is distinguished from the New by this among other things, that the Holy Spirit was "not given to every believer, but to Israel as a nation," whilst, under the New, He is given to all believers! There were, then, "*believers*" under the Old Testament to whom the Spirit was not given, and, consequently, "*believers*" whose faith was not a fruit of the Spirit. It is not unnatural to ask, was this faith of these Old Testament "believers" saving faith? If it was, whence did it arise? Was the natural estate of man, or the estate of the natural man, under that dispensation, so widely diverse from what it is under the present dispensation, that there was no need for the regenerating agency of the Holy

Ghost? The question put by our Saviour to Nicodemus does not seem to be out of place here: "Art thou a master (ὁ διδάσκαλος, a teacher) of Israel, and knowest not these things?" If Nicodemus, *as a teacher of Israel*, should have known these things,—should have known that a man can neither see nor enter the kingdom of God except he be born again, except he be born of the Holy Spirit,—then it must have been true of every individual of that nation of which Nicodemus was a teacher, of every man in Israel, that without the new birth he could not be saved. To say, then, as our author does, that "the Holy Spirit was not given to every believer in Israel," is simply to say that the private membership of the nation were not born again, which is all one with saying that such were not saved, as the Scriptures count salvation. How closely this view of the status of the people of God under the Old Testament is related to the Romish doctrine of a *Limbus Patrum*, it is unnecessary to inquire.

Doctrine of a Collective Organic Spiritual Inhabitation.

But the author, whilst denying that the Holy Spirit was given to believers individually, in Old Testament times, teaches that He was given "to Israel *as a nation*," and that instead of residing in each He resided "in chosen organs, especially in the prophets, who are, *par excellence*, 'men of the Spirit,' and He 'was also given to David.'"

The following passages are cited to prove this collective inhabitation through a chosen organ: "But they rebelled, and vexed His Holy Spirit: therefore He was turned to be their enemy, and He fought against them. Then He remembered the days of old, Moses, and His people, saying, Where is He that brought them up out of the sea with the shepherd of His flock? where is He that put His Holy Spirit within him?" (Isa. lxiii. 10, 11). "The days of visitation are come, the days of recompense are come; Israel shall know it: the prophet is a fool, the spiritual man is mad, for the multitude of thine iniquity, and great hatred" (Hos. ix. 7). "Then Samuel took the horn of oil, and anointed him in the midst of his brethren; and the Spirit of the Lord came upon David from that day forward" (1 Sam. xvi. 13). "The Spirit of the Lord spake by me, and His word was in my tongue" (2 Sam. xxiii. 2).

This Doctrine examined, and proved Unscriptural.

Now it will be observed that the instances given of this national inhabitation through chosen organs are instances, without exception, of the supernatural gifts of the Holy Spirit bestowed upon men to qualify them for the execution of extraordinary functions as leaders and instructors of Israel. The first passage refers to the gift of the Spirit to Moses, the last two to the gift of the Spirit to David, and the second passage to the prophets in general. As it is a clearly revealed doctrine of Scripture that these supernatural gifts, given for such purposes, do not *necessarily* imply a gracious saving operation of the Holy Ghost, either upon the immediate subjects of them or upon others through their agency, it is manifest that if this were all that the Holy Ghost effected for Israel, by this *mediate* national inhabitation, His people whom He redeemed from the bondage of Egypt were never made the subjects of His saving grace. If it was as true of Moses and the prophets as it was of Paul and Apollos, that "neither he that planteth is anything, neither he that watereth, but God that giveth the increase," then if the Holy Ghost did not Himself give, by His own *immediate* agency, the increase, the Mosaic planting and the prophetic watering must have been in vain. Surely the critical theory that leads to such conclusions respecting the salvation of Israel cannot be Biblical.

Romish cast of the Doctrine.

But there is another feature of this doctrine of the *mediate* inhabitation of the Holy Spirit which cannot but strike any one who is at all acquainted with the Romish controversy. The doctrine here avowed regarding the relation of the Holy Spirit to the Church under the Old Dispensation, bears a very close resemblance to the doctrine of Rome regarding His relation to the Church under the New. The Romish doctrine is, that the Holy Spirit dwells in the external organization and operates through chosen organs, especially the bishops or chief pastors; the doctrine of our author is, that He dwelt in Israel as a nation, residing in chosen organs, especially the prophets. The Romish doctrine, however, ascribes to the Spirit, as the efficient cause, the efficacy of the "intervening ritual sacrament;" while our author acknowledges no "ritual sacrament," and his views regarding the result, upon the Old Testament worshippers, of the indwelling of the Spirit in the prophets and others appointed over them as administrators, are exceedingly obscure and indefinite. The fact is, that when his note on p. 417 is read in connection with what he says respecting the worship of Israel and the subject of prayer, noticed elsewhere in this review, the impression produced is very painful. One feels that it must be all but impossible to accept the theory, and continue to believe that the people of God under the Old Testament, the true Israel,—Israel κατὰ πνεῦμα, and not Israel κατὰ σάρκα,—were in possession of spiritual life or had fellowship with God.

Summation.

In fact, this post-exilic theory of the authentication of sacrifice has compelled its advocates to take up a position of antagonism to the historical facts of the Biblical record. Its sole reliance is placed upon a few statements such as those already examined, while the concurrent Torahs of all pre-exilic times, so far as they allude to Israel's worship and her immemorial practice, and the institutions of the wilderness and of the residence in Canaan, proclaim, with one united voice, its condemnation, and leave its advocates without the shadow of an excuse.

The position, therefore, that the Pentateuchal Torah did not originate with Ezra or his contemporaries, and that the law he brought from Babylon was, from times immemorial, the "religious and municipal code" of Israel, is established by historical evidence which nothing save absolute historical scepticism will venture to call in question. The species of criticism by which it is sought to disprove the pre-exilic existence of this Torah would, if applied to the history of Scotland, shake the confidence of the people of North Britain in the history of the Scottish Reformation. It were just as easy to prove that John Knox never spoke what he is said to have spoken before the Queen and the nobility of Scotland, as to prove that Moses never uttered what the Pentateuch credits him with uttering, in presence of the elders and before the whole congregation of Israel. The criticism that can rifle Moses of all ascribed to him in the Pentateuch save the two tables of the law, could as easily prove that while John Knox was, in sentiment and principle, a reformer, he nevertheless did not give to Scotland her Presbyterian constitution.

CHAPTER V.

THE NEWER CRITICISM AND THE TEXT.

PASSING from the question of the origin of the Pentateuchal Torah, then, there remains for examination the question of the transmission of it by the scribes. Granting that they received an accurate text, did they faithfully transmit it?

Author summoned as a Witness to the Faithfulness of the Scribes.

In proof of the faithfulness with which they executed this task of transmission, it is peculiarly gratifying to be able to place our author himself in the witness-box. After admitting "that the text of the Hebrew Old Testament which we now have is the same as lay before Jerome 400 years after Christ; the same as underlies certain translations into Chaldee called Targums, which were made in Babylon in the third century after Christ; indeed, the same text as was received by the Jewish doctors of the second century, when the Mishna was being formed, and when the Jewish proselyte Aquila made his translation into Greek,"—our witness testifies, that "the Jews, in fact, from the time when their national life was extinguished and their whole soul concentrated upon the preservation of the monuments of the past, devoted the most strict and punctilious attention to the exact transmission of the received text, down to the smallest peculiarity of spelling, and even to certain irregularities of writing." So punctilious were these transcribers, as is well known, and as our author testifies, that "when the standard manuscript had a letter too big, or a letter too small, the copies made from it imitated even this, so that letters of an unusual size appear in the same place in every Hebrew Bible. Nay," he adds, "the scrupulousness of the transcribers went still further. In old MSS., when a copyist had omitted a letter, ... and when the error was detected, as the copy was revised, the reviser inserted the missing letter above the line, as we should now do with a caret. If, on the other hand, the reviser found that any superfluous letter had been inserted, he cancelled it by pricking a dot above it." All this, our witness admits, "shows with what punctilious accuracy the one standard copy was followed." This carefulness is still further evinced "in the few cases in which it was thought necessary to suggest a correction on the reading of the text." In such cases "the rule was laid down, that you must not on that account change the text itself." The course adopted was, "the reader simply learned to pronounce, in reading certain passages, a different word from that which he found written; and in many MSS. a note to this effect was placed on the margin. These notes are called *Keris*, the word *Keri* being the imperative 'read!' while the expression actually written in the text, but not uttered, is called *Kethîb* (written)." The author admits still further, "that such a system of mechanical transmission could not have been carried out with precision if copying had been left to uninstructed persons." Hence he tells his readers that it became the speciality of a guild of technically trained scholars, called Massorets, or "possessors of tradition, that is, of tradition as to the proper way of writing the Bible." ... "The final result of this labour," which extended over centuries, "was a system of vowel-points and musical accents, which enable the trained reader to give exactly the correct pronunciation, and even the correct chanting tone, of every word of the Hebrew Old Testament" (pp. 69–72).

Our witness still further admits (p. 73), that "all the evidence of variations and quotations later than the first Christian century points to the received text as already existing practically as we have it, but (that) we cannot follow its history beyond that time." Notwithstanding this confession, our author tries to pass "beyond that time," and to prove, or conjecture, various readings in earlier Hebrew MSS. The chief sources of proof on which he relies are the Samaritan Pentateuch and the Septuagint.

Date of the Samaritan Pentateuch inconsistent with a Post-exilic Torah.

With regard to the former, to help out the theory of the post-exilic origin of the Levitical system, he makes it bear date 430 B.C., and tries to support this view by an argument, in the *Notes*, p. 398, which simply contradicts the account given (2 Kings xvii.) of the instruction of the Samaritans by a priest sent back from Assyria at their request, "in the law and commandment which the Lord commanded the children of Jacob," even "the statutes and the ordinances, and the law, and the commandment which He wrote for you." On referring to the argument advanced in this note, the reader will not be surprised to find that it is the author's chief argument when he wishes to prove the non-existence of a law, viz. the fact that the law in question was not observed. The argument is simply this: "the Samaritans worshipped images, and did not observe the laws of the Pentateuch (2 Kings xvii. 34, 41). The Pentateuch, therefore, was introduced as their religious code at a later date; and it could not be accepted except in connection with the ritual and priesthood which they received from Jerusalem through the fugitive priest banished by Nehemiah"! This conjecture is backed up by an interpretation of a passage in Josephus (*Antiq.* xi. 8), in which it is related that Manasseh, the son-in-law of Sanballat, fled from Jerusalem to Samaria, and founded the schismatic temple on Mount Gerizim, with a rival hierarchy and ritual. Suffice it to say, that the premises do not warrant the conclusion. Even though it were proved that the Samaritan temple dates from the advent of the fugitive priest, it would not follow that the Samaritans had not previously received the Pentateuch. "Their persistent efforts to establish relations with the Jewish priesthood, and secure admission to the Temple at Jerusalem," which our author admits in this note, would seem to point to a very different conclusion. These "persistent efforts" may have arisen from their knowledge of the Pentateuch, and its laws respecting the priesthood and the central sanctuary.

So far as the chief aim of the author is concerned, this reference to the Samaritan Pentateuch has proved a mistake. The passage in 2 Kings xvii. proves that the laws of the Pentateuch were known to the Samaritans, for they were blamed for the non-observance of them, more than 240 years before the date of their reception of it as given by our author. If the Samaritans had the Pentateuch, Israel of the ten tribes must have had it 300 years before Ezra read it to the children of the captivity "in the street that was before the water-gate" in Jerusalem.

Author's Faculty of Generalization.

The witness adds a partial modification of his testimony to the punctilious accuracy of the transcribers, and their reverential treatment of the sacred text: "In earlier times, according to the statement of the

Rabbinical books, a certain small number of alterations, chiefly on dogmatical grounds, was made even upon the writing of Scripture. These changes are called the 18 *Tikkûnê Sopherim* (corrections or determinations of the scribes)." (See Turretin, *De Scriptura*, quæst. x., t. xii.) These instances the author makes the basis of the generalization, " that the early guardians of the text did not hesitate to make small changes in order to remove expressions which they thought unedifying;" and adds, that "no doubt such changes were made in a good many cases of which no record has been retained;" and then proceeds to make out an instance on his own account from the variation in the name of Saul's son and successor as given in the Books of Samuel and in 1 Chron. viii. 33. (Pp. 78, 79.)

Author's Accusations of the Scribes met by himself.

Our author has the unhappy faculty of adducing evidence and then exaggerating it, and then neutralizing the evidence even in its exaggerated dimensions. The eighteen corrections of the scribes in his hands become the evidence of a very general correctional habit, of whose operation he can discern other instances than those pointed out by the Rabbins, which are sufficient to prove that these guardians of the text were not sound critics; but when he has stated these formidable premises, he abandons them, and tells us "that the standard copy which they ultimately selected, to the exclusion of all others, owed this distinction not to any critical labour which had been spent upon it, but to some external circumstance that gave it a special reputation. Indeed," he continues, "the fact which we have already referred to, that the very errors and corrections and accidental peculiarities of the MS. were kept just as they stood, shows that it must have been invested with a peculiar sanctity; if, indeed, the meaning of the so-called extraordinary points—that is, of those suspended and dotted letters, and the like—had not already been forgotten when it was chosen to be the archetype of all future copies" (p. 80).

It would seem difficult to find even among the oddities of Talmudic argumentation anything to match this. The scribes who were the guardians of the text are to be proved incompetent or untrustworthy; and the proof is, that only in eighteen instances have they ventured to touch, by change, the sacred text! Our logician, it is true, conjectures other instances besides these; but as soon as this conjecture is advanced, it is met and neutralized by the admission of a reverence for the sacred text, cherished by these same transcribers, which led them to transmit, "just as they stood, the very errors and corrections and accidental peculiarities of the MS." from which they copied!

Text to be transmitted was without Vowel-Points.

To enhance our conceptions of the difficulty of the task of these scribes, and to shake our confidence in the correctness of the resultant record, our attention is called by this representative of "the newer criticism," to the character of the text with which they had to deal. "They had," he says, "nothing before them but the bare text denuded of its vowels, so that the same words might often be read and interpreted in two different ways." What the lecturer meant to say here was, that the vowel sounds were not represented in the text at that time, an idea which the word "*denuded*" would scarcely convey, as that term necessarily implies their presence in the text at a previous time. As an example of the equivocal character of such a text, he mentions the historic reference in Heb. xi. 21, to Jacob leaning upon the top of his "staff," and points out the fact, that "when we turn to our Hebrew Bible, as it is now printed (Gen. xlvii. 31), we there find nothing about the 'staff'—we find the 'bed.' Well," he proceeds, "the Hebrew for 'the bed' is 'HaMMiTTaH,' while the Hebrew for 'the staff' is 'HaMMaTTeH.' The consonants in these two words are the same, the vowels are different; but the consonants only were written, and therefore it was quite possible for one person to read the word as 'bed,' as is now the case in our English Bible, following the reading of the Hebrew scribes, and for the author of the Epistle to the Hebrews, on the other hand, to understand it as a 'staff,' following the interpretation of the Greek Septuagint" (pp. 50, 51).

Vowelless Text all the easier of Transmission.

This critique on the "ambiguous" character of the text, as it is designated p. 51, with this illustration annexed, is fitted to shake confidence in the text transmitted to us, but only in the case of those who will not take pains to weigh the facts in the scales of common sense. The question raised by the facts submitted is simply this, Which is the more difficult of accurate transmission, a text consisting exclusively of consonants, or a text consisting of both consonants and vowels? Take as our example the one selected by our critic himself, this word which may mean either "the bed" or "the staff," according to the pronunciation given to it by the reader. A reference to the word as given above will settle the question at once; for it will be seen that while the word without the vowel-points embraces only six characters, the same word with the vowel-points embraces nine characters. The question, then, comes to this, Which is easier of accurate transcription and transmission,—a word of nine letters or a word of six? This question is one to be settled by actual experiment; and if the auditors who listened to this critique upon "the bare text denuded of its vowels"—and who, if they caught the spirit of the criticism, must have all but concluded that "the bed," which had proved to be a bed of death to the patriarch Jacob, was likely to become the death-bed of our present Hebrew text—had but taken the trouble of writing out the word commented on, with, and without, the vowels, even in our own current English characters, they would have reached the very opposite conclusion to that aimed at by the orator of the hour. It might be put down as a canon of transcription, that the fewer the characters to be transcribed, the less liable is the scribe to make mistakes.

Ignorance of Import not a Foe to accurate Transmission.

But our critic is ready with another difficulty in the way of accurate transcription and transmission: " Beyond the bare text, which in this way was often ambiguous, the scribe had no guide but oral teaching. They had no rules of grammar to go by. The kind of Hebrew which they themselves wrote often admitted grammatical constructions which the old language forbade; and when they came to an obsolete form or idiom, they had no guide to its meaning, unless their masters had told them that the pronunciation and sense were so and so" (p. 51).

The question here is, What effect would this alleged unacquaintance of the scribes with the *meaning* of the words they were transcribing have upon the accuracy of the transcription? This also is a question not very difficult of settlement. It may be laid down as a canon applicable to such a case, that the transcription would be affected only when a scribe attempted to give a meaning to a word of whose meaning he was ignorant. Even ignorance requires conditions for its operation; and the scribe's ignorance of the meaning of a word could affect his transcription of it only when, instead of simply copying the symbols of the unknown term, he tried to indicate his interpretation of it by other signs than those presented in the MS. he was copying. Recurring to the example already given,—Jacob's bed,—and assuming that the scribe found before him "the bare text *denuded*" (as our author expresses it) "of its vowels," and could see nothing save HMMTTH, and did not know whether it meant "the bed" or "the staff," would the ambiguity of the expression, or even his utter ignorance of its meaning, prevent him from transcribing it correctly? Beyond intelligent challenge, neither in the one case nor in the other could error in transcription arise save when the scribe would attempt the execution of a function which did not belong to him as a scribe, arrogating to himself the prerogatives of an interpreter. While he kept by the textual characters of that "bare text denuded of its vowels," he could work no mischief on the record. Only when, in order to interpret, a thing which his task as a transcriber did not embrace, and which the great reverence for the Hebrew text, admitted by the author to exist, forbade, he betook himself to the insertion of those vowels of which, according to the expression employed, the text had been "*denuded*," could he by any possibility fall into error, except he substituted another word for the one before him. But, according to the representation made by the lecturer, the system of vowel-points was the final result of the labours of a guild of technically-trained scholars, called the Massorets, or "possessors of tradition,—that is, of tradition as to the proper way of writing the Bible. These Massorets laboured for centuries, and their task was not completed till at least 800 years after Christ" (p. 72). This is strong testimony in favour of the position already mentioned, viz. that during the intermediate period between the time of Ezra and the rise of the Massorets, the sacred text was not very likely to be changed by the introduction of the chief disturbing element—to wit, the vowel-points. During all that period HMMTTH was most likely to remain HMMTTH, unmodified by an "*a*," or an "*i*," or an "*e*." Hence our author concedes (p. 73) that "all the evidence of variations and quotations later than the first Christian century points to the received text as already existing practically as we have it, but we cannot follow its history beyond that time."

Competency of the Massorets to vocalize the Record.

But the question remains, and it is one of deep interest, Were these Massoretic doctors competent to the task of giving voice to the bare consonantal text transmitted by their predecessors? Are we sure that the vowel-points introduced by them, not only above and below the consonants, as this book alleges, but also in their bosom at times, fairly enunciate the words of the sacred text, or rather, do they give a true grammatical interpretation of it? As we have already seen from the illustration given by the author, to vocalize HMMTTH is neither more nor less than to give a meaning to it. By inserting "*a*," "*i*," "*a*," these signs become "the bed;" and by inserting "*a*," "*a*," "*c*," they are transformed into "the staff." A process by which such changes can be wrought in the meaning of a word, may work vast transformations on a record. How, then, are we to determine whether the Massorets have employed their science of *punctuation* with intelligence and fidelity in the discharge of the sacred trust reposed in them? This, after all, is not a very difficult question. It is not very different from the question, How are we to determine whether King James's translators, or the recent revisionists of their labours, have translated the New Testament intelligently and with fidelity? The cases are not widely different, for it is just as true of a Greek word, that it may stand for more than one thing, as it is of a particular combination of Hebrew consonants. On turning to a Greek Lexicon, one may find that the word he is about to translate has half a dozen or more meanings; how is he to ascertain which of all these he is to select as the representative of that word in his translation? The only guide he has is his own common sense, and the effect of the selected meaning upon the sentence taken as a whole and upon the context. If the selected meaning be necessary to the sense, and makes the sentence read well, and does not place it at war with its immediate environment, the presumption is that the selected meaning is the true one. And as it is with translation, so is it with Massoretic vocalization. The Massorets have vocalized the Hebrew text so as to make it read well, and the vowel-points they have inserted are necessary to the enunciation and interpretation of its consonantal combinations. It is true Hebrew has been read, and may still be read, without these points; but only by the use of certain Hebrew letters called, in consequence of their *quasi* vocal nature, and the help they afford in enunciation, *matres lectionis*, and with the aid of vowel sounds which the reader has been instructed to employ where the *matres lectionis* are not available. It is also true, as our author states, that the synagogue rolls are unpunctuated to this day. But, nevertheless, it still holds good that these Massorets have proved themselves such masters of their language, that the ablest Hebraists of our day rarely find it necessary to change the punctuation they have adopted and transmitted to us.[1] So unquestionable are the results of their labours, that, as we have already seen, our author has to confess, despite all his criticisms, that "the

---

[1] *Delitzsch's Confidence in the Accuracy of the Vowel-Points.*—This estimate of the knowledge possessed by those old Hebraists is in accordance with that entertained by the best Hebrew scholarship in Europe. In his Commentary on Habakkuk, Delitzsch speaks of it as follows:—"How is the enigma to be resolved, that the punctuator shows (as always elsewhere) the deepest insight into the relation of these words to the preceding, as well as into their meaning, whilst the Targums, Talmud, and Midrash have wholly lost the key and vent the silliest stuff? The tradition which the Targumist had at his command reaches back certainly beyond the Christian era, and yet we are to believe the punctuation of the text to be the work of the school at Tiberias! One, who is acquainted with the expositions of Scripture

final result of their labour was a system of vowel-points and musical accents which enable the trained reader to give exactly the correct pronunciation, and even the correct chanting tone, of every word of the Hebrew Old Testament" (p. 72).

in the Targums and Talmud, will scarcely think possible such a fixing of its sense by written signs at a time when scriptural interpretation had long been converted by the Midrash into the plaything of a capricious fancy" (*Der Prophet Habakuk ausgelegt von Franz Delitzsch*, p. 202). Without giving any opinion regarding the antiquity of the vowel-points, this verdict respecting their accuracy may be accepted.

CHAPTER VI.

THE NEWER CRITICISM AND THE DOCTRINE OF SACRIFICE.

AS we have already seen again and again, "the newer criticism," as developed in these lectures, "denies that these things (sacrifice and ritual) are of positive divine institution, or have any part in the scheme on which Jehovah's grace is administered in Israel," prior to the exile. This is the interpretation which our author puts upon the language of the pre-exilic prophets referred to above. We are to understand the prophets as teaching by such language, that Jehovah has not enjoined sacrifice. "This," however, we are told, "does not imply that He never accepted sacrifice, or that ritual service is absolutely wrong. But it is at best mere form, which does not purchase any favour from Jehovah, and might be given up without offence. It is," he says, "impossible to give a flatter contradiction to the traditional theory that the Levitical system was enacted in the wilderness. The theology of the prophets before Ezekiel has no place for the system of priestly sacrifice and ritual" (p. 288).

It is not necessary to discuss over again the import of those utterances of Isaiah, and Jeremiah, and Amos, and Hosea, and Micah, on which this negative doctrine of God's attitude toward sacrifice and ritual, in pre-exilic times, is so confidently based. The interpretation on which its advocates proceed is contradicted by the spirit, and in some instances by the language, of the context, while it arrays the prophets before the exile against the prophets of post-exilic times, and against the divinely appointed institutions of their own times, and makes some of these pre-exilic prophets contradict themselves. So long as it is admitted that the first Temple, with its characteristic furniture, was a divinely authorized and authenticated institution, there would seem to be no possibility of denying, at least with any show of reason, that sacrifice and ritual had, during its continuance, positive divine sanction.

Worship by Sacrifice, and all that belongs to it, uncommanded prior to the Exile.

What we have to consider at present, however, is not the import of these texts, but the import of this theory of uncommanded yet accepted sacrifice and ritual. The doctrine is, that the notion that God's favour may be secured by sacrifice and ritual service, is of natural, and not of supernatural, origin. "What is quite certain is that, according to the prophets, the Torah of Moses did not embrace a law of ritual. Worship by sacrifice, and all that belongs to it, is no part of the divine Torah to Israel. It forms, if you will, part of natural religion, which other nations share with Israel, and which is no feature in the distinctive precepts given at the Exodus. There is no doubt," our author continues, "that this view is in accordance with the Bible history, and with what we know from other sources. Jacob is represented as paying tithes; all the patriarchs build altars and do sacrifice; the law of blood is as old as Noah; the consecration of firstlings is known to the Arabs; the autumn feast of the vintage is Canaanite as well as Hebrew; and these are but examples which might be largely multiplied. The true distinction of Israel's religion lies in the character of the Deity who has made Himself personally known to His people, and demands of them a life conformed to His spiritual character as a righteous and forgiving God. The difference between Jehovah and the gods of the nations is that He does not require sacrifice, but only to do justly, and love mercy, and walk humbly with God. This standpoint is not confined to the prophetic books; it is the standpoint of the ten commandments, which contain no precept of positive worship. But, according to many testimonies of the pre-exilic books, it is the ten commandments, the laws written on the tables of stone, that are Jehovah's covenant with Israel. In 1 Kings viii. 9, 21, these tables are identified with the covenant deposited in the sanctuary. And with this the Book of Deuteronomy agrees (Deut. v. 2, 22)" (pp. 298, 299).

This extract puts our author's doctrine beyond doubt. During the whole pre-exilic period, "worship by sacrifice, and all that belongs to it, is no part of the divine Torah to Israel." Sacrifice, it is true, was offered, and there is nothing in the language of the prophets implying that it was never accepted (p. 288); but it was never enjoined during all that vast period of Israel's history. During all this time, God's dealings with them, so far as there was any express or positive indication of His will, were upon the basis of the ten commandments. In other words, salvation, or, to use a more appropriate expression (as salvation on such a basis is out of the question), acceptance with God, was, during that period, by the works of the law and not through the righteousness of faith! This system, too, is very old. It pervades the Bible history, running back through the whole patriarchal age even to Noah. The basis of the covenant with Israel is the ten commandments; and God's acceptance of Israel depended not upon the expiation of their sins through "the blood of bulls, or of goats, or the ashes of an heifer sprinkling the unclean," but upon their doing justly, loving mercy, and walking humbly with Him! In a word, the way of acceptance (for it were a perversion of language to call it salvation) prior to Josiah's day, or prior to the exile, was purely Socinian!

To make this sketch absolutely correct, the only modification necessary is that (in all likelihood) God was moved to the acceptance of these pre-exilic worshippers, despite their legal shortcomings, by a sacrifice and ritual which He had never enjoined!

The Theory assumes the Human Origin of Sacrifice.

The first question raised by this series of assertions is the question respecting the origin of sacrifices. Our author does not *formally* raise it or discuss it. He simply assumes that sacrifices belong to the religion of nature. The question, however, is one which he was under special obligation to raise, and under very special obligation to discuss and settle, before proceeding one step with his argument in support of the post-exilic theory of the divine authentication of sacrifice. That theory stands or falls with the theory that sacrifice is of human and not of divine origin. It is only by assuming that men devised this mode of worship, and practised it from Adam to Ezra, without any intimation from God that sacrifice was an essential element in worship, that the advocates of its post-exilic origin, as a divinely authenticated institution, can even claim to be heard. As they do not deny that both Israel and the nations practised sacrifice, and regarded it as an important element, and indeed a fundamental element, in worship, it must follow that if this mode of worship was not of human origin, it must have been originated by God, and therefore must have had pre-exilic and ante-patriarchal sanction—a sanction antecedent to all sacrificial worship, and coeval with the first sacrifice. It was therefore a question which "the newer criticism" should have placed in the forefront of its appeal to "the Scottish public." Our author, in making his appeal, should have said to the *Christian element* of "the Scottish public:" "Brethren, I belong to a school of criticism whose views of the way of acceptance with God differ somewhat from the use-and-wont of Scottish theology. Holding with this school, I do not regard sacrifice as an essential condition of the acceptance of the worshipper with God. Consistently with this view, I look upon all sacrifices presented in patriarchal times, and antecedently to the close of the Babylonish exile, as unauthorized and destitute of divine sanction. I admit and teach that from the days of Ezra this mode of worship was formally adopted by Jehovah, but I hold that, prior to that epoch in the history of Israel, His attitude toward sacrifice (although I do not say that He never accepted it, or that ritual service is absolutely wrong) was simply negative, and I deny that 'sacrifice or ritual had any part in the scheme on which Jehovah's grace was administered in Israel.' This, of course, implies that sacrifice is the offspring of man's reason, and this I hold myself bound to establish at the outset."

Some such avowal of the doctrine of sacrifice held by the school in whose name our author claims to speak, was about as little as the Christian portion of the Scottish public could have expected. Instead of this, however, the appellant passes by this question as if it did not merit formal discussion, and merely tries to sustain the theory of the human origin of sacrifice by hints which imply it. To these hints attention is requested.

The Author's First Assertion.

The first hint is, that "it forms, if you will, part of natural religion, which other nations share with Israel" (p. 298). This hint amounts simply to this, that the fact of the universal prevalence of sacrifice among the nations proves that sacrifice was of human and not of divine origin! This assertion, of course, rests upon the assumption that the universality of a doctrine or practice can be accounted for only by assuming that it has its foundation in the constitution of man, or is so clearly revealed in external nature that all men have, of necessity, come to see its appropriateness, and been led to adopt it. On the former of these assumptions, the doctrine of sacrifice must belong to the category of primary beliefs, or beliefs which are the necessary outcome or offspring of the nature of man; on the latter, there must be such a revelation of it in external nature that no nation has failed to make the discovery. Consistently with these alternative hypotheses, it may be held that sacrifice, discovered in one or other of these ways by our first father, who lived nearly one thousand years to establish this form of worship, may have been to his posterity a matter of tradition, confirmed by the findings of their religious consciousness, or by external nature.

Universal Prevalence of Sacrifice consistent with a Divine Origin.

At the outset, it must be manifest that this theory of the universal prevalence of sacrifice is purely gratuitous. It is just as easy to account for the universal prevalence of this mode of worship among the nations by referring it to a divine revelation, as by referring it to a constitutional prompting, or to indications of it given in the constitution of external nature. An original revelation to Adam on this subject would be as likely to gain universal acceptance, and pass into universal practice, as an original Adamic discovery. The theory, therefore, has no advantage over the ordinary doctrine. So far as the universal prevalence of this mode of worship is concerned, it would be as readily accounted for by assuming a divine as by assuming a human origin of sacrifice. The posterity of Adam would be as likely to hold fast the tradition in the one case as in the other.

Human Origin of Sacrifice not reasonable.

But passing from these merely *a priori* considerations, let us look at the two theories in the light of reason. Is it reasonable to suppose that the human mind would ever devise a sacrificial system as a mode of divine worship? Could it ever occur to any rational being that he could render himself acceptable to God by taking away the life of His creatures? Would the very opposite conclusion not be much more reasonable? Might he not more reasonably conclude, that by slaughtering God's innocent creatures, and rending them in pieces, and pouring out their life's blood, and burning them upon an altar, he would incur the divine displeasure? Reason reveals itself in the adoption of means which have a natural tendency to secure the end aimed at; but here the means adopted have no connection, discernible by human reason, with the end proposed, while, on the other hand, so far as reason can judge, the means adopted are fitted to expose the worshipper to the divine rebuke.

Argument from the fact that Sacrifice preceded the Use of Animal Food.

This consideration gains force when account is taken of the fact that worship by sacrifice prevailed before man had been authorized to slaughter animals for food. At the time Abel brought of the firstlings of his flock, and of the fat thereof, this permission had not been given, and man had therefore no authority to destroy animal life. As the dominion over the animal creation given to man, at that stage of his history, did not embrace the power of life and death, it is much more reasonable to assume that a pious man, such as Abel was, would conclude that he had no right to put the sheep that God had given him to death in any form. or for any purpose. This, at least, would seem to be beyond dispute, that the reasonableness of approaching God by means of sacrifice, in the days of Abel, is not so clear as to warrant the conclusion that this mode of worship was a device of human reason. The whole circumstances point to the opposite conclusion. The natural conclusion is, that Abel "brought of the firstlings of his flock, and of the fat thereof," in accordance with a divine command.

Argument for Divine Origin from Abel's Offering.

Indeed, this conclusion would seem to follow, of necessity, from the fact that Abel's offering was made in faith and met with divine acceptance. Faith is correlative to faithfulness, and, in this case, to the faithfulness of God, and hence implies a divine promise. But the faith that comes to God through sacrifice must be correlative to a faithfulness pledged in a promise connected with sacrifice; and this is all one with saying that God had, at that time, revealed His purpose of mercy in connection with a sacrificial system, and had promised to accept those who came before Him in that appointed way. The faith that is acceptable to God is not a blind faith. It is a faith that believes God; and a faith that believes God must have hold of a word which God has spoken. Between this conclusion and the doctrine that Abel's sacrifice was an act of will-worship there is no middle ground. Nor is it unworthy of note that the acute Dr. Priestley, who at one time attributed the rise of sacrificial offerings to anthropomorphic conceptions of God, was led to change his views, because of the unlikelihood of Cain and Abel being influenced by such considerations, and to give it as his opinion, in treating of their offerings, that, "on the whole, it seems most probable that men were instructed by the Divine Being Himself in this mode of worship."

Now, one thing which adds great force and significance to this case of Abel's offering is, that it is the only instance of public worship mentioned in the history of the entire antediluvian age, a period of over sixteen hundred years. So far as Scripture sheds light on the subject of the mode of public worship during that period, there is every reason to believe, and no reason to doubt, that there was no other mode of *public* worship known to man or acceptable to God. The way in which the solemn transaction is introduced, implying a previous use-and-wont of the same kind, the mention of the divine acceptance of the offering, and the subsequent reference to it in the New Testament, bespeak a ceremony divinely instituted and devoutly observed.

Argument from Noah's Sacrifice.

The case of Noah seems to confirm this conclusion. Noah was a preacher of righteousness, and was singled out by God as a singular monument of His grace. He was warned of God to prepare an ark to the saving of his house, and was admitted into His secret counsel respecting the impending doom of a guilty world. Are we to suppose that God would be careful to reveal to him with such minuteness of detail everything about the mode of the temporal deliverance, while at the same time He was careful to conceal from him the mode in which the great spiritual redemption promised through the bruising of the woman's seed was to be achieved? The whole history of God's dealings with him and his family, and the whole transaction on Ararat, are irreconcilable with such a view. It seems inconceivable how any one can read the account of Noah's first act of worship on coming out of the ark, and yet hold, as our author does, that God's attitude towards his burnt-offerings was simply negative or neutral. God was manifestly pleased with Noah's offerings, for we are told by the sacred historian, who tells us so little about antediluvian worship, that "the LORD smelled a sweet savour; and the LORD said in His heart, I will not again curse the ground any more for man's sake, . . . neither will I again smite any more every thing living as I have done. While the earth remaineth, seed-time and harvest, and cold and heat, and summer and winter, and day and night, shall not cease. And God blessed Noah and his sons," etc. (Gen. viii. 21–ix. 1). Surely this is no mere negative attitude. Could an act of worship, as to its mode, be more emphatically sanctioned? It is not simply that God accepts Noah, and blesses the earth, and blesses both Noah and his sons, but that He does so on smelling his burnt-offerings. The Lord, we are told, "smelled a sweet savour," and the mention of this fact must be intended to teach us that the Lord took cognizance of the mode as well as of the spirit of the worship, and that the mode had His sanction. Now, as it cannot be for a moment imagined that the odour of burning flesh is acceptable to God, who is a Spirit, or that the reason of man, or the promptings of his religious consciousness, would ever lead him to invent such a means of rendering himself or his worship acceptable to his Creator, the only inference which seems at all in consonance with reason or common sense is, that the smell of the burnt-offering was acceptable to God because of the relation which that burnt-offering, as a type, sustained to the great Antitype of all the sacrifices offered by God's people throughout all dispensations, whether pre-exilic or post-exilic.

The Author's Second Assertion.

With the second argument, or assertion rather, viz. "that sacrifice and its accompanying ritual formed no part of the distinctive precepts of the exodus," it is unnecessary to deal further than has been done already. The argument or assertion, as has been shown before, overlooks the fact that "the distinctive precepts of the Exodus" embrace the commandments connected with the institution of the Passover, which was a truly sacrificial ordinance. This baseless assertion is surely sufficiently met by this counter assertion, which is based on the Scripture account of the Exodus.

The Author's Third Assertion.

The third argument, or assertion, or hint, reduces God's covenant with Israel at Sinai to a covenant of works, representing, as it does, that covenant as consisting of the ten commandments written on the two tables of stone, apart from any "precept of positive worship," or any symbol of satisfaction demanded by the law. This account of the transaction at Mount Sinai is, of course, a direct contradiction of the account given, Ex. xxiv., which informs us that the covenant at Mount Sinai was sealed with sacrificial blood, which was sprinkled on the altar and on the people, as the blood of the covenant, before the ten commandments were written on the tables of stone, Moses proclaiming the connection of the blood with the covenant in words that cannot be mistaken, "Behold the blood of the covenant which the LORD hath made with you concerning all these words." According to the sacred narrative, the blood was correlative to the "ten words," and symbolized the satisfaction of their penal claims.

Argument confirmed by the Epistle to the Hebrews.

Of course this argument from Ex. xxiv. will not have much weight with "the newer criticism," as, according to the progressive analytic methods of that school, it is quite easy to show that this section of the chapter belongs to the priests' codex, and is of post-exilic origin. (See note, p. 433.) It is, however, a codex recognised by the author of the Epistle to the Hebrews, chap. ix. 18–22, whether "the newer criticism" will recognise it or not; and its testimony sets aside the doctrine of our author's third assertion as utterly out of harmony with the nature of the covenant into which God entered with Israel, and with the spirit of the whole economy inaugurated with burnt-offerings, and peace-offerings, and sprinkling of blood at Sinai.

Stripped, then, of all rhetorical garniture, the doctrine underlying this account of the Sinaitic covenant is simply this, that it was a covenant of works. Our author does not come out candidly and tell the Christian public of Scotland that this is the view of that covenant held by "the newer criticism," but that such is the doctrine here taught in this reduction of that covenant to the ten commandments set forth as the basis of God's intercourse with Israel is beyond question. The motto of the whole period is, "This do and thou shalt live." Such were the terms of the only covenant of God with Israel!

To Abraham's seed, then, but not to himself (!), were the promises of this covenant made; but we find that God made a very different covenant with Abraham, and that, too, a covenant which the law referred to by our author, as the sole covenant of God with Israel, could not disannul so as to make the promise of none effect. "For if the inheritance is of the law," as our author alleges, "it is no more of promise; but (and this is the condemnation of his naturalistic theory) God hath granted it to Abraham by promise."

Wherefore then serveth the Law?

But our author may ask, "What then is the law?" He may say, "Did not God covenant with Israel at Sinai on the basis of these ten commandments? and am I to be told that God's intercourse with Israel and His acceptance of them did not turn upon their fulfilling the terms of that covenant enshrined in the ark?" "Wherefore then serveth the law?" is a very natural question, and merits an answer; and the best answer is that given by the apostle, who seems to have anticipated the difficulties of the Scottish school of "the newer criticism." His answer is, "It was added because of transgressions, till the seed should come to whom the promise was made; and it was ordained by angels by the hand of a mediator."

Such is the apostle's account of the relation of the law to the covenant; but it is very different from the account of this relationship given in these lectures. According to the apostle, the law was added to the covenant; according to "the newer criticism," the law is itself the covenant.

It would be difficult to frame a theory of Old Testament history, or of God's revelation of the way of life, more antagonistic to the economy of redemption, or evincing less acquaintance with the relation of the economy of grace to the economy of law, than our author has revealed in these lectures. In dealing with such anti-evangelical dogmatism, one is at a loss to know where to begin. The author is right in alleging that the ten commandments "are identified with the covenant" (p. 299). Identified with it they are, beyond all doubt. They exhibit the terms on which alone God will hold intercourse with Israel. Such are the terms of the covenant, but, as our author himself confesses, they "contain no precept of positive worship" (p. 299). It is not the business of the law to reveal the way of escape from the condemnation it utters, or the way in which the transgressors of it (and all are transgressors of it, for all have sinned and come short of the glory of God) may find forgiveness and acceptance with God. "By the law is the knowledge of sin," not the knowledge of salvation. By its verdict, reiterated by conscience, every mouth is stopped, and all the world brought in guilty before God. By deeds done by fallen man in satisfaction of its claims, there shall no flesh be justified in His sight. This is a truth not simply for the Romans, or for Paul's day, or for post-exilic times. "No flesh" must be taken in its widest scriptural comprehension, as embracing the whole posterity of Adam, and Adam himself.

These are among the A, B, C, of the truths of the Bible, and are we to be told that the revelation of them was reserved for post-exilic times? Is it to be proclaimed from the bosom of the Free Church of Scotland, that it was by doing justly, loving mercy, and walking humbly with God, that the men of pre-exilic times were justified? Are we to be told, in the face of the apostle's express declaration, that Abraham was justified by faith and not by works, that he was saved by works of justice, and mercy, and humility? Is this the gospel that was preached before unto Abraham? Is it come to this, that it is necessary to sound in the ears of the men of the present generation, what Paul uttered in the ears of the Romans eighteen hundred years ago, that if Abraham were justified by works he had whereof to glory, but not before God? Must the generation next after Chalmers and Cunningham be told, that "as many as are of the works of the law are under the curse"? It is surely not possible that well-nigh one-half of the ministers and elders of the Free Church of Scotland claim for those who hold such views of the history of redemption, as given in the Bible, the right to proclaim them from her Theological Halls.

Uncommanded Worship Unconfessional Doctrine.

But let us look at this theory of uncommanded yet accepted pre-exilic sacrifice, in the light of the Sinaitic covenant as sketched by "the newer criticism" itself. This covenant consisted, we have seen already, of the laws written on the two tables of stone, and it is alleged that these "contain no precept of positive worship" (p. 299). These ten commandments, nevertheless, do contain a very important precept about worship. As interpreted by the Westminster divines, whose doctrinal formularies our author has subscribed, one of these commandments "forbiddeth the worship of God by images, or in any way not appointed in His word." According to this interpretation of the second commandment (and it must be regarded as the interpretation of all who have subscribed our Confession of Faith and Catechisms), it is a breach of it to worship even the true God in a way which He has not appointed in His word. This is, of course, all one with saying that it was a breach of the Sinaitic covenant, as held by "the newer criticism," to worship God by sacrifice prior to the days of Ezra, for "the newer criticism" teaches that this mode of worship was uncommanded, and therefore not appointed, in pre-exilic times.

Uncommanded Worship a Breach of the Sinaitic Covenant.

Here, then, "the newer criticism" has prepared for itself another dilemma. Either worship by sacrifice was appointed by God in pre-exilic times, or it was not. If it was not appointed in pre-exilic times (and "the newer criticism" says that it was not), then worship by sacrifice during that entire period, at least from the inauguration of the Mosaic economy, must have been a breach of the Sinaitic covenant, and all such acts of worship must have been regarded by God as idolatrous. This, of course, is the only horn of the dilemma which the advocates of the post-exilic theory can lay hold of, and it is manifestly, in the case of those who have subscribed our standards, a last resort. They must, when they reflect on their own recognised interpretation of the second commandment, feel when they take hold of this horn very much as Joab did, when, holding by the horns of the altar (for altars were sacred in Joab's section of the pre-exilic period), he saw Benaiah, the son of Jehoiada, approaching him the second time.

Nor is it open to our author to reply, "I see another horn, a very little one, it is true, but still a horn, where the sword of Benaiah cannot reach me. It is the horn of 'non-injunction,' or, to speak plainly, if not reverently, the horn of non-committal, for my doctrine is that 'Jehovah has not enjoined sacrifice.' I have never said, nor does my school hold, that 'He has never accepted sacrifice, or that ritual service is absolutely wrong'" (p. 288). This reply, however, is not available, nor can this little horn prove a refuge from the Westminster Benaiah. This messenger of the king is not up in the distinctions of "the newer criticism," and cannot discriminate between "has not enjoined" and "has not appointed," and is as sure to slay the refugee at the little horn of non-injunction as at the other horn, which yet is not another, of non-prohibition.

In a word, the doctrine of the Sinaitic covenant, as held by "the newer criticism," cannot be reconciled with their doctrine of the non-injunction of sacrifice during the pre-exilic period of the history of God's covenant people. A covenant embracing the second commandment must have precluded the possibility of God's standing towards the sacrifices of Israel in an attitude of indifference. According to that commandment, He must have approved or condemned, and if we are to accept the interpretation of it given in our standards, He could not have accepted Israel's sacrifices unless He had commanded them. To say, as our author does (p. 288), that a service never enjoined by God may nevertheless be sometimes "accepted of Him," and that a service uncommanded is nevertheless "not absolutely wrong," is simply to contradict the interpretation already referred to, which makes the divine appointment essential to acceptance. This, it will be observed, is not a question about a "circumstance" of an established ordinance of worship; for it is readily admitted, and our standards and common sense teach, that "there are some circumstances concerning the worship of God, and government of the Church, common to human actions and societies, which are to be ordered by the light of nature and Christian prudence, according to the general rules of the word, which are always to be observed" (*Conf. of Faith*, chap. i. § vi.). The service of praise is commanded, but the tunes, etc., are left to be ordered by the light of nature. Preaching is a divine ordinance, but the Scriptures do not reveal a science of homiletics. The fact that the circumstances are left to man, under the aforesaid conditions, however, does not warrant the conclusion that men may frame distinct ordinances of worship, or devise modes of approach unto God, independently of His appointment. This latter, however, is the doctrine of this book; and this one feature of it strips it of all claim to Confessional or Scriptural authority, so far as one of the fundamental questions of divine worship is concerned.

CHAPTER VII.

THE NEWER CRITICISM AND THE DOCTRINE OF SACRIFICE
—*continued.*

IT is no marvel that our author, after such a sketch of Old Testament pre-exilic theology, should feel that his position creates a difficulty. "If it is true," he asks, "that they (the prophets) exclude the sacrificial worship from the positive elements of Israel's religion, what becomes of the doctrine of the forgiveness of sins, which we are accustomed to regard as mainly expressed in the typical ordinances of atonement?" (p. 301). This is a very natural question, and our author thinks it "necessary, in conclusion, to say a word on this head," and on a question of such interest it is but proper that he should speak for himself. He has reached the crucial test of his system, for, as he says (p. 305), "it is more important to understand the method of God's grace in Israel than to settle when a particular book was written" (although he settles the dates of most of the books of the Bible by what they teach regarding the method of God's grace). Having taken the ground that, whatever the age of the Pentateuch as a written code, the Levitical system of communion with God the Levitical sacraments of atonement, were not the forms under which God's grace worked, and to which His revelation accommodated itself, in Israel before the exile, it has become imperative to show that by taking away the doctrine of atonement he has not, with it, abolished the doctrine of the forgiveness of sins. He feels that "the newer criticism" is on its trial, and here is his defence: "When Micah, for example, says that Jehovah requires nothing of man but to do justly, to love mercy, and to walk humbly with God, we are apt to take this utterance as an expression of Old Testament legalism. According to the law of works, these things are of course sufficient. But sinful man, sinful Israel, cannot perform them perfectly. Is it not therefore necessary for the law to come in with its atonement to supply the imperfection of Israel's obedience? I ask you," he says, "to observe that such a view of the prophetic teaching is the purest rationalism, necessarily allied with the false idea that the prophets are advocates of natural morality. The prophetic theory of religion has nothing to do with the law of works. Religion, they teach, is the personal fellowship of Jehovah with Israel, in which He shapes His people to His own ends, impresses His own likeness upon them by a continual moral guidance. Such a religion cannot exist under a bare law of works. Jehovah did not find Israel a holy and righteous people; He has to make it so by wise discipline and loving guidance, which refuses to be frustrated by the people's shortcomings and sins. The continuance of Jehovah's love in spite of Israel's transgressions, which is set forth with so much force in the opening chapters of Hosea, is the forgiveness of sin.

"Under the Old Testament the forgiveness of sins is not an abstract doctrine, but a thing of actual experience. The proof, nay, the substance, of forgiveness is the continued enjoyment of those practical marks of Jehovah's favour which are experienced in peaceful occupation of Canaan and deliverance from all trouble. This practical way of estimating forgiveness is common to the prophets with their contemporaries. Jehovah's anger is felt in national calamity; forgiveness is realized in the removal of chastisement. The proof that Jehovah is a forgiving God is that He does not retain His anger for ever, but turns, and has compassion on His people (Micah vii. 18 seq.; Isa. xii. 1). There is no metaphysic in this conception, it simply accepts the analogy of anger and forgiveness in human life.

"In the popular religion the people hoped to influence Jehovah's disposition towards them by gifts and sacrifices (Micah vi. 4 seq.), by outward tokens of penitence. It is against this view that the prophets set forth the true doctrine of forgiveness. Jehovah's anger is not caprice, but a just indignation, a necessary side of His moral kingship in Israel. He chastises to work penitence, and it is only to the penitent that He can extend forgiveness. By returning to obedience the people regain the marks of Jehovah's love, and again experience His goodness in deliverance from calamity and happy possession of a fruitful land. According to the prophets, this law of chastisement and forgiveness works directly, without the intervention of any ritual sacrament. . . . According to the prophets, Jehovah asks only a penitent heart, and desires no sacrifice; according to the ritual law, He desires a penitent heart approaching Him in certain sacrificial sacraments. . . . And so the conclusion is inevitable, that the ritual element which the law adds to the prophetic doctrine of forgiveness became part of the system of God's grace only after the prophets had spoken" (pp. 301–304).

Exposition of the Author's Theory of Forgiveness.

Such is our author's answer to the question which he sees arises inevitably out of his doctrine respecting "the forgiveness of sins, which we are accustomed to regard as mainly expressed in the typical ordinances of atonement." The prophets, he tells us, know of no such condition of forgiveness as we have been accustomed to assume. The law is not, "the priest shall make an atonement for him, and it shall be forgiven him;" but Jehovah shall chastise him, and thus work penitence in him, and his sins shall be forgiven him. The sole condition of forgiveness is penitence and a return to obedience.

Then, again, forgiveness is not what we have been accustomed to think it is. It is not an abstract doctrine, but a thing of actual experience; and the proof, nay, the substance, of it is the continued enjoyment of those practical marks of Jehovah's favour, such as Israel enjoyed in Canaan! As regards the difficulties in the way of God's extending forgiveness to the transgressor, there do not seem to be any. There are no difficulties in its pathway which "this inalienable divine love," which is the ground of forgiveness, cannot overcome. The analogue of the divine forgiveness is found in the forgiveness which men extend to one another in the intercourse of life. As one man can forgive another, and should forgive another, upon the manifestation of penitence for an offence, "without the intervention of any ritual sacrament," so can God forgive sinners, without conditioning His forgiveness on the shedding or sprinkling of the blood of bulls or of goats.

Estimate and Classification of the Author's Theory of Forgiveness.

"These results," as our author says (p. 305), "have much larger interest than the question of the date of the Pentateuch." They raise, as he acknowledges, the question of "the method of God's grace in Israel." They raise, in fact, the questions discussed by Socinus and Grotius, questions involving the discussion of the fundamental principles of the economy of redemption. According to Socinus, there is nothing in the nature of sin, nothing in the nature or attributes of God, and nothing in the nature of the divine government, requiring the punishment of sin. According to Grotius, there is nothing in the nature of sin, and nothing in the nature or attributes of God, requiring the punishment of sin; but there is something in the nature of the divine government which requires that sin be punished. This something is the justice of God, not regarded as an essential attribute, but as a rectoral quality. According to our author, there is nothing in the nature of sin, nothing in the nature of God, requiring the punishment of sin; but there is something in the relation of Jehovah as the Moral Governor of Israel, requiring, not punishment, but chastisement.

On first sight, this theory of the method of God's grace seems to resemble the Grotian, or governmental theory, as it finds a reason for the infliction of suffering on sinners in God's relation as a Moral Governor. On closer inspection, however, this is seen to be a mistaken view of our author's doctrine. Grotius found in God's rectoral relation a necessity, not simply for chastisement, but for punishment; and held that the punishment demanded was demanded by the law and rectoral justice of God, and was regarded as a *solutio pœnarum*, serving the twofold purpose of a satisfaction of law and a deterrent from further acts of rebellion against the divine government. Our author's theory is widely diverse from this. It differs from it both in regard to the thing demanded, and the ground of the necessity for demanding it. The thing demanded, in our author's view, is not, as with Grotius, punishment, but chastisement; and the ground of the necessity of such a demand is not the claims of law or justice, but the relation of chastisement to forgiveness, the chastisement being inflicted simply to bring the sinner to the tender, regretful estate of penitence, which is represented as the sole condition of pardon and the returning favour of God.

This representation of the method of God's grace, in one of its fundamental points, is simply that given by Socinus. The only obstacle in the way of forgiveness, according to both, is subjective—the subjective obstacle existing not in God, but in man, and consisting in the hardness and impenitence of man's heart. The character of this obstacle determines the character of the economy of grace. According to Socinus, the means adopted are, such an exhibition of divine love as shall melt down and conquer all enmity, and bring the sinner to repent of his sin and sue for pardon. This estate of soul is the one requisite for the exercise of the divine prerogative of pardon. The means adopted for the exhibition of this all-mastering, all-constraining love, are the gift of God's own Son, and the sufferings He endured in life and in death. When the sinner apprehends the love of God thus displayed, so as to feel its power, he turns with penitential sorrow to a forgiving God, and finds himself in the embrace of the divine forgiveness. The means whereby the same, or at least a similar, estate of soul is reached, according to our author, are the varied castigatory instrumentalities and agencies employed by God in the exercise of "a just indignation, a necessary side of His moral kingship in Israel. He chastises to work penitence, and it is only to the penitent that He can extend forgiveness. By returning to obedience the people regain the marks of Jehovah's love, and again experience His goodness in deliverance from calamity and happy possession of a fruitful land. According to the prophets, this law of chastisement and forgiveness works directly, without the intervention of any ritual sacrament."

While the theory of our author very closely resembles that of Socinus, it differs from it in a very important particular, and that, too, in a particular which places the Socinian immensely above it. While both agree that God's love to sinners is revealed through suffering, and that the design of the suffering is to remove the subjective obduracy of the sinner's heart, and bring him to a proper subjective estate for the reception of the meditated forgiveness, they differ widely in regard to the subject on whom the suffering is inflicted. According to Socinus, the suffering is inflicted upon the Father's beloved Son; according to our author, it is inflicted upon the sinner himself. According to Socinus, there is a Mediator; according to our author, there is none. According to Socinus, there is at least the mediation of a suffering internuntius; according to our author, "this law of chastisement and forgiveness works directly, without the intervention of any ritual sacrament," either typical or symbolical, foreshadowing a Mediator, or indicating a mediation. According to Socinus, there is need for the agency of Christ to produce the requisite subjective estate; according to "the newer criticism," the same result was brought about, at least in pre-exilic times, by Philistia, or Syria, or Babylon. What is wrought through the agency of the Son of God, according to Socinus, was wrought, according to our author, through the agency of Benhadad, or Rabshakeh, or Nebuchadnezzar.

Simply one of the many Subjective Theories of Salvation.

Our author's theory is, after all, but one of the modern subjective theories of the atonement with Christ left out, the special providence of God toward Israel in pre-exilic times answering all the ends served by the Levitical system from Ezra to Christ, and, if this theory of forgiveness be true, all that is effected even by the death of Christ Himself. Here, then, according to "the newer criticism," is the result of critical scholarship, so far as the theology of pre-exilic times is concerned. "Whatever the age of the Pentateuch as a written code, the Levitical system of communion with God, the Levitical sacraments of atonement, were not forms under which God's grace worked, and to which His revelation accommodated itself before the exile" (p. 306).

Gravity of the Question thus raised.

In weighing this theological result, one cannot wonder, as has been already observed, at the author's conclusion, that "these results have a much wider interest than the question about the date of the Pentateuch," as "it is more important to understand the method of God's grace in Israel than to settle when a particular book was written" (p. 305). There can be no second opinion about the gravity of the conclusion reached. It must be a matter of no ordinary interest to the Church of Christ, either in Scotland or elsewhere, be it Presbyterian or not, whether God's grace from Adam to Ezra worked on the assumption that the sole obstacle in the way of forgiveness was to be found in the subjective state of the sinner himself; or, in other words, whether, during the whole history of our world prior to the Babylonish exile, the grace of God was administered upon Socinian principles as modified by "the newer criticism."

Author's Theory of Pre-exilic Grace seems to determine his Theory of the Date of the Pentateuch.

Still it is difficult to avoid the impression that the author's theory of the pre-exilic economy of God's grace has determined his theory regarding the date of every book which associates that grace with sacrifice, or "Levitical sacraments of atonement;" and it is equally difficult to see any other reason for referring those sacrifices, whose pre-exilic occurrence cannot be challenged, to the religion of nature. The critical method pursued throughout is to relegate all books, or parts of books, which ordain sacrifice or prescribe ritual, to post-exilic times, and to treat such sections as cannot, with any show of reason, be thus proscribed and postponed, as the offspring of natural religion.

But whatever may be the relation of his critical theory to his theory of the pre-exilic method of grace, the fact is, as has been already shown, that his views on this momentous question are neither more nor less than a modification of the doctrine of Faustus Socinus, derived from the elder Socinus, and that, too, a modification immensely inferior to the original Socinian scheme, as it dispenses with all mediatorial intervention between the sinner and an offended God, while the Socinian scheme gives to Christ the *quasi*-mediatorial position of an internuntius.

The Theory denies what the Confession affirms.

As our author claims, at the opening of Lecture XI., that these results " are not critical, but historical, and, if you will, theological," he cannot well object to their being subjected to historical and theological tests. To begin with the historical; it is manifest that, in the view of the Westminster divines, the covenant of grace, though " differently administered in the time of the law and in the time of the gospel," is nevertheless the same identical covenant under all dispensations. " Under the law it was administered by promises, prophecies, sacrifices, circumcision, the paschal lamb, and other types and ordinances delivered to the people of the Jews, all fore-signifying Christ to come, which were for that time sufficient and efficacious, through the operation of the Spirit, to instruct and build up the elect in faith in the promised Messiah, by whom they had full remission of sins, and eternal salvation; and is called the Old Testament" (*Conf.* chap. viii. § v.). This statement is at once historical and theological. Its theology is federal, and the claim it advances for this federal theology is, that it covers the whole historic ground of the Old Testament dispensation. It proclaims a covenant of grace as the form in which the divine purpose of mercy was revealed, and it teaches that the method in which this covenant was administered embraced the very elements which our author's history and theology leave out for more than three thousand years, or relegate to the religion of nature. According to the Westminster divines, this covenant "was administered by promises, prophecies, sacrifices, circumcision, the paschal lamb, and other types and ordinances;" according to our author, the covenant had nothing to do with sacrifice or anything belonging to it. "What is quite certain is, that, according to the prophets, the Torah of Moses did not embrace a law of ritual. Worship by sacrifice, and all that belongs to it, is no part of the divine Torah to Israel. It forms, if you will, part of natural religion, which other nations share with Israel, and which is no feature in the distinctive precepts given at the Exodus. There is no doubt that this view is in accordance with the Bible history, and with what we know from other sources" (p. 298).

Now to say, as our author says here, that "the law of Moses did not embrace a law of ritual," and "that worship by sacrifice, and all that belongs to it, is no part of the divine law to Israel," is about as flat a contradiction of the foregoing statement of the Confession of Faith as can be framed. The two statements are manifestly contradictory and irreconcilable. The very method of administration which the Confession says was in operation under the law given to the Jews, is the method which, if we are to accept the teaching of this book, was no part of the divine law to Israel. "The standpoint of the prophetic books," in which alone we are to look for the method of the divine administration in pre-exilic times, "is the standpoint of the ten commandments, which contain no positive precept of worship, and these ten commandments written on the two tables of stone are Jehovah's covenant with Israel" (p. 299). In the one statement, the covenant is indissolubly joined to positive ordinances of worship, including sacrifices; in the other, all positive precepts of worship are discarded and repudiated, that the grace of God may work directly through chastisement, "without the intervention of any ritual sacrament" (p. 303).

So far, then, as our author's historico-theological theory, in its chief positive feature, is concerned, there can be no doubt that it is not only destitute of Confessional authority, but that it is directly contradictory of the doctrine of the Westminster divines.

The Theory omits what the Confession asserts.

But besides, his theory differs from the Westminster

doctrine of the method of the divine administration under the pre-exilic period in what it omits, and this, too, in regard to the vital question of an administrator. It finds no place, as has been already shown, for the mediator of the covenant, while the Westminster divines teach that all the blessings enjoyed, embracing the remission of sins and eternal salvation, were conditioned upon faith in the promised Messiah, through whom alone these blessings were conferred.

Further Justification of this Charge.

The justice of this charge of departure from the Westminster doctrine of the covenant of grace, and the method of its administration under the law, is still further confirmed by the next section of the same chapter (§ vi.): "Under the gospel, when Christ the substance was exhibited, the ordinances in which this covenant is dispensed are, the preaching of the word, and the administration of the sacraments of Baptism and the Lord's Supper; which, though fewer in number, and administered with more simplicity and less outward glory, yet in them it is held forth in more fulness, evidence, and spiritual efficacy, to all nations, both Jews and Gentiles; and is called the New Testament. There are not, therefore, two covenants of grace differing in substance, but one and the same under various dispensations."

The doctrine here is, that there is but one Testament or Covenant, and that this one Covenant has been administered differently under various dispensations, Baptism and the Lord's Supper taking, under the New Dispensation, the place of circumcision, sacrifices, and the paschal lamb, mentioned in the preceding section as the administrative ordinances of the Old. This, of course, is all one with saying that "the ritual sacraments" of the Old Testament sustained to the covenant of grace under that dispensation the same relation that the sacraments of Baptism and the Lord's Supper sustain to it under the New. As the language employed leaves no room for doubt on this point, it must be obvious that the Westminster divines did not hold the doctrine avowed in these lectures, viz. that during the pre-exilic period "Jehovah asks only a penitent heart and desires no sacrifice" (p. 304). The men who penned the seventh chapter of our Confession would have listened with astonishment to a member of that venerable assembly who, rising in his place, would have given forth such utterances as the following: "The difference between Jehovah and the gods of the nations is, that He does not require sacrifice, but only to do justly, and love mercy, and walk humbly with God" (pp. 288, 289). "According to the prophets, this law of chastisement and forgiveness works directly, without the intervention of any ritual sacrament" (p. 303). "The prophets altogether deny to the law of sacrifice the character of positive revelation; their attitude to questions of ritual is the negative attitude of the ten commandments, content to forbid what is inconsistent with the true nature of Jehovah, and for the rest to leave matters to their own course" (p. 305).

Statements of this kind would certainly have excited surprise among the theologians assembled at Westminster, and their surprise would have been nothing the less when informed that they were the sentiments of a countryman of the learned and accomplished theologian, George Gillespie, and of the heavenly-minded, reverential Samuel Rutherford. Had they reached that stage of their proceedings, they would very likely have referred such an anti-sacrificial theologian to their interpretation of the second commandment, and read him a lecture on the subject of will-worship, if, indeed, they did not demand his immediate expulsion from their counsels. As the result of an historical investigation (and our author claims that it is historical), there could be no theory of the covenant, and the method of its administration during the pre-exilic period, more palpably antagonistic to the Westminster account of the history of the covenant of grace.

The Confession does not admit the Author's Distinction of the Economy into Pre-exilic and Post-exilic.

Nor can our author exculpate himself from this very grave charge, by alleging that he holds with the Westminster divines that the grace of God ran in the sacramental channel of sacrifice and ritual from the time the law entered, the sole point in dispute between him and them being as to the time at which the law came in, or, as he says St. Paul puts it in Rom. v. 20, the time at which "the law came in from the side (νόμος δὲ παρεισῆλθεν)." This will not serve as an exculpation, nor does it at all make the divergence charged one whit the less, for the Confession recognises no pre-exilic period, long or short, during which the covenant of grace was not sacramentally administered. This is clear from the fact that it represents the covenant as Abrahamic, and teaches that it was administered by promises, prophecies, and circumcision, as well as by sacrifices, etc. And our Saviour tells the Jews that circumcision was not of Mosaic origin, but of the fathers (John vii. 22).

Meaning of the term Law in the Epistle to the Romans.

It is noteworthy, in passing, that the meaning our author has attached to the term *law* in the passage he cites from Paul, Rom. v. 20, is not the meaning attached to it by the apostle himself. Throughout this Epistle the law is pre-eminently the moral law, and not the ceremonial as a distinct institution. It is the law that reveals itself by its works written in the heart, the law to which conscience bears witness, the law which is not made void through lack of circumcision, and whose claims are not met by circumcision alone, apart from obedience; it is the law by which every mouth is stopped, whether of Jew or Gentile, and whereby all the world becomes guilty before God. It is the law by which we have the knowledge of sin, the law whose claims were met by the propitiation made by Christ, the standard in accordance with which God acts when He justifies him that believeth in Jesus; it is the law that is not made void but established by faith. It is the law that worketh wrath; it is the commandment which was ordained unto life, and which the apostle found to be unto death; it is the law which is holy, and just, and good; it is the law of sin and death, the law whose righteousness is fulfilled in the justified, who walk not after the flesh but after the Spirit; it is the law to which the carnal mind neither is, nor can be, subject. It is therefore not alone ". the law of commandments contained in ordinances," which our author alleges " came in from the side," and whose entrance marks the inauguration of the Levitical system, but the Mosaic economy as a whole, embracing both the moral and the ceremonial law.

This interpretation of the term law in this passage is all the more singular, as the context shows that it was given by Moses, *i.e.* given with a fulness and explicitness previously unknown in the history of God's dealings with men. If this be true (and if our author's argument has any intelligible meaning, this law, which he says came in from the side, must have been given by Moses), then it is manifest that our author has completely circumvented himself, for his position in these lectures, and elsewhere, is that Moses left no written law save the ten commandments. If so, it would seem that this law must have been not the ceremonial but the moral law.

If Moses gave no Priestly Torah, how can the Levitical System be developed from Mosaic Principles?

Nor can it be said in reply, that the law given by Ezra, or some one else, at the end of the exile, may still be said to have been given by Moses, as it is but a development of the principles of the Mosaic legislation; for if Moses simply gave the ten commandments, the ceremonial law cannot be regarded as a development of Mosaic principles. If, as our author states (p. 298), "the Torah of Moses did not embrace a law of ritual;" and if, as he says in the next sentence, "worship by sacrifice, and all that belongs to it, is no part of the divine Torah to Israel;" and if, as he tells us on the next page, the ten commandments contain no precept of positive worship, by what process of development can there be evolved, from such a Torah, a law of ritual, embracing every detail of priestly orders, and priestly attire, and priestly actions; and every detail of sacrificial Torah, embracing the most minute particulars respecting the species, qualities, age, etc., of the victims? In his article "Bible" in the *Encyclopædia Britannica*, our author's account of the process is that ancient writers were not wont to distinguish between historical data and historical deductions; but the problem to be solved does not admit of such extempore solutions. It is not: given the necessary historical *data*, to deduce therefrom a given historical system. On the contrary, it is: given, in a particular historical legislative system, nothing save exclusively moral *data* (and of set purpose exclusively moral), to deduce therefrom a given historical legislative system which shall be absolutely ceremonial! Such is the problem which "the newer criticism" has to face, and compared with it the problem submitted to the science of the age by Darwin and his coadjutors is simplicity itself.

Historical Deductions from the Ten Words of Moses.

That the dimensions of this problem, and the magnitude of the difficulties involved in the solution of it, may be estimated, let us look at some of the historical deductions which we are informed were drawn forth from the ten words of Moses in the days of Josiah, and, at a later stage, in the days of Ezekiel or Ezra:—

"Unto the place which the LORD your God shall choose out of all your tribes to put His name there, even unto His habitation shall ye seek, and thither thou shalt come: and thither ye shall bring your burnt-offerings, and your sacrifices, and your tithes, and heave-offerings of your hand, and your vows, and your free-will offerings, and the firstlings of your herds and of your flocks. . . . Take heed to thyself that thou forsake not the Levite as long as thou livest upon the earth. . . . Thou shalt offer thy burnt-offerings, the flesh and the blood, upon the altar of the LORD thy God: and the blood of thy sacrifices shall be poured out upon the altar of the LORD thy God, and thou shalt eat the flesh" (Deut. xii.). Such is one phase of the evolutionary process as exhibited in one of the arches of that Deuteronomic bridge by which the Mosaic Torah is connected with the Levitical system. How the pre-exilic side of the arch is made to rest on the two tables of stone is not as yet explained. As modern masonry, in obedience to modern engineering, has succeeded in transforming sand into stone, and by this means has laid substantial foundations even in quicksands, so it may be that "the newer criticism" has been able to devise, through its knowledge of arts lost for ages, some material whereby it has managed to fill up the chasm which, up to the days of Josiah, separated the Mosaic tables from the Levitical Torah.

Other Arches of the Ceremonial Viaduct.

But let us look at the Ezekielian and Esdrine arches of this ceremonial viaduct. In Ezekiel we have the following description of a section of it as seen by him in vision in one of the mountains of Israel: "And it shall come to pass that when they (the priests) enter in at the gates of the inner court, they shall be clothed with linen garments; and no wool shall come upon them whiles they minister in the gates of the inner court and within. They shall have linen bonnets upon their heads, and shall have linen breeches upon their loins. . . . . Neither shall they shave their heads, nor suffer their locks to grow long; they shall only poll their heads" (Ezek. xliv.). Next in order is the Esdrine arch, the pattern of which he brought from Babylon: "And Moses brought Aaron and his sons and washed them with water. And he put upon him the coat, and girded him with the girdle, and clothed him with the robe, and put the ephod upon him, and he girded him with the curious girdle of the ephod, and bound it upon him therewith. And he put the breastplate upon him: also he put in the breastplate the Urim and the Thummim. And he put the mitre upon his head; also upon the mitre, even upon his forefront, did he put the golden plate, the holy crown; as the LORD commanded Moses" (Lev. viii.).

The Bridge does not reach all the Way across.

It will be seen at once that there is no difficulty in connecting the Ezekielian arch with the Deuteronomic on the one hand, or in connecting it with the Esdrine on the other. The sole difficulty, as has been already seen, lies on the other side of the bridge. The problem is, "How the traveller, when he has got as far as the Mosaic side of the Deuteronomic arch, is to effect a landing on the tables of the Mosaic Torah." When he has reached that point, let it be observed, he is still standing on the Levitical Torah, surrounded by altars, and priests, and sacrificial offerings, and carnal ordinances. Thus he stands, and as he looks toward the terminus to which "the newer criticism" told him the bridge would without fail conduct him, he discovers, to his amazement, a vast chasm digged by "the newer criticism" itself, and can hear, with still increasing astonishment, the Scottish herald of the school proclaiming, "You cannot get across; Moses spake no precept of positive worship. That Levitical structure on which you have made your way so far is no part of the divine Torah to Israel, and you must just abide where you are."

CHAPTER VIII.

THE NEWER CRITICISM AND THE DOCTRINE OF SACRIFICE—*continued*.

TO return to the figure of development, as the bridge must be abandoned, the problem propounded by "the newer criticism" is no ordinary one. It is neither more nor less than to trace the development of ceremonial *results* out of purely moral *data*. There is manifestly no other way of connecting this so-called post-exilic ceremonial legislation with the Mosaic Torah; and if the process of development cannot be shown, it ought not to be assumed; and if it cannot be shown nor assumed, "the newer criticism" cannot justify itself in claiming that the Levitical system has been historically, or otherwise, deduced from the principles of the Mosaic Torah. The question of historical development, therefore, is for "the newer criticism" a question of life and death. It has staked upon it not only its own character, but the character of all the sacred writers who have had anything to do with the alleged post-exilic legislation, so far as it is fathered by them upon Moses. The principle of the solution, as given in the article "Bible," has been already stated. At that time, however, the author seems not to have availed himself of all the adminicles furnished by "the newer criticism" for smoothing down and mitigating the charge of fraud which is implied in the claim of Mosaic authorship for post-Mosaic compositions. In these lectures he has returned to the subject, and placed before the Scottish public what, it is to be presumed, he regards as a more satisfactory vindication of these writers for the liberties which they have apparently taken with the name of the great lawgiver of Israel. As the theory is here at one of the gravest of the many crises which it is called upon to pass, even at the risk of tediousness, our author's newer or fuller explanation of this nice ethical point must be given at sufficient length to place it fairly before the reader. It runs as follows :—

"That the whole law is the law of Moses does not necessarily imply that every precept was developed in detail in his days, but only that the distinctive law of Israel owes to him the origin and principles" (original principles, probably ?) "in which all detailed precepts are implicitly contained. The development into explicitness of what Moses gave in principle is the work of divine teaching in connection with new historical situations.

"This way of looking at the law of Moses is not an invention of modern critics: it actually existed among the Jews. I do not say that they made good use of it; on the contrary, in the period of the scribes it led to a great overgrowth of traditions, which almost buried the written word. But the principle is older than its abuse, and it seems to offer a key for the solution of the serious difficulties in which we are involved by the apparent contradictions between the Pentateuch on the one hand and the historical books and the Prophets on the other.

"If the word Mosaic was sometimes understood as meaning no more than Mosaic in principle, it is easy to see how the fusion of priestly and prophetic Torah in our present Pentateuch may be called Mosaic, though many things in its system were unknown to the history and the prophets before the exile. For Moses was priest as well as prophet, and both priests and prophets referred the origin of their Torah to him. In the age of the prophetic writings the two Torahs had fallen apart. The prophets do not acknowledge the priestly ordinances of their day as a part of Jehovah's commandments to Israel. The priests, they say, have forgotten or perverted the Torah. To reconcile the prophets and the priesthood, to re-establish conformity between the practice of Israel's worship and the spiritual teaching of the prophets, was to return to the standpoint of Moses, and bring back the Torah to its original oneness. Whether this was done by bringing to light a forgotten Mosaic book, or by recasting the traditional consuetudinary law in accordance with Mosaic principles, is a question purely historical, which does not at all affect the legitimacy of the work" (pp. 310, 311).

The Import of all this.

Here, then, is our author's solution of the problem of ritualistic development out of purely ethical legislation, a legislation which uttered no precept of positive worship (p. 299), and which knew nothing of worship by sacrifice or anything belonging thereto (p. 298). Such were the author's views when he penned these latter pages; but when he reaches pages 310, 311, he has forgotten all this, and tells us that "Moses was priest as well as prophet, and both priests and prophets referred the origin of their Torahs to him." Nor is this all; for these two Torahs were once blended together, as appears from our author's statement on the last-mentioned page, where he says "that in the age of the prophetic writings the two Torahs had fallen apart." To an ordinary person not skilled in the methods of "the newer criticism," it would appear from this account of the matter that Moses did give something more than the purely moral Torah exhibited in the ten commandments. It would, indeed, be very singular that one who combined in his own person the two offices of prophet and priest should repress and hold in abeyance the priestly (which, if we are to credit "the newer criticism," is ever coming to the front and asserting itself to the repression of the prophetic), and content himself with executing the less illustrious functions of a prophet. It would appear, then, that originally there was but one Torah, which was both priestly and prophetic, and somehow or other (as it would seem, through priestly forgetfulness or priestly perversion, p. 311) the two elements of this one Mosaic Torah were divorced, and the Deuteronomic or the post-exilic reformation did but return to the standpoint of Moses, and bring back the Torah to its original oneness!

To our author this may seem explanation: to all men, save himself and the school he represents, it is more likely to seem self-contradiction. It amounts simply to this, that while the post-exilic Torah, with its Levitical priestly system, cannot be traced to Moses as a prophet, it can be traced to him as a priest. Now, as the thing to be traced back is pre-eminently priestly, it is obvious that its priestly elements must have existed in the priestly department of the one original undivided Mosaic Torah. If this be so, and so it must be, on our author's own showing, then how can it be said, as our author has taught throughout this book, that "the Torah of Moses did not embrace a law of ritual," and that "worship by sacrifice, and all that belongs to it, is no part of the divine Torah to Israel" (p. 298)?

How does the Author know that Moses was a Priest, or that his Torah had Priestly Elements?

But the question now arises, How does our author know that Moses was a priest, and that this original Mosaic Torah contained priestly elements? Whatever sources of information in regard to these two points "the newer criticism" may profess to have discovered, the sole reliable source, available or accessible, is the books of the Bible. With regard to external sources, two things may be said: first, that they are not contemporaneous, and therefore not of equal historical authority; and, secondly, that in no instance do they contradict the testimony of the Bible itself on the question at issue. Now these Biblical records, even when our author, under the guidance of Nöldeke and Wellhausen (see Note 4, Lect. xi.), has eliminated from them all traces of a Levitical Torah on which he can venture to lay his hand, still exhibit traces of a priestly Torah which he finds it impossible to delete, and traces, too, on which he has ultimately to rely for evidence when he is claiming for the post-exilic Levitical Torah an embryonic existence in the Mosaic legislation. Apart from these persistent, irrepressible testimonies, which bid defiance to the instruments and methods of "the newer criticism," he finds that there are no Mosaic priestly *data* from which to draw historical priestly deductions, and that without them he cannot trace to a Mosaic Torah the post-exilic priestly Levitical system. But when, in palpable contravention of the whole spirit and aim of the school with which he would fondly identify Biblical criticism in Scotland, he recognises these sections as authentic and genuine parts of the historic record, he brings his school into fatal collision with their own original thesis,—that the Torah of Moses was purely ethical, and "that a law of sacrifice is no part of the original covenant with Israel"

(p. 370). Verily Nöldeke and Wellhausen, and the "other recent" analyzers of "the Levitical legislation," have brought our author into deep waters. Genuine Biblical scholarship, however, will not allow the advocates of "the newer criticism" thus to play fast and loose with the sacred record, as Nöldeke or Wellhausen or others may list, now ignoring, now adoring, now exscinding, now remanding, selected sections of it, according to the exigencies of their shiftless and ever-shifting theories. That scholarship, sustained by common sense and common honesty, will compel these critics to give a reason for accepting so much of these sections as will serve to prove that Moses was a priest, and delivered to Israel an elemental priestly Torah, while they reject other sections historically blended with these accepted ones; and except they can give more cogent reasons than those furnished by our author in these lectures and elsewhere, the friends of true Biblical science, whether theological, historical, or critical, will reject their critical conjectures as the offspring of an unbridled unscientific imagination.

In justification of this verdict upon our author's attempt, it is but necessary to refer the reader to the book itself. The chief and ever-recurring reason for his sectional evisceration of the priestly portions of the Pentateuch, as has been already shown, is that the priests, and judges, and kings, and prophets, could not have known of the existence of these parts; and the proof of this, again, is that they did not live, or act, or speak, in accordance with the fully developed Torah they reveal!

It is unnecessary to say anything in addition to what has been already said in refutation of this argument. To argue from the action of Eli and his sons, or from the action of Ahaz and Urijah, that the fully developed Levitical Torah did not exist in their days, is about as reasonable as to argue that Eli did not know the fifth commandment, and that his sons knew neither the fifth nor the seventh, and that neither Ahaz nor Urijah was aware of the existence of the second. And to argue from the utterances of the prophets the non-existence of the Levitical system, is as much against "the newer criticism," in its final stand upon an elemental pre-exilic Mosaic Torah, as it is against a fully developed Mosaic Levitical Torah, since the language of the prophets relied on to prove the non-existence of the latter, is equally available to prove the non-existence of the former. The reader will be surprised to find, as he may on examination, that when these two classes of arguments, with their collateral supports, are eliminated from these lectures and the appendix, the book is reduced to an absolute chaos, and left in about as hopeless a state of disorganization as its author has sought to inflict upon the Pentateuch.

The Theory of Development demands what our Author cannot admit save at the Sacrifice of his Fundamental.

Let it be observed, then, that to preserve and retain in the Pentateuch a pre-exilic Mosaic priestly *nucleus*, out of which it may be possible to develop the so-called post-exilic Levitical Torah, "the newer criticism" is compelled to confess that Moses was a priest, and was the author of at least an elemental priestly Torah; and all this after having laid it down as a clearly established position, by the laws of an unquestionably scientific criticism, that "what is quite certain is that, according to the prophets, the Torah of Moses did not embrace a law of ritual," and that "worship by sacrifice, and all that belongs to it, is no part of the divine Torah to Israel" (p. 298). Is it possible to retain the priestly *nucleus*, and accept this result of this so-called scientific criticism? If it be "quite certain," and *the* thing which "is quite certain," that "the Torah of Moses did not embrace a law of ritual," and equally certain that "worship by sacrifice and all that belongs to it, is no part of the divine Torah to Israel," it must also be "quite certain," not simply that "the Torah of Moses" and "the divine Torah to Israel" did not contain a fully developed Levitical system, but that neither the one Torah nor the other, neither the Torah as Mosaic nor the Torah as divine, contained even the *nucleus* of the Levitical system. The Levitical system, as fully developed, reveals two things, viz. sacrifice and ritual, and if these were not in the *nucleus*, the system cannot claim to have been developed from it. But, if we are to credit "the newer criticism," no such elements are to be found in the original elemental Mosaic Torah, and consequently the post-exilic Levitical legislation, themselves being judges, can have no connection, either historical or logical, with the Mosaic Torah.

The Charge of Fraud still remains.

Neither the article "Bible," therefore, nor the present series of lectures, can be regarded as freeing the author from the grave charge of ascribing fraud to the author or authors of the post-exilic legislation. In fact, this recent attempt at explanation has but served to make the justice of the charge all the more manifest. The only possible vindication would have been that which has been here advanced, had the theory, taken as a whole, admitted of it. The credit of the sacred writers, on our author's theory, might perhaps have been saved could he have shown, what he has asserted without proof, viz. that they developed the Torah of the post-exilic times out of a pre-exilic Mosaic *nucleus;* but by denying the existence of sacrifice or law of ritual in this Mosaic Torah, they have stripped themselves and the sacred writers of even this defence, and left these holy men of God, who spake as they were moved by the Holy Ghost, to lie under the grievous charge of a fraud, which their proposed explanation only renders the more palpable.

Our author's theory of the pre-exilic unpriestly, unsacrificial Torah therefore remains, and refuses any righteous adjustment, and, thus abiding, carries with it, as an inevitable consequence, the rejection of our Confessional doctrine of "the scheme on which Jehovah's grace was administered in Israel" during the pre-exilic period. It is impossible to reconcile the two schemes. If the Westminster divines are right in teaching that the covenant of grace, under the law, was administered by circumcision, sacrifice, and the paschal lamb, etc., the doctrine of this book, which excludes "the intervention of any ritual sacrament" from the economy of grace during the same period, must be wrong; and the wrongness of it becomes all the more patent when its inventors try to eke it out by asserting, in apology for the sacred writers, what the theory at the very outset denies, and what the great body of this book aims at disproving,—to wit, that Moses was the author of a priestly as well as of a prophetic Torah, and that it is only when the prophetic and the priestly Torahs are reconciled that the worship of Israel "returns to the standpoint of Moses" (p. 311).

Principles at Stake in this Discussion.

As has been already shown, the scheme propounded as the one "on which Jehovah's grace was administered in Israel" in pre-exilic times, is simply a modification of the subjective scheme of Socinus. The arguments against the one, therefore, are equally available against the other. The fundamental questions for settlement in dealing with both are the same, and are the fundamental questions raised in connection with the constitution and administration of the economy of redemption. One's estimate of the scheme will be determined by his views of the nature, attributes, and prerogatives of God, and of His relations to finite moral agents; also by his views of the nature of sin and holiness; also by his views in regard to free agency, and the ability of a man, simply under the influence of chastisement, to come to a truly penitent estate, and render an obedience such as the holy, omniscient, omnipresent, righteous Jehovah could accept. In connection with the questions which at once spring up around these determining points, it will be found impossible to avoid the question of mediation. In the very forefront stands the momentous question: "How shall One possessing the attributes of vindicatory justice, and holiness, and truth, take Abel, or Enoch, or Noah, or Abraham into fellowship with Himself, and sustain toward them, or any of the fallen, guilty, unholy sons of men, the relations which God is represented in the Scriptures as sustaining to Israel?" To this question the human mind, constituted as it is, must demand an answer; and it is the question of all times,—exilic, or pre-exilic, or post-exilic. It is simply the question put by the man of Uz, "How should man be just with God?" (Job ix. 2). Job could see the necessity for a Goel; but we are told that Job lived in post-exilic times. It is, however, not unlikely that if the book that bears his name had not laid such stress on piacular sacrifices for his sons and for his friends, there would have been no hint given of a post-exilic date. At any rate, Job's question has its well-spring in man's heart; and it insists on an answer, and will accept of none which does not proclaim the Goel apprehended by the patriarch of Uz. If sin from its inherent nature merits punishment, and if God, because of His own unchangeable nature, as an infinitely holy and righteous Being, must punish it, then the pardon of sin, and the acceptance of the sinner as righteous, must be impossible apart from the intervention of a Goel, who shall meet, for the transgressor, the claims of the law and justice of God. Penitential tears, even though the unregenerate heart of man could shed them, cannot erase the dreadful record of past transgression; and no future acts of obedience, even though the natural man could perform them, can atone for previous disobedience, or justify God in justifying the penitent. If God must be just in justifying, and if His law is not to be made void in accepting the ungodly as righteous, then there must be an atonement for sin, and a perfect obedience rendered by one who is *competent* and *authorized* to do both.

These are among the primary, fundamental principles of the economy of redemption, and cannot be regarded as peculiar to any one dispensation. They are principles for all times, whether pre-exilic or post-exilic. The economy is based upon them, and is based upon them because of the nature of sin and the character of God. If, therefore, sin was forgiven under the Old Testament, or, to put it otherwise, if Abel, and Enoch, and Noah, and Abraham, and David were justified, then justification must have proceeded upon these principles. If these men were justified, their iniquities must have been assumed by a Daysman, and laid upon him by Jehovah Himself; and this Daysman must have taken their place before the law, and undertaken to meet all its demands upon them, whether preceptive or penal. As the latter class of its claims demanded satisfaction made to the divine justice, the Daysman must suffer in their room.

The Theory Unreasonable.

Now, it seems most unreasonable, if such were the character of the economy of redemption, to be disclosed in all its glory and matchless grace in the fulness of the times, that no hint at all of this, its fundamental feature and chief glory, as an expression at once of the love and the justice of "a redeeming God," should have been given, with divine sanction, through all the vast period of our world's history covered by the term "pre-exilic times." Yet, if we are to credit "the newer criticism," such is the fact. Abel was saved under this economy, and worshipped by sacrifices foreshadowing mediatorial sufferings, and yet he knew it not. Enoch walked with God, and prophesied about the advent of his Lord, and the doom of the ungodly, and never obtained a hint of his indebtedness to the Mediator for his acceptance and the fellowship he enjoyed. Noah was chosen from the midst of an ungodly generation as a subject of the sovereign grace of God, and was delivered from the doom of his wicked contemporaries, and, at the close of that fearful outpouring of the divine vengeance, worshipped, as Abel did, by sacrifice, and yet had no knowledge of the import of these sacrificial acts enacted by himself on Ararat. Abraham, too, walked with God, and was justified by faith and not by works, and was informed that in his seed, who was to descend not from Ishmael, but from Isaac, all the families of the earth should be blessed; but if the theory that the grace of God in pre-exilic times wrought, not *mediately* through the intervention of any ritual sacrament, but *directly* through the law of chastisement and forgiveness, he must have lived and died in ignorance of the doctrine of salvation through the sufferings or merits of the promised seed. And this Abrahamic ignorance will appear all the more strange when it is borne in mind that Abraham was in the habit of worshipping by sacrifice, and was actually taken formally into covenant relation with God by sacrifice; and stranger still, when Christ's testimony to the faith of Abraham is considered: " Your father Abraham rejoiced to see my day; and he saw it and was glad " (John viii. 56). The conversation between Abraham and his son Isaac, as they drew near to Mount Moriah on that awful errand, proves conclusively that worship by sacrifice was no strange thing to father or son. How natural, how simple, and yet how instructive, on this point, is that affecting dialogue! " And Isaac spake unto Abraham his father, and said, My Father: and he said, Here am I, my son. And he said, Behold the fire and the wood; but where is the lamb for a burnt-offering? And Abraham said, My son, God will provide Himself a lamb for a burnt-offering: and so they went both of them together." This incident carries us into the family history of Abraham at Beer-sheba. Isaac knew what the fire and the wood meant, but was at a loss to know where his father should find a lamb for a burnt-offering. He could not have known the import of the preparatory elements, or have asked about the missing element, had he not been accustomed to sacrificial ceremonies at home. And when the son is released from that awful agony of expected sacrificial doom, and the father's heart relieved from the no less poignant anguish of inflicting it, by the direct interposition of God, Abraham knows how to proceed with the sacrifice of the divinely-provided substitute, and offers up the ram " for a burnt-offering *in the stead of* his son." Verily these men of the pre-exilic times knew a little more about the way of access to God than " the newer criticism" gives them credit for. The child Isaac connected sacrifice with worship because he had been accustomed to that mode of worship at home.

This incident sheds great light not only on Abrahamic, but on patriarchal and early pre-exilic worship, and warrants the conclusion that the grace of God in Abraham's day did not, as our author would have the Free Church of Scotland believe, work directly by " the law of chastisement and forgiveness, without the intervention of any ritual sacrament," but, on the contrary, that it revealed itself through the medium of atoning sacrifices, which kept before God's people their own personal unworthiness, and the conditions of pardon and acceptance, as embracing expiation by the blood of an atoning substitute. If our author had been as careful to generalize such incidental references to pre-exilic custom in the matter of sacrificial worship, as he shows himself to be in every instance where, by sheer straining of the record, it can be made to teach that the Pentateuchal Torah was unknown in pre-exilic times, he would never have written or published these lectures.

Another instance of the Author's proclivity for Generalization.

There is one instance of this spirit of adverse generalization which merits special notice. Speaking of the covenant into which the children of the captivity entered in the reformation of Ezra, he says: "It was not merely a covenant to amend certain abuses in detailed points of legal observance; for the people, in their confession, very distinctly state that the law had not been observed by their ancestors, their rulers, or their priests up to that time (Neh. ix. 34); and in particular it is mentioned that the Feast of Tabernacles had never been observed according to the law from the time that the Israelites occupied Canaan under Joshua,—that is, of course, never at all (Neh. viii. 17)" (p. 56). There is a generalization worthy of a scientific critic! "Since the days of Joshua the son of Nun unto that day," in which Israel under Ezra kept the Feast of Tabernacles, means "never"! The time covered by the one expression is the time covered by the other! As Israel had not kept the Feast of Tabernacles since the days of Joshua, they had never kept that feast according to the law at all! A more unwarrantable inference, a more unjustifiable generalization, could scarcely be imagined. It might be true that from the days of Joshua they had not observed that feast in any shape or form, and yet it would not follow that they had never observed it at all. It might have been that the feast was duly and legally observed till Joshua the son of Nun died; and that after his death, and the death of the elders who overlived him, the children of Israel, ever prone to backslide and forget both God and His law, neglected to give due attention to the ceremonies prescribed for the observance of this great annual feast. This interpretation is in harmony with the character of Israel; but there is nothing in the history of Israel, and nothing in the language of Nehemiah, that will warrant the sweeping generalization of our author,—a generalization of the expression, *since the days of Joshua the son of Nun*, into a period comprehending the whole history of Israel!

Nor is this all. Not only is this generalization unwarrantable, but the interpretation on which it proceeds makes Nehemiah contradict Ezra, who testifies (chap iii. 4) that the children of the captivity, ninety years before the instance mentioned by Nehemiah, had "kept the Feast of Tabernacles, *as it is written, and offered the daily burnt-offerings by number, according to the custom, as the duty of every day required.*"

Here, then, again our author, as his wont is, makes one sacred writer contradict another. He makes Nehemiah say that the Feast of Tabernacles had never been observed according to the law at all, while Ezra affirms that it had been observed ninety years before, and that the observance was *according to the writing and the custom,* thus implying that the observance was no novel thing in Israel. He has counselled his readers to cease sifting tradition, and accept the instructions of Ezra and Nehemiah; and, when his advice is accepted, he makes these guides contradict each other! And this, we are to believe, is scientific criticism!

This Adverse Generalization becomes eventually adverse to the Author.

But when he has achieved this scientific feat, what is the fruit of it? How does it help him in establishing his doctrine of the Esdrine or post-exilic doctrine of the origin of the Pentateuchal Torah? Instead of aiding or abetting his theory, it furnishes a flat contradiction of it. If this Torah did not come into existence till the days of Ezra, or till post-exilic times, it is not very wonderful that the Feast of Tabernacles had not been kept in accordance with it since the days of Joshua, even though we give that expression the all-comprehending import of "never at all." The only wonderful thing about the whole transaction is, that Ezra, and Nehemiah, and the people, and their princes, should have taken the matter so much to heart, and that they should have blamed not only themselves, but their fathers also, for the imperfect observance of a Torah which had only then come into being, and of which neither they nor their fathers had ever before heard. So wonderful, indeed, is this thing, that no one outside the circle of "the newer criticism" will believe it. All men of common sense will conclude that if Israel, moved by Ezra and Nehemiah, confessed their trespass, and the trespass of their fathers, in this matter of the observance of the law, the law must have existed during the lives of their fathers, and been obligatory at least since the days of Joshua.

On the assumption of the Torah, through which these reformers evoked this confession from their brethren of the captivity, being a new Torah, a very grave question regarding the morality of the procedure is raised. This question has been raised and discussed already, but it is ever cropping up because of its inseparable connection with a theory which is, at all its distinctive points, in antagonism with the history of the covenant and the mutual relations of its several parts. The question is simply this: "How could Ezra and Nehemiah stand up before the God of Israel, as His commissioners, and call upon His people to make confession of their sins, and the sins of their fathers, for their transgression of a Torah which they knew in their hearts neither the men then before them nor their fathers had ever heard of?" As there is no room for a second opinion regarding the morality, or rather the immorality, of this procedure, on the theory of "the newer criticism," it is better to raise a cognate question, and ask, How can one who has read these books of Ezra and Nehemiah stand up before audiences of Bible-reading Scotland, in its chief centres of intelligence, and affirm that the Torah which evoked such confession was then for the first time made known to Israel? As this cognate question also admits of but one answer, it were a work of supererogation to discuss it. Silence is sometimes charitable as well as golden.

It is not without good grounds, therefore, that the charge of a proclivity for adverse generalization, coupled with the opposite propensity of extreme frugality in the exercise of this faculty where the material would warrant a favourable generalization, has been preferred against the author of these lectures. Like the school he represents, he balances his theory upon small points and petty criticisms. So accustomed has he become to the use of the microscope of "the newer criticism," that he cannot any longer use both his eyes, or take in a horizon of wider diameter than the field covered by this narrowest of all critical instruments.

A Crucial Question to be answered by our Author.

But there is a collateral question arising out of the author's doctrine of sacrifice, to which those who are asked to accept it are entitled to demand a reply. As it appears from the Epistle to the Hebrews that this pre-exilic popular worship, with its Tabernacle and priesthood, its ritual and calendar, afterwards appropriated and endorsed by the God of Israel, was the shadow of which Christ is the substance, its priesthood the shadow of Christ's priesthood, its sacrifice the type of Christ's sacrifice, its atonements the type of His all-expiating death, its very Tabernacle with its mercy-seat a type of heaven itself with its throne of grace, into which our great High Priest has entered, not with the blood of others, but with His own blood, having obtained eternal redemption for us—as such typical relations subsist between the Levitical system and the economy of grace on earth and the estate of glory in heaven, the question necessarily arises, and must be answered, How comes it that there is such a correspondence—such a correspondence as can exist only between type and antitype—in all these detailed elements of the economy of redemption? Such correspondence can be accounted for only on one or other of the following hypotheses:—1. That the so-called natural system, as a typical system, was devised by God, and revealed at first to mankind. Or, 2. That the nations, including Israel, independently of supernatural instruction, forecast the whole constitution of the economy of redemption, with its priestly sacrificial Torah, and had such insight into its mysteries, that their vision outran its earthly manifestations, and penetrated into the *arcana* of the sanctuary in the heavens. Or, 3. That Jehovah, in devising the economy of grace, adapted its constituent elements, both in the sphere of the terrestrial and the celestial, to the preconceptions of mankind, making the earthly and human not simply the types, but the archetypes of the heavenly and divine. Or, 4. That the coincidence and wonderful concurrence of the human preconception and the divine counsel were purely fortuitous, and undesigned by either God or man. These hypotheses seem to exhaust the possibilities of the case, and there cannot be much difficulty in judging of their respective claims to acceptance. As regards the second, if, as we are informed in the New Testament, the redemption of the Church by Christ Jesus is designed, among other ends, to make known to the principalities and powers in heavenly places the manifold wisdom of God, it cannot be true that such a scheme was foreseen in all its essential elements by human wisdom. A scheme which human wisdom could devise, cannot, by any possibility, be set forth as revealing, not simply human wisdom, but divine wisdom in all its fulness and manifoldness.

Turning to the third hypothesis, it is found equally objectionable. Like the doctrine of conditional decrees, it makes the divine purposes and plans contingent upon the determinations of finite moral agents; and such a conception of the relation of the divine will to the human cannot be accepted, either in the economy of nature or of grace. Especially objectionable is such a conception when the economy foreshadowed by the rites and ceremonies of this so-called natural religion, is an economy whose mysteries have been hid in God before all worlds, mysteries which angels desire to look into, mysteries which even the prophets, who prophesied of the grace that should come unto us, sought and searched diligently to understand, and failed to fathom. Indeed, this latter fact is peculiarly pertinent to this case, for one of the things of which these prophets testified was *the sufferings of Christ*, the very thing which *the sacrifices* of this so-called natural religion came, by the divine *ex post facto* endorsement, to typify. Is it possible that any one, yea, that even the author of these lectures, can believe that an economy, which the very men who aforetime were inspired to predict it did not understand, could have been conditioned upon an economy which men, without divine instruction, were able to devise? So far are men in their natural estate from being able to devise such an economy, that we are told, on the authority of an apostle, that they cannot receive or know its mysteries even when they are revealed, and are informed by Christ Himself that except a man be born again he cannot see, or enter, the kingdom to which these mysteries pertain.

The mere statement of the fourth possibly conceivable hypothesis, is all that is needed to warrant and secure its rejection. No one can accept, even as a hypothesis, the conception that the coincidence between the sacrificial system of Jew and Gentile and the economy of redemption as presented in the New Testament, is fortuitous and undesigned, either on the part of God or man. Not until men have come to believe that the universe, with all its accurately balanced mechanical adjustments, and all its marvellous organic and inorganic interdependencies and mutual adaptations, has sprung into being through the fortuitous concurrence of atoms destitute of intelligence or life, can they be induced to entertain the belief that the coincidence, or the harmony of that ancient sacrificial system with the economy of redemption, is the offspring of chance.

The only Theory of the Coincidence in Harmony with God's Attributes.

These, then, are all the possible views of this unquestionable coincidence that can be taken; and the only view that any one who entertains Biblical views of Jehovah, or of the economy of grace, can possibly accept, is the first. It is the only one that can be reconciled with the attributes and prerogatives of One who is infinite, eternal, unchangeable in His being, wisdom, power, holiness, justice, goodness, and truth. But with the failure of the other hypotheses there is connected—inevitably connected—the failure of the central theory of this book, viz. that access to

God by the intervention of sacrifice, or " ritual sacrament," as a mode of approach positively sanctioned by Him, was unknown prior to the return of the Jews from Babylon. This conclusion necessarily follows; for if man's wisdom could not devise a scheme which is the highest manifestation of the wisdom of God that has ever been made even to the principalities and the powers in the heavenly places, then the typical system which so accurately foreshadowed it cannot have been a thing of human device. As this so-called naturalistic system did exist in pre-exilic times, and did, beyond all question, embrace the types and symbols of the divine economy afterwards, in the fulness of time, so gloriously revealed, there is no alternative left, to any intelligent mind, but to hold that these types and symbols were of divine devising, and were divinely revealed and authenticated to man. If so, then there never was a time in the history of sacrifice in Israel when it could be said, as " the newer criticism " says, that the divine attitude toward sacrifice or ritual was merely negative ; for, as we have seen, apart from a divine revelation of such a scheme, it never could have come into existence at all. In a word, a book which relegates those parts of the Pentateuch in which the economy of redemption is prefigured, by sacrificial types and symbols, to postexilic times, is, *ipso facto*, condemned as inconsistent with the divine origin, structure, and design of the economy of grace.

CHAPTER IX.

THE NEWER CRITICISM AND THE DOCTRINE OF WORSHIP.

OUR author's views on this subject merit special notice. On pp. 223, 224, he gives the following account of this deeply interesting and vital matter:—"To us worship is a spiritual thing. We lift up our hearts and voices to God in the closet, the family, or the church, persuaded that God, who is spirit, will receive in every place the worship of spirit and truth. But this is strictly a New Testament conception, announced as a new thing by Jesus to the Samaritan woman, who raised a question as to the disputed prerogative of Zion or Gerizim as the place of acceptable worship. Under the New Covenant, neither Zion nor Gerizim is the Mount of God. Under the Old Testament it was otherwise. Access to God—even to the spiritual God—was limited by local conditions. There is no worship without access to the deity, before whom the worshipper draws nigh to express his homage. We can draw near to God in every act of prayer in the heavenly sanctuary, through the new and living way which Jesus has consecrated in His blood. But the Old Testament worshipper sought access to God in an earthly sanctuary, which was for him, as it were, the meeting-place of heaven and earth. Such holy points of contact with the divine presence were locally fixed, and their mark was the altar, where the worshipper presented his homage, not in purely spiritual utterance, but in the material form of the altar-gift. The promise of blessing, or, as we should now call it, of answer to prayer, is in the Old Testament strictly attached to the local sanctuary. 'In every place where I set the memorial of my name' (literally, rather, where I cause my name to be remembered or praised), 'I will come unto thee and bless thee.' Every visible act of worship is subjected to this condition. In the mouth of Saul, 'to make supplication to Jehovah' is a synonym for doing sacrifice (1 Sam. xiii. 12). To David, banishment from the land of Israel and its sanctuaries is a command to serve other gods (1 Sam. xxvi. 19; compare Deut. xxviii. 36, 64). And the worship of the sanctuary imperatively demands the tokens of material homage, the gift without which no Oriental would approach even an earthly court. 'None shall appear before me empty' (Ex. xxiii. 15). Prayer without approach to the sanctuary is not recognised as part of the 'service of Jehovah;' and for him who is at a distance from the holy place, a vow, such as Absalom made at Geshur in Syria (2 Sam. xv. 8), is the natural surrogate for the interrupted service of the altar. The essence of a vow is a promise to do sacrifice or other offering at the sanctuary (Deut. xxvii.; 1 Sam. i. 21; compare Gen. xxviii. 20 seq.). This conception of the nature of divine worship," we are told, " is the basis alike of the Pentateuchal law and of the popular religion of Israel, described in the historical books and condemned by the prophets."

The Theory tested by Historical Facts.

If such were the conception of the nature of divine worship, it is no wonder the prophets rebuked the worshippers and condemned the worship. But the question is, Was this the conception of divine worship which is the basis alike of the Pentateuchal law and of what this book describes as the popular religion of Israel? Are we to believe that the saints of God under the Old Testament had no access to God save at some local sanctuary? Is it true that David, when he was banished from the land of Israel, and was living with Achish at Gath, in the land of the Philistines, or at Ziklag, had no access to Jehovah? It is true he used the ephod, but we are not told that he approached a local sanctuary, or offered sacrifice; and yet he had remarkable access, and received a remarkable answer, and had proof of Jehovah's acceptance in the direction of his band to the rendezvous of the Amalekites, and in the signal victory by which he smote and scattered their forces, and recovered both the captives and the spoil. David's inquiry by the ephod was worship, and it was made on the assumption that God would hear him at Ziklag in Philistia, as well as in Israel, and that He would hear him where he was, as well as at a local sanctuary, for he sent to Abiathar the priest, Ahimelech's son, to bring the ephod to him, and it was made on the assumption that He would hear him without his approaching, on all occasions, by sacrifice. David's view of the consequences of banishment from the land of Israel and from its sanctuaries, therefore, however those who drove him out might regard it, or whatever interpretation "the newer criticism" may put upon his language to Saul in the passage quoted above, evidently does not imply that during the term of his banishment he might not approach God as an inquirer, or seek counsel and guidance at His hands, except at some local sanctuary, and invariably through the shedding of sacrificial blood. With regard to the employment of the ephod in the inquiry, all that can be said is, that very little is revealed respecting the mode in which the request for information was made, or regarding the way in which the answer was returned. What is known in connection with the case is sufficient to prove that God could be worshipped (for inquiry was a form of worship) outside the land of Israel, apart from local sanctuaries, and apart from sacrificial rites performed, or interim vows made, in connection with every prayer, or other act of worship.

The argument based on the language of Saul (1 Sam. xiii. 12) simply furnishes another proof of our author's proclivity for adverse generalization. In his apology to Samuel for offering sacrifice before his arrival at the camp, "Saul said, Because I saw that the people were scattered from me, and that thou camest not within the days appointed, and that the Philistines gathered themselves together at Michmash; therefore said I, the Philistines will come down upon me to Gilgal, and I have not made supplication unto (before) the Lord; I forced myself, therefore, and offered a burnt-offering." Surely it must be manifest that Saul does not here refer to an ordinary act of supplication. The Philistines are preparing to attack Israel, and Israel and their king are waiting for Samuel that he may intercede for them by sacrifice before they engage in battle with their foe. Wearied with waiting, Saul orders the sacrificial rite to proceed; and this form of approach he calls supplication; and so it was. No doubt, if ever Saul prayed, he prayed as the smoke of his burnt-offering ascended before God. But to infer from this transaction that Saul regarded the expression " to make supplication " as " a synonym for doing sacrifice," is altogether unjustifiable. Every act of sacrifice is an act of supplication, but every act of supplication is not therefore a sacrificial act.

Arguments in support of the Theory based upon Erroneous Interpretations of Scripture.

Nor is this theory of worship sustained by the reference made to the conditions of worship at the sanctuary. It does not follow because Israel, in approaching God in His sanctuary, were required not to "*appear before Him empty,*" that is, without a gift, that God's people in their homes, or in their closets, might not draw near without gift or sacrifice. Especially out of place does this quotation appear when the context of this command is considered. This command (Ex. xxiii. 15) has reference to Israel's appearing before the Lord three times in the year, on the occasions of the great appointed feasts of the Lord. Nothing but an irrepressible proneness to generalization could impel any one to translate a command of such manifest speciality into a universal law, designed to regulate and condition all acts of worship, whether in public or in private. It is simply doing violence to all righteous exegesis to represent such special restrictions (intended, beyond all question, to apply only to stated occasions), as liturgical canons, to be observed in all acts of family worship, and in all the private devotions of every member of the household. This, however, is what is taught in these lectures. The generalization reached is, that "prayer without approach to the sanctuary is not recognised as part of the service of Jehovah!" The provision made (by the author) "for him who is at a distance from the holy place," is "a vow such as Absalom made at Geshur in Syria" (2 Sam. xv. 8). Absalom never offered a prayer during the three years he was at Geshur, and the proof is, that he vowed a vow, or at least told his father that he had done so!

Two obstacles, according to this generous science of criticism, were in Absalom's way. He was outside the land of Israel, and he was at a distance from the sanctuary. Gifts he could have presented, but he was too far off to give them in. What was true of Absalom, we are to believe, was true of the thousands of Israel under like circumstances; however they might multiply their vows while at a distance from the sanctuary, even though they might not be at Geshur, or elsewhere in other lands than Israel, there was one thing they might not do—they might not pray! As the mass of the nation, save when they were present at the great feasts of the Lord, were at a distance from the sanctuary, the conclusion, of course, is that, except on these occasions, prayer must have all but ceased throughout the nation. This conclusion would be modified on the theory of interim approaches at local centres of worship, but only somewhat modified; for even were it true that these local centres could be visited by all Israel once a week, which few will be apt to regard as a probable or a possible custom for a whole nation, still there remains an interim of the restraining and suspension of prayer, in fact, an embargo laid upon its exercise which cannot be brooked by any one who knows that the life ingenerated by the Spirit of God, when a man is born again, is a life manifested and sustained by prayer.

If it be alleged that the *vow* was regarded as a provisional basis for a prayer then and there offered, it is easy to reply, that the thing alleged, as already shown, is unsupported even by the instances on which our author relies, while it is contradicted by the whole history of prayer. The fact that men made vows, whether with or without prayer, whether in Old Testament or New Testament times, is no proof that they regarded their vows as the condition of the acceptance of their prayers. We find that even the Apostle Paul had a vow upon him, in conformity with which he had his head shorn in Cenchrea (Acts xviii. 18). It were surely a strange procedure to cite this historical incident to prove that the apostle of the Gentiles, full twenty years after his conversion, regarded a vow as "the natural surrogate" for that sacrifice upon whose efficacy even the intercession of Christ Himself depends.

As a Theory of Prayer the Doctrine is incredible.

Such, according to our author, was the worship which is "the basis alike of the Pentateuchal law and of the popular religion of Israel, described in the historical books and condemned by the prophets" (p. 225). If such it was, one cannot wonder that the prophets condemned it; nor does it seem strange that it was popular with Saul or Absalom; but it is certainly puzzling to think that it was popular with the others indicated in the textual references submitted in evidence. It is difficult to believe that such "a conception of the nature of divine worship" could have found favour with Jacob, or Hannah, or David. It taxes one's credulity rather much to accept a theory which carries with it the implication that none of these ever prayed to the God of their fathers except when they visited some local sanctuary,—that Jacob never prayed during his twenty-one years' residence in Padan-aram, save when he was in the neighbourhood of some extemporized Bethel; that Hannah never prayed at home; and that David never prayed at Ziklag, or during all his fugitive wanderings, when driven out from the reach of all local sanctuaries by the cruel jealousy of Saul!

Argument from the Book of Jonah.

The Book of Jonah, although not ranking with our author as veritable history, may nevertheless be accepted by him as shedding some light upon the views entertained by ancient mariners in relation to the connection between sacrifice and prayer. The men who sailed with Jonah evidently did not hold the views on this subject charged upon the men of their day by "the newer criticism." They did not wait to sacrifice before "they cried every man to his god." They held the doctrine of sacrifice, as is shown by their subsequent conduct; for when the sea, according to the prediction of Jonah, "ceased from her raging" after he was thrown overboard, "they feared the LORD exceedingly, and offered a sacrifice unto the LORD, and made vows." And Jonah seems to have held similar views, for we are told that he "prayed unto the LORD his God out of the fish's belly," believing, as the mariners did, that sacrifice would be as legitimate after prayer as before it.

If it be alleged in palliation or mitigation, that it would have been impossible for Jonah to sacrifice under the circumstances, the impossibility is readily admitted; but the concession lends no relief to our author's theory, for we find Jonah engaging very earnestly in prayer without sacrifice at Nineveh, where there was no hindrance to his adopting such a mode of approach.

Argument from Psalm cvii.

The doctrine of Jonah and of the men who sailed with him finds eloquent expression in Ps. cvii.: "They that go down to the sea in ships, that do business in great waters; these see the works of the Lord, and His wonders in the deep. For He commandeth, and raiseth the stormy wind, which lifteth up the waves thereof. They mount up to heaven, they go down to the depths: their soul is melted because of trouble. They reel to and fro, and stagger like a drunken man, and are at their wit's end. Then they cry unto the LORD in their trouble, and He bringeth them out of their distresses." Here, again, we have prayer without the contemporaneous offering of sacrifice. Neither these mariners nor the psalmist held the doctrine that men might not pray to God save when their prayers were mingling with the smoke of their sacrifices.

But when the theory is placed in the light of the history of the captivity in Babylon, it stands out, not only as an indefensible, but as an utterly inexcusable, conception of the religion of Israel. It is unnecessary to go into any detail of the historic facts and circumstances. Suffice it to say that, according to "the newer criticism," prayer in Israel must have ceased for seventy years!

Views of the Ancient Heathen on this Theory of Prayer.

This school of criticism must have strange conceptions of the nature of religion, to imagine that it could be sustained in the soul of any man, whether in pre-exilic or post-exilic times, by such infrequent approaches to God as this theory demands. The fact is, that the natural religion, which they allege was common to the surrounding nations, and practised by them as well as by Israel, should teach them better. Our author, especially, is fond of ruling our conceptions of everything Biblical, whether historical, or doctrinal, or critical, by the use and wont of ancient times. With such regard for ancient usage, it is singular that he has not consulted it on the subject of the connection between sacrifice and prayer. The doctrine current among the Greeks in Homer's day is indicated in the prayer addressed to the Sminthian Apollo by the old disconsolate priest Chryses, whom Agamemnon had dishonoured, and to whom he had refused to restore his beloved daughter. The prayer, as recorded by the poet, is very brief, but it covers the question at issue :

" Κλῦθί μευ, ἀργυρότοξ', ὃς Χρύσην ἀμφιβέβηκας
Κίλλαν τε ζαθέην Τενέδοιό τε ἶφι ἀνάσσεις,

Σμινθεῦ, εἴποτέ τοι χαρίεντ' ἐπὶ νηὸν ἔρεψα,
ἢ εἰ δή ποτέ τοι κατὰ πίονα μηρί' ἔκηα
ταύρων ἠδ' αἰγῶν, τόδε μοι κρήηνον ἐέλδωρ·
τίσειαν Δαναοὶ ἐμὰ δάκρυα σοῖσι βέλεσσιν."

"Hear me, O thou of the silver bow, who hast protected Chrusa and the sacred Killa, and dost rule mightily over Tenedos; O Smintheus, if *at any time* I have roofed for thee a beautiful temple, or if *at any time* I have burnt to thee fat thigh-pieces of bulls or of goats (that is, have offered to thee burnt-offerings), grant me this request: let the Greeks atone for my tears through thy weapons."

As the old priest, heart-stricken because of the dishonour done him by the son of Atreus, and oppressed with grief for the loss of his beloved child, went musing over the insult and bereavement along the shore of the loud-roaring sea, he did not think it necessary *there* and *then* to offer a sacrifice to his god before calling upon him in prayer. Enough for him that he was one of Apollo's worshippers, who was in the habit of honouring him with burnt-offerings of bulls and of goats, and erecting temples to his name. Such was the conception of Chryses, and if our views of the current "natural religion of ancient times" are to be regulated by the testimony of ancient writers, here we have it. The heathen of whom Homer sung did not regard their prayers as restricted to the times when they were standing by their altars and watching the smoke of their sacrifices ascending to their gods. In the interval of sacrifice, whether longer or shorter, the worshipper could, at any time, and in any place, whether by the shore of the barren sea or elsewhere, approach his god in prayer.

Origin of this Conception.

This conception which ruled the heathen mind and regulated their acts of worship was doubtless a lingering ray of the Noachian revelation. This Homeric incident, fairly interpreted, brings out distinctly the Scripture doctrine, that prayer, for acceptance, depends upon sacrifice; but it teaches also the scriptural doctrine that those who have made their peace by sacrifice, can pray at all times, and in all places. Our critic's appeal to natural religion, as he terms it, therefore, is not sustained by the history of that religion as practised by other nations than Israel. The heroes of Homer, as well as the priest of Apollo, are found calling upon their gods in every emergency. Achilles addresses Thetis, his goddess mother, without the intervention of sacrifice, and is heard by her. But it is unnecessary to multiply instances. Tried by his own critical canon, our author's theory of the necessity of the synchronism of the acts of prayer and sacrifice, must be rejected; while it cannot for a moment bear the test of its chosen Scripture references, nor approve itself to the understanding and heart of any man who knows by experience what prayer is.

The Theory implies Changeableness in Jehovah.

Nor does it relieve one's perplexity very much to be told that this conception of prayer, and its resultant or concomitant religion, condemned by the prophets up to the very hour of Israel's deliverance from Babylon, was then accepted by Jehovah, and enjoined upon the nation as the religion of priest, and prophet, and people, to be enforced with all the rigid exactitude of the perfected Levitical system, for a period of more than four hundred years! In fact, it is this latter element of the theory that ensures its condemnation not only in the court of Christian criticism, but in the court of conscience itself. Where conscience has not been perverted, it will be found impossible to believe that the holy, just, and true Jehovah, who is as unchangeable as He is holy, and just, and true, should, by the mouth of His prophets speaking in His name, continue to condemn a form of worship during all pre-exilic times, and that then, abandoning the attitude of antagonism and condemnation, He should frame a most elaborate system, embodying the entire scheme which for ages His prophets had been commissioned to denounce! It is not inconsistent with the revealed character of Jehovah to abrogate a system of positive enactments, issued under His own authority, in the exercise of His unquestionable sovereignty. Indeed, such abrogation is necessarily implied in the very nature and manifest design of such a system. But the case is very different where a system of human origin, which, as in the present instance, has, we are taught by "the newer criticism," been placed under ban by Jehovah Himself for centuries, is afterwards taken under His protection, and fortified by specific enactments, accompanied by sanctions involving, in some instances, the forfeiture of life itself. The difficulty of accepting such a theory is enhanced beyond solution, when we are asked to believe that this human system is not only sanctioned, but adopted as a typical economy to foreshadow the economy of redemption, with its one great High Priest and His one all-atoning sacrifice, and that its very Tabernacle is adopted as a figure of "a greater and more perfect Tabernacle, not made with hands."

One would think that the man who can accept such a theory of Old Testament worship, with its pre-exilic condemnation and its post-exilic *ex post facto* divine appropriation and endorsement, and its extraordinary parsimony of prayer, might be able to believe that Moses left on record more than the ten commandments, and might even believe that he was the author of the Pentateuch itself, including not only its "historical *data*," but even its "historical deductions."

CHAPTER X.

THE NEWER CRITICISM AND THE DESIGN OF THE MOSAIC ECONOMY.

THE fundamental error of the critical system represented in these lectures, arises from an utter misapprehension of the central idea of the Mosaic economy. No one having right conceptions of the design of that economy could speak of it as if the chief object of the mission of Moses, after the deliverance of Israel from bondage, was to put them in possession of the ten commandments. That economy, it is true, was intended to proclaim authoritatively and emphasize the moral law; but this in connection with a clearer revelation than had hitherto been made of the way in which the claims of that law were, in the fulness of time, to be met. The keynote of the economy is struck at the very hour in which Moses receives his commission. That interview at Horeb is a fair type of the whole dispensation which he is to introduce. At the very outset he is reminded of the holiness of Israel's God. The salutation, "Draw not nigh hither: put off thy shoes from off thy feet, for the place whereon thou standest is holy ground," precedes the gracious announcement of His covenant relation to father Abraham, and, through him, to Moses himself: "I am the God of thy father, the God of Abraham, the God of Isaac, and the God of Jacob" (Ex. iii. 5, 6). Thus spake the angel of the covenant from the midst of the burning bush to the future lawgiver of Israel, and in the spirit of this interview the whole economy proceeds. If Israel is to be delivered, the deliverance must not be achieved at the sacrifice of the claims of the Holy One who had taken them into covenant relation four hundred years before, and who, remembering His covenant, had now come down to fulfil His promise made to Abraham and his seed. (Compare Ex. ii. 24 with Gen. xv. 13–21 and Luke i. 68–79.) It is to assert and vindicate these claims that the ceremonial law is instituted.

Symbolic Import of the Passover.

The Passover is not a casual incident, or a mere family feast or national festival, as our author would have us believe. It is instituted to teach Israel, in the very hour of their emancipation, that they owed their deliverance from bondage not to their own moral pre-eminence over their Egyptian oppressors, but to the sovereign grace of their covenant God. Hence, and for this reason, the stroke that humbled the haughty Pharaoh was averted from the first-born of Israel by the interposition of sacrificial blood. The Passover was the ordained memorial not simply of their departure out of Egypt, and the breaking of the bonds wherewith their cruel taskmasters had bound them, but it was the memorial of the passing of the Angel of the Lord over their houses when he slew the first-born of Egypt. Throughout their generations the children of Israel were to be reminded that they had been shielded from the vengeful sword of the divine justice by the blood of the heaven-appointed victim. The memorial of their deliverance would impress them with the love of their redeeming covenant God; but it was such a memorial as must, at the same time, impress them with His holiness and wrath, and make them sensible of their just exposure to His righteous vengeance, which, if unaverted and unappeased by the blood of any interposing sacrifice, must have fallen upon them as well as upon their oppressors. The moral impression theory of God's dealings with Israel advocated in this book will not bear the test furnished by this unquestionably typical redemption of Israel out of Egypt; and it is no wonder that our author tries, by an unwarrantable limitation of the Hebrew word "*bashal*," to represent the paschal victim as non-sacrificial, although he has to do so in contravention of the history of the institution itself, and of the express teaching of our Saviour and His apostles.

It is true that the ceremony connected with the Passover was fitted to impress Israel with a sense of the love of their Redeemer, who made such a distinction between them and the Egyptians; but surely it must have been impossible for any Israelite to witness that ceremony without being deeply impressed with the momentous truth, which lies at the basis of the whole Mosaic dispensation, viz. that there was wrath to be averted as well as love to be revealed. The command was, "None of you shall go out at the door of his house until the morning;" and the reason assigned was, "For the LORD will pass through to smite the Egyptians; and when He seeth the blood upon the lintel, and on the two side posts, the LORD will pass over the door, and will not suffer the destroyer to come in unto your houses to smite you." No Israelite could hear that strict command uttered, or obey it, without receiving the impression—(1) that there was wrath to be manifested that night in Egypt; (2) that it was a wrath to which Israel was exposed in common with their neighbours; (3) that the exemption of Israel was due to the sovereign grace of their covenant God; and (4) that their exemption was connected with the interposition of sacrificial blood.

Sacrificial Character of Paschal Lamb recognised by Christ and His Apostles.

As already intimated, the sacrificial character of the paschal victim, although denied by our author (and his denial of it is essential to his whole theory of the purely moral and anti-sacrificial character of the Mosaic economy), is clearly established not only by the fact that Christ ordained, as the antitype of the Passover, an institution commemorative of His own death, but by the express declaration of the Apostle

Paul (1 Cor. v. 7), in which he affirms that "Our Passover also hath been sacrificed, *even* Christ." By the institution of His Supper in connection with that ancient sacramental feast of Israel, our Lord would have His Church to know that His blood alone averts from His people the merited wrath of a righteous God, and consequently that what His death is to His people was prefigured by the death of the paschal lamb. This relation of Christ's death to the death of that victim were out of the question if that victim had not been regarded by Christ as sacrificially slain. If Christ's death was sacrificial, so must the death of the paschal lamb have been; and if the paschal lamb was not a sacrificial victim, Christ cannot be regarded as teaching, by the institution of His Supper, that His body, given and broken for many, was given and broken for the remission of sins, or that the cup which He gave to His disciples in that solemn hour was the symbol of sacrificial blood shed in ratification of the covenant of redemption. In like manner, if the paschal lamb did not die as a sacrifice dieth, Christ in His death— which it is to be hoped our author still holds to have been sacrificial—could not have been designated our Passover. If Christ, as sacrificed, is called our Passover, as He is by Paul in the passage cited above, then the Passover must have been a true and proper sacrifice; and as that sacrifice is the first efficient, or rather meritorious cause in the redemption of Israel, and gives character to the entire economy which it triumphantly inaugurates, there must be great lack of theological and economic balance among the advocates of "the newer criticism," who deny to it a sacrificial character, and who would strip the entire economy, of which it is the primary exemplar, of all sacrificial or ritual elements throughout the whole pre-exilic history of its administration.

Anti-economic Separation of the Ceremonial from the Moral Law.

This separation of the ceremonial from the moral is one of the worst features of this book, and betrays great unacquaintance with that true doctrine of economic development which teaches, that throughout the whole process, from the delivery of the *protevangelion* (Gen. iii. 15), and in every stage of its history, all the essential elements of the redemptive work of the promised Seed are to be found. It were unwarrantable to say that in every type of the Mosaic economy we have a full exhibition of all that is found in the great Antitype, or that in every symbol or symbolical act we have a full exhibition of the corresponding gospel truth. The truth is this, that in the economy, taken in its entirety, we have an outline— an outline and shadow, however, and not a full delineation—of the Messiah and His redemptive work. Of such an outline or shadow, as a positively authenticated scheme, "the newer criticism" knows or recognises nothing before the close of the Babylonish exile! And this one fact ought to ensure its rejection not only by every scientific investigator of the Biblical revelation, but by every Christian, however moderate his literary qualifications.

A Fundamental Economic Question.

Let us then look intelligently at this fundamental question: "Does the Mosaic economy exhibit the ceremonial law in correlation with the moral law as given from Sinai in the ten commandments?" The Mosaic legislation teaches that the moral law, as contained in the Decalogue, was the test and standard of all righteousness, and the centre around which the whole economy revolved. The doctrine held on this subject is not simply that the moral law was the standard by which a man who sought justification by his works (or, as our author puts it, "by doing justly, loving mercy, and walking humbly with God") was to be judged; but also that it was the standard by which the remedial system, through which those who are unable of themselves to meet the claims of that law are to be saved, was itself to be judged. The Mosaic economy, as given in the Bible, and not as it is eviscerated by a superficial carping criticism, teaches—(1) that the law sits in judgment upon the work of the sinner himself; and (2) that it sits in judgment on the work of his substitute. The sinner himself is adjudged and condemned by the law; and the work whereby he is, notwithstanding this condemnation, pronounced righteous, *i.e.* pardoned and accepted as righteous, is also subjected to the scrutiny of this same law, and presented before it for approval or rejection.

The Moral Law states the Conditions of Life under all Dispensations.

As to the former of these points, it is scarcely necessary to enter upon any formal proof. The law written and engraven on tables of stone was written there for Israel. Its commandments were obligatory on the chosen people, and the transgressor was exposed to its penalty. In the days of our Saviour the Jews acknowledged that the law was the standard of righteousness, and that in order to gain life it was necessary to love the Lord our God with all our heart, and soul, and strength, and mind, and our neighbour as ourselves. To this standard our Saviour always referred the self-righteous, who were acting in His day on our author's theory of the way of life for preexilic times. "If thou wilt enter into life, keep the commandments," was a statement of the conditions of life from which no Jew did, or could, dissent. Trained under a system whose sanctions found expression in that all-comprehending anathema, "Cursed is every one which continueth not in all things which are written in the book of the law to do them," he could recognise no other standard of righteousness or rule of obedience. What the law whose works are written in the heart is to the Gentile, such was that same law, as fully proclaimed from Sinai, and written and engraven on stone, to Israel. To both it announced of old, as it announces now, the rule of righteousness and the condition of life.

The Moral Law applies to the Substitute as well as to the Principal.

Equally manifest is the second proposition mentioned above. It is just as clear that the moral law took cognizance of the substitute and its work, as it is that it took cognizance of the principal and his. It is evident that the standard by which the righteousness of the Israelite was judged was the moral law, and it is no less evident that this same moral law was the standard by which the satisfaction rendered by his substitute was measured. The law which pronounced sentence of death upon the transgressor, was the very law which demanded the life's blood of his substitute as the condition of his release and pardon, and the ground of his acceptance.

The Ceremonial Law correlative to the Moral.

It is important that this reference of the sacrificial system of the Mosaic economy to the moral law (a reference for which "the newer criticism" has no place in pre-exilic times) should be clearly apprehended; for even apart from the theory which has no place for the ceremonial elements of the Mosaic economy before the return from Babylon, there seems to be a vague indefinite notion, very widely prevalent, that the sacrifices which were under the law were correlative to the ceremonial law, and were necessary only as demanded by it. In a word, they are not unfrequently regarded as required under an arbitrary arrangement, typical, it is true, but typical merely as foreshadowing the general truth that the sufferings of Christ were to be of the nature of an expiation. This representation is true, but it is indefinite and defective. It does not express the one great central truth of that typical economy, viz. the reference of the ceremonial system to the moral law. To this point attention is earnestly asked. The position to be established is, that the whole ceremonial system by which, under the Mosaic economy, provision was made for the reconciliation of a transgressor to God, had reference to the moral law.

Arguments in Support of this Position.

1. This relation of the ceremonial to the moral is implied in the order observed in the original institution of the Mosaic dispensation. When God descended on Sinai to inaugurate that dispensation, He, at the very outset, proclaimed the moral law. By asserting the claims of this law, whilst at the same time He revealed Himself as the covenant God of Israel, who had brought them out of the land of Egypt, out of the house of bondage, He would have them understand that in entering into covenant with them He

was not acting inconsistently with His character as a righteous God, or ignoring that standard of righteousness which has its ultimate foundation in His own all-perfect and immutable nature. He would, in fact, teach them that the only way in which they could hold fellowship with Him, or He with them, was by satisfying the demands of His holy law. The announcement of such a law, on such an occasion, involved of necessity, and implied, the doctrine that the economy about to be inaugurated must have respect to the moral law.

2. This reference of the ceremonial to the moral law is implied in the place assigned to the two tables of stone on which the Decalogue was written. That position certainly gives no countenance to the idea that there was no relation or bond of connection between the moral law and the economy instituted by Moses. The ark of the covenant, or ark of the testimony, as it was also called, containing the moral law, written by the finger of God, had the singular pre-eminence of being the first article connected with the Tabernacle which Moses was commanded to make. Of all the sacred things, there was nothing which, in point of sacredness, could be compared with the ark. The chamber in which it was deposited was the holy of holies, and over it hung the august symbol of the divine presence. Everything in that chamber pointed to the ark as the central object of regard. The cherubim stretched their wings as a canopy over it, and gazed upon the mercy-seat which covered it. It

sat not in the most holy place as in a place of safety, but it was there as, under God, the chief object of interest, towards which all the symbols even of the holy of holies pointed, itself the pledge and symbol of the safety of the chosen race. And in the most solemn of all the ceremonies of the year, on the great day of atonement, when the offerings of sacrifice and of incense for the year were completed, the highest function of the high priest was to sprinkle the blood of the atonement upon and before the mercy-seat, that covered it, seven times, and to offer incense, which ascending might cover the mercy-seat.

Reason of the Sacredness of the Ark.

As the sacredness of the ark is manifest, so also is the cause of that sacredness. This is found not simply in the fact that God manifested Himself over it, and from its cover, as a mercy-seat, held communion with Moses and His people Israel, but in the fact that it was the ordained receptacle of the moral law. All else was correlative to the ark, and the ark was correlative to the law. After instructing Moses regarding the dimensions and form of the ark, God indicates the design of it: "And thou shalt put into the ark the testimony which I shall give thee" (Ex. xxv. 16). "Thou shalt put the mercy-seat above upon the ark; and in the ark thou shalt put the testimony that I shall give thee. And there I will meet with thee, and I will commune with thee from above the mercy-seat, from between the two cherubim which are upon the ark of the testimony, of all things which I shall give thee in commandment unto the children of Israel" (Ex. xxv. 21, 22).

Reason of the Appointment of the Ark as the Seat of the Divine Administration.

There can, therefore, be no doubt that the sacredness of the ark arose from its relation to the law; nor can there be any doubt that God appointed the place in which the ark rested as the place where He would meet with His servant Moses, in order that He might teach Israel that fellowship with Him could be maintained only on the basis of that holy law. As He was revealing Himself as the covenant God of those who were confessedly transgressors of that law, it was most fitting and most necessary that its claims upon such should be recognised, and the satisfaction of its claims symbolized, by the sprinkling of atoning blood upon and before the ark which contained it. Even under the typical economy God would teach men that in justifying the ungodly He was not unjust, and that in holding intercourse with the violators of His most holy law, He was not unmindful of its claims.

Whatever subordinate ends, therefore, the ceremonial law served, it is manifest that, in its grand fundamental idea, its object was to impress men with the exceeding sinfulness of sin, and to shadow forth the way of reconciliation. If, as we have seen, the economy annually reached its culmination on the great day of atonement, when the high priest sprinkled the mercy-seat with the atoning blood, it must have been the design of God, in the institution of the economy, to keep Israel mindful of the claims of His most holy law. In a word, then, the Mosaic economy, in its great fundamental idea, was designed to assert the majesty of the moral law, and to reveal, by types and symbols, the way in which its claims were afterwards to be met by Him who is the great Antitype of all.

Bearing of these Facts upon the Character of the New Testament Dispensation.

The bearing of these unquestionable facts upon the subject of the nature of the atonement made by Christ is obvious. If the Mosaic economy, in its great central institution and fundamental idea, was correlative to the moral law, *i.e.* was designed to set forth its claims upon transgressors, and at the same time to foreshadow the way in which these momentous claims were to be met and satisfied, then it must follow, if the Mosaic economy was typical of the gospel, that the work of Christ must be correlative to the moral law, and designed to meet its claims upon those with whom God enters into covenant relationship. There is, and there can be, no way of escape from this conclusion except by denying one or both of the premises. He who admits that the Mosaic economy was correlative to the moral law, and that it was the shadow of which the gospel is the substance, must also admit that the gospel is correlative to the moral law. As the former of these positions has been established, it only remains necessary to establish (and this merely with somewhat more fulness than has been done already) the latter, viz. that the Mosaic economy was typical of the work of Christ.

Extent of the Typology of the Mosaic Dispensation.

On this point a few specimen passages may suffice. In his Epistle to the Colossians, chap. ii. 17, the Apostle Paul teaches that even the distinctions of meats and drinks, and holy days, and new moons, and sabbath days, were a shadow of good things to come, the body or substance of which is Christ. The author of the Epistle to the Hebrews makes a similar statement in regard to the whole Mosaic economy, Heb. x. 1, 2: "For the law having a shadow of good things to come, and not the very image of the things, can never with those sacrifices which they offered year by year continually make the comers thereunto perfect. Else would they not have ceased to be offered? because the worshippers, having been once cleansed, would have had no more conscience of sins." Speaking of the Tabernacle (chap. ix.), he represents it as being "a figure, *for the time then present*" (not for post-exilic times simply, but for the time of its continuance), "in which were offered both gifts and sacrifices, that could not make him that did the service perfect as pertaining to the conscience;" and in the 11th and following verses of the same chapter, to the 14th verse, he introduces Christ and His Tabernacle and sacrifice as the substance foreshadowed by these temporary institutions.

Thus we are taught that the Tabernacle, the high priest, and all the transactions which took place in connection with the sanctuary, were typical of Christ and His work. It is true that our Saviour is contrasted with the priests that were under the law, in regard to His priesthood, His sacrifice, and the sanctuary in which He officiates; but the points of contrast are those which obtain between the shadow and the substance. He differs from the Aaronic priests (even Aaron himself, who, it is to be presumed, lived in pre-exilic times, being a type), but the difference consists not in this, that whilst Aaron and his successors were priests, Christ was not a priest, or only a priest in a figurative sense; but herein consists the difference, that their priesthood was but the figure of which His was the reality and substance. Their sacrifices could never take away sin, whilst by His one sacrifice He has perfected for ever them that are sanctified. His Tabernacle differs from theirs (and it is not too much to presume that their Tabernacle was pitched in pre-exilic times) as the antitype differs from its types, as the heavenly and enduring differs from the earthly and temporal, as that which was pitched by the Lord Himself differs from that which was constructed by the hands of man—by Aholiab and Bezaleel, or by Hiram and Solomon.

Conclusion from the foregoing Facts.

As the premises are now established, the conclusion is inevitable. As the Mosaic economy, with its "sacrificial system, and all that belongs to it," was on the one hand correlative to the moral law, and was on the other typical of Christ and His redemptive work, it must follow that the work of Christ was correlative to the moral law, and designed to meet and satisfy its claims upon His people. This is no strained inference, but a conclusion flowing inevitably from the very central idea of the entire Mosaic dispensation. A work claiming to be the antitype of that economy, taken in its entirety, which did not recognise and satisfy the claims of the moral law, would certainly fail to establish its claims. No such work could be regarded, by any one who entered into the spirit of that typical economy, as meeting or presenting the great essential features of the dispensation so elaborately prefigured.

Bearing of these Facts upon the Post-exilic Theory of "the Newer Criticism."

The bearing of the facts now brought out, upon the post-exilic theory of the Levitical system, is manifest. The current and constant representation of that theory is, that in pre-exilic times the intercourse of God with Israel was direct, *i.e.* as we have seen again and again, "without the intervention of any ritual sacrament" (p. 303), or, as it is put (p. 288), "Worship by sacrifice, and all that belongs to it, is no part of the divine Torah to Israel." According to this theory, God and Israel stood face to face, and held intercourse independent of any "sacrifice," or ceremony, or "ritual sacrament." The sole condition of this intercourse was "to do justly, love mercy, and walk humbly with Him" (pp. 288, 289). In other words, as the last reference covers the whole Decalogue, the condition of acceptance in those anti-sacrificial, anti-ritual, anti-sacramental pre-exilic times, was observance of the ten commandments! To sustain this conception of the worship and religion of Israel, it is, of course, necessary to keep the moral law as widely separate from the ceremonial law as possible, and hence the latter is projected into the indefinite future, finding no place till some fragments of it are allowed entrance in the days of Josiah, and this, too, in a place whose very structure and furniture and office-bearers implied its pre-existence and regulative authority. Thus separated from the ceremonial, the moral law, in all its inexorable nakedness, engraven on stone, without the intervention of any mediatorial agency, is left behind to regulate God's intercourse with Israel throughout the whole pre-exilic period, the only remedy for Israel's delinquencies being the law of chastisement! Such is the pre-exilic gospel of "the newer criticism"!

In view of the positions now established,—positions which a man cannot challenge and yet claim to accept the express teaching of the New Testament,—one may say to such theorists, "What God has joined together, let not man put asunder." The Sinaitic legislation proclaimed two things which are in direct antagonism with this post-exilic theory: 1. That, on the basis of that fiery law which went out from God, Israel could hold no *direct* intercourse with Him. 2. That Israel's covenant God would hold intercourse with Israel through the typical mediator, whose intervention the proclamation of that law had led them to invoke. This, of course, is all one with saying that the Sinaitic arrangement for intercourse was not the one sketched in this book. Place beside it the arrangement of "the newer criticism," "to do justly, love mercy, and walk humbly with God," and the contrast is of itself sufficient refutation. In a word, the very circumstances connected with the giving of the only pre-exilic Torah which "the newer criticism" will allow as the *life* Torah to Israel, prove that the intercourse of God with Israel is not "*direct*" but *mediatorial*. Even that moral Torah "was ordained through angels by the hand of a mediator" (Gal. iii. 19).

Mediation in Pre-exilic Times is still found even in the Minimum of Record acknowledged by "the Newer Criticism."

The fact is, it fares with "the newer criticism" as

it fares with those who deny the deity of our Saviour; no matter how ruthlessly they deal with the record, there yet remains, after they have done their worst, enough to prove that the doctrine they wish to get rid of is still interwoven with those portions over which they have not dared to invert their critical *stylus*. When they have reduced the Pentateuch to a minimum, the sacrificial typical Torah is still there.

It appears plainly enough, then, that even though there were nothing left of Exodus save the 20th chapter, which represents Israel as so terrified in the presence of God proclaiming the fiery Torah of the Decalogue, that they withdrew and stood afar off, and besought Moses to act as mediator between them and God, there would nevertheless remain quite enough to overthrow the doctrine of a direct non-mediatorial intercourse between Himself and Israel. So long as the fact of the mediation of Moses abides, so long as it remains on record that "the people stood afar off, and Moses drew near unto the thick darkness where God was," the theory which makes the intercourse direct cannot be entertained. That moral law, be it ever remembered, was, when engraven on stone, given into the hand of a mediator. Our author therefore gains nothing, even though he were able to prove that the Torah of Moses did not embrace a law of ritual, so long as he must confess that Moses, through whom the alleged purely moral Torah was delivered to Israel, was constituted a mediator between them and God. He may tell us that whatever is more than the words spoken at Horeb (meaning thereby the ten commandments) "is not strictly covenant" (p. 299); but he has to face the contextual statement (Deut. v. 22–28), which reveals this mediatorial arrangement, and thereby subverts the theory of direct intercourse between Israel and Israel's God. The subsequent history shows that the mediatorial office held by Moses was part of the economy, and that its functions were executed by him with fidelity and great unselfishness. He is ever ready to interpose between an offended God and a stiff-necked, stubborn race. One of the most affecting incidents in the wondrous history of that man of God is his intercession for Israel when they had sinned in the matter of the golden calf. "And Moses said unto the people, Ye have sinned a great sin: and now I will go up unto the LORD; peradventure I shall make an atonement for your sin. And Moses returned unto the LORD, and said, Oh, this people have sinned a great sin, and have made them gods of gold. Yet, now, if Thou wilt forgive their sin—; and if not, blot me, I pray thee, out of Thy book which Thou hast written" (Ex. xxxii. 30–32). Here is veritable mediation, conducted by a veritable mediator, ordained by God to mediate, and so long as the history of it abides as an unchallengeable part of the sacred record, it must continue to testify against the purely legal doctrine of the pre-exilic way of life taught in these lectures. Moses, the mediator, is connected with the moral law; it is placed in his hands, and his mediation is correlative to it. Israel has broken its second commandment by making to themselves gods of gold, and Moses, in the spirit of his mediatorial office, intercedes for them, specifying this particular breach, and confessing it as a great sin before their covenant God.

The Theory needs to rid the Pentateuch not only of Mosaic Authorship, but of Moses himself and his Mediation.

"The newer criticism," therefore, has not as yet completed its task. It cannot afford to leave untouched by its instruments of mutilation, or relegation, the first twenty-one verses of this 20th chapter of Exodus. It must get rid even of this section of this chapter with its ordinance of Mosaic mediation, or all its labour is in vain. It is not enough that it rid itself of his Pentateuchal authorship; it must get rid of Moses himself, for so long as he is recognised as a historical verity, by whomsoever the history has been written, his official relations to Israel and the divine Sinaitic Torah, must thwart the counsels of all men, whether of the school of Socinus or of "the newer criticism," with its Scottish modifications, who would place any section of the human race under the covenant of works, whether in pre-exilic or post-exilic times. He being dead yet speaketh, and his words, as has been shown before, are reiterated by an apostle in order to dissuade men from adopting the very same doctrine regarding the way of life as is taught in this book as the gospel of pre-exilic times. That reiteration is as authoritative to-day in North Britain as it was in Paul's day in Galatia: "As many as are of the works of the law are under the curse; for it is written, Cursed is every one that continueth not in all things which are written in the book of the law to do them" (Gal. iii. 10). And the context shows that it was not a doctrine peculiar to New Testament times, for the apostle confirms it by a quotation from a pre-exilic prophet (Hab. ii. 4), which, according to his interpretation both in Galatians and Romans, proves that salvation by works is impossible, and that righteousness is by faith alone.

CHAPTER XI.

THE NEWER CRITICISM AND THE MOSAIC INSTITUTIONS—
THE ARK, THE AARONIC PRIESTHOOD.

AS another obstacle in the way of this post-exilic theory, stands the ark of the covenant. Even though our theorists could succeed in disposing of the great lawgiver of Israel, their scheme must be regarded as very far from being established or fortified, so long as the ark and its history remain. This task our author can scarcely be said to have formally essayed in these lectures. His references to the ark are exceedingly rare, and generally not very explicit. On page 357 he remarks: "It is very noteworthy, and, on the traditional view, quite inexplicable, that the Mosaic sanctuary of the ark is never mentioned in the Deuteronomic code. The author of this law occupies the standpoint of Isaiah, to whom the whole plateau of Zion is holy; or of Jeremiah, who forbids men to search for the ark or re-make it, because Jerusalem is the throne of Jehovah (Jer. iii. 16, 17)." On this remark it might be remarked, with a little more propriety, that it is very noteworthy, and, on the post-exilic view, quite inexplicable, that this Mosaic sanctuary of the ark, which, we are told by the author, is never mentioned in the Deuteronomic code (although it is expressly stated (Deut. xxxi. 25, 26) that "Moses commanded the Levites, which bare the ark of the covenant of the LORD, saying, Take this book of the law, and put it in the side of the ark of the covenant of the Lord your God, that it may be there for a witness against thee"), and which, according to our author, Jeremiah enjoins Israel neither to search for nor re-make, was, within a few years after Jeremiah's decease, about to become the divinely sanctioned centre of that Israelitish worship inaugurated in the Levitical Torah! If prophetic denunciation of Israel's sacrifices in pre-exilic times proves that sacrifice in pre-exilic times was without positive divine sanction, surely prophetic prohibition of the ark in post-exilic times should prove that the ark was not divinely authorized after the exile. If Jeremiah can be quoted again and again, as he is by our author (see pp. 117, 225, etc. etc.), against the pre-exilic sanction of "the altar and the altar gifts, and the solemn feasts, and the tithes, and the free-will offerings," there certainly can be no show of reason for holding that when Jeremiah speaks in similar strains against the sanctuary of the ark, and against the ark itself, in reference to post-exilic times, his language has not the same significance, and that it was not intended to convey the idea that the ark, after the exile, was an institution of will-worship, unsanctioned and unapproved by Jehovah. It confounds all one's ideas of consistent exegesis to find a critic, who claims to interpret the Bible on the most strictly scientific principles, drawing conclusions diametrically opposite from identical premises.

Ceremonies connected with the Ark unsanctioned until the Ark was lost!

Nor is one's confusion or surprise diminished when he takes into consideration the fact intimated by our author in his quotation from Jeremiah (p. 117), that this ark of the covenant which, notwithstanding the prohibition of one of the LORD'S prophets, is about to become the very sanctuary and centre of Israel's worship, and that, too, by express divine appointment, has disappeared, and is not to be sought for, or re-made! While the ark existed, the ark received no sanction— no divine sanction, for one thousand years; but when the ark is lost, and a prophetic prohibition issued against the re-making of it, then the Levitical Torah, which turns on the ark as its hinge and centre, is to come into operation with all the authority wherewith the divinely commissioned post-exilic prophets can invest it! In the history of critical speculation, save in the oddities of "the newer criticism" itself, it would be difficult to find anything to match this. Within the latter, the only thing like to it, which occurs just now, is that point in its theory of the all-but-post-exilic origin of the Deuteronomic code, according to which rules are laid down for the election of the first king in Israel, and for his guidance in the administration of his kingdom, one hundred years after the kingdom of the ten tribes was carried into captivity, and the kingdom had absolutely ceased for ever to exist!

The Theory in conflict with the References to the Ark in the Epistle to the Hebrews.

But this theory of the post-exilic sanction of the ark and its accompaniments is not only embarrassed with such manifest contradictions and absurdities as the foregoing; it has to face and deal with the solemn fact that it contradicts the express teaching of the New Testament. While it teaches that the Levitical system, which unquestionably revolved around the ark, was not divinely authorized until the return of Israel from Babylon, the Epistle to the Hebrews (addressed to men who knew as much about their own institutions as the author of these lectures does) teaches that "even the first covenant had ordinances of divine service, and a worldly sanctuary. For there was a Tabernacle prepared, the first, wherein were the candlestick, and the table, and the shew-bread; which is called the Holy Place. And after the second veil, the Tabernacle which is called the Holy of Holies; having the golden censer, and the ark of the covenant overlaid round about with gold, wherein was the golden pot that had manna, and Aaron's rod that budded, and the tables of the covenant, and above it the cherubim of glory overshadowing the mercy-seat," etc. (Heb. ix. 1–5). It will be difficult to reconcile the post-exilic theory of the authentication of that system in which the ark was absolutely enshrined, and from which it was inseparable, with the teaching of this epistle. The exegetical critic who alleges that the passage now quoted is descriptive of the worship of Israel after the exile, and under the second Temple, and denies that it was intended to apply to the worship of pre-exilic times, or the ordinances of the Tabernacle or first Temple, simply sets all laws of righteous interpretation at defiance. The language employed in this great epistle leaves no room for a second opinion. The sanctuary described is neither the first nor the second Temple, but the Tabernacle, and the Tabernacle was not a post-exilic structure. This one fact settles the whole controversy; for in this confessedly pre-exilic sanctuary, as the passage affirms, there was a service conducted, which is described as a *divine* service, and whose parts, as the eighth verse shows, were designed by the Holy Ghost to shadow forth the great leading doctrines of the New Dispensation, and in the midst of all the types and symbols of the coming economy, the ark of the covenant holds pre-eminence as the seat whence God administers, as from a throne, the blessings of His grace.

The Ark necessary from the time the Moral Law was given.

Indeed, were we left without the light of the New Testament, we might be led to the conclusion that the ark, from the outset, must have been divinely sanctioned. Once it is admitted that Moses received the sacred deposit of the law engraven by the finger of God, the conclusion seems to be inevitable, that provision would be made for its safe keeping. The estimate of its importance, which led to its being so engraven, and engraven on such material, would, one might think, lead to the institution of special arrangements for its preservation. It is hard to conceive of those two tables, prepared by express divine instruction, and engraven by the immediate act of God Himself, being left without some such repository as Moses was directed to make (Ex. xxv.). If there was an ark at all, there would seem to be no reason for believing that it was not ordained from the very time at which, we are told in Exodus, Moses was commissioned to make it; nor is there any reason for doubting that, with its sacred contents, it was made from the first the centre of the worship of Israel, and its cover the mercy-seat from which God held communion with the typical mediator of His covenant people. This view, which the very nature of the case would seem to demand, is just the view given in the Pentateuch; and, as has been already shown, the position, both economic and chronological, or historical, thus assigned to the ark of the covenant is essential to a right apprehension of the Mosaic dispensation in its relations to the moral law on the one hand, and to the New Testament dispensation on the other.

Question of Fraud raised again by the Post-exilic Theory.

But these facts and principles being premised, a question of very grave interest arises. If the Levitical system, with its ark of the covenant,—which was professedly of Mosaic origin, and which, both in the Pentateuch and the New Testament, is represented as inaugurated in the Tabernacle, the Holy Ghost, as we are informed, thereby signifying that the way into the holy place was not yet made manifest, while as the first Tabernacle was yet standing,—was notwithstanding not divinely sanctioned till after the return from Babylon, the question cannot be repressed, How are Ezra and his companions, who introduced that system as a divine institution, to be defended against the charge of perpetrating a fraud upon their brethren of the captivity? and how is the author of the Epistle to the Hebrews to be defended against the charge of endorsing and perpetuating the Esdrine deception? "The newer criticism" has had to encounter a precisely similar difficulty in connection with their theory of the origin of the Deuteronomic code, and to that difficulty this other must now be added. Our author's solution of the ethical problem in the case of Deuteronomy was, that in ancient times men did not distinguish between historical *data* and historical deductions, and it is likely some such solution would be tendered in the present case. But the Epistle to the Hebrews was not written in those ancient times, when men had such confused notions, as our author alleges, on the subject of historical composition; nor can the position be successfully challenged by any one who, without any theoretic bias, will read those portions of the Pentateuch in which the Levitical system is fully developed, that if such a system was first introduced in post-exilic times, the introducers of it must have deceived the children of the captivity. Indeed, it is difficult to believe that it was possible to make the very next generation after the men who built and dedicated the second Temple accept this Esdrine Torah, as has been shown already, if it were not the Torah under which their fathers erected the house of the Lord and ordered its service. On the assumption that the Torah which Ezra brought with him from Babylon was a new Torah, we must conclude that the Jews, whom he induced to make confession of their own sins and the sins of their fathers for violating its statutes and judgments, were ignorant of the laws under which their fathers had lived, or that they had joined in a transaction which it is impossible to vindicate.

Special Insuperable Difficulties of the Theory arising from the acknowledged Loss of the Ark during the Exile.

However viewed, then, whether under the light of the Old Testament or the New, or of the circumstances under which the moral law was given, the ark must be regarded as inseparable from the Mosaic economy. The Levitical economy, which "the newer criticism" alleges was not introduced before the close of the

Babylonish exile, implies and proclaims its existence; and if that system was then for the first time established, as the author of this book teaches, it was not introduced, even on his own confession, till after the ark, which was the very centre of it, was lost! Can any reader of the Old Testament or the New believe this? Is it possible for any one who accepts the Bible as a revelation from an "All-wise Author" to believe that the mercy-seat, before and upon which the atoning blood was to be sprinkled, was lost before God sanctioned the sprinkling? He who accepts the teaching of this book must believe that in the days of Josiah, the Lord, referring to the restoration, spake unto Jeremiah as follows: "And it shall come to pass, when ye be multiplied and increased in the land, in those days, saith the Lord, they shall say no more, The ark of the covenant of the LORD: neither shall it come to mind: neither shall they remember it; neither shall they visit it; neither shall that be done any more," or, as it is sometimes rendered, "neither shall it be made any more," or, as our author renders it, "re-made;" and he who accepts its teaching must also believe that in the days of Ezra, when the restoration was an accomplished fact, and not till then, the whole Levitical system, with the ark as its centre, was inaugurated in Israel by the express command of Jehovah! That is, what God promises through His servant Jeremiah, immediately before the captivity of Judah, as in store for her on her restoration to her own land, He takes special pains, through His servant

Ezra, to render impossible, by the institution of an elaborate system of sacrifice and ritual, having as its chief symbol that which was not to be named, or thought of, or visited, or re-made! Such is one of the grand generalizations of the scientific criticism over which handkerchiefs are waved by young ladies, and in honour of which public breakfasts are given by men affecting to represent the culture and the Biblical scholarship of the Free Church of Scotland! With such, the system which arrays prophet against prophet, and, as in this case, priest against priest, and even the Jehovah of pre-exilic times against the Jehovah of post-exilic times, may pass for Biblical science; but in the estimation of the true representatives of that grand old church, and in that of the genuine piety and culture of Christendom, it will be regarded as neither more nor less than the science of Biblical disparagement. Like the men of Ashdod, its worshippers may set the ark before it, but they will find, as did their prototypes, that in its presence their Dagon cannot stand. The only hope for the idol is to send back the ark of the covenant to pre-exilic times, and even this alternative is perilous unto theoretic death.

Aaron and his Sons.

But even though the ark of the covenant were dismissed, "the newer criticism" would not be freed from all embarrassment. There is no difficulty arising from the inauguration of the Levitical system after the loss of the ark, which does not necessarily arise from the inauguration of it after the death of Aaron and his sons. Under his third group of laws our author ranges the Levitical legislation (p. 317); and this legislation contains a law for "the consecration of Aaron and his sons" (p. 318). Turning to Exodus xxviii. 1–xxix. 35, we find this law, which is introduced as follows: "And take thou unto thee Aaron thy brother, and his sons with him, from among the children of Israel, that he may minister unto me in the priest's office, even Aaron, Nadab and Abihu, Eleazar and Ithamar, Aaron's sons. And thou shalt make holy garments for Aaron thy brother for glory and for beauty." Then follows a most minute description of the garments of Aaron and of his sons, with a detailed consecration ritual. Now, it will be seen at once that in these two chapters we have the foundation and top-stone of the whole Levitical legislation. We have the distinctive priesthood of Aaron and his sons, by which he and his sons are separated from the children of Israel, of whatsoever tribe; and we have the high-priesthood of Aaron, by which he is distinguished from, and raised above, the other priests, his sons. In the fortieth chapter we have an account of the actual consecration of Aaron to his office and of his sons to theirs, and of the rearing up of the Tabernacle, and of the descent upon it of the cloudy symbol of the divine presence.

Account of the Consecration of Aaron and his Sons pronounced not Historical.

Such, in brief, is the apparently historical, and, as will be seen on reference to these closing chapters of Exodus, most graphic account of the inauguration of the Tabernacle and of the consecration of the Aaronic priesthood. But, in the estimation of "the newer criticism," this is not history at all, or at least is not all history. In fact, its characteristic factors are not historic. All that signalizes this part of the sacred record pertains to a period separated from the days of Aaron and his sons by more than one thousand years! "The law for the consecration of priests," says our author, "is given in a narrative of the consecration of Aaron and his sons. The form is historical, but the essential object is legal. The law takes the form of recorded precedent. There is nothing," he remarks, "surprising in this. Among the Arabs, to this day, traditional precedents are the essence of law, and the kadhi of the Arabs is he who has inherited a knowledge of them. Among early nations, precedent is particularly regarded in matters of ritual, and the oral Torah of the priests doubtless consisted in great measure of case law. But law of this kind is not history. It is preserved, not as a record of the past, but as a guide for the present and future. The Pentateuch itself shows clearly that this law, in historical form, is not an integral part of the continuous history of Israel's movements in the wilderness, but a separate thing" (pp. 318, 319).

The reader is now in a position to judge of the author's theory, and of the style of argument by which he endeavours to sustain it. The story of the consecration of Aaron and his sons is not veritable history; for if it were, Graf and Kuenen, and their brethren of the Scottish school of "the newer criticism," must abandon their theory. No one who believes that Aaron and his sons were called of God, and separated from their brethren of the children of Israel, and even from their brethren of the tribe of Levi, as this narrative seems to teach, can believe, with these critics, that the Aaronitic priesthood was a thing of gradual development, reaching its culmination at the close of the Babylonish captivity, and formally inaugurated by Ezra. According to the narrative in Exodus, and according to the interpretation of all men whose minds have not been warped and biassed by the principles of this rationalistic school, the Aaronic orders were instituted by the express command of God, through His servant Moses, and their commission bears date from the institution of the Tabernacle itself. Hence the necessity of proving that the closing chapters of Exodus should not be interpreted in a historical sense, but that they should be regarded, as the Arabs are wont to regard such narratives, as mere traditional precedents. This, however, is assertion, not proof; nor does it obviate the difficulty which this narrative of the consecration of Aaron and his sons casts in the pathway of this post-exilic theory of the Levitical legislation. It is true that the legal precedents of a nation do not make up the whole national history. It is true, however, that without history there can be no precedent. If, as our author states in the passage quoted above, "the oral law of the priests consisted in great measure of case law," it must be manifest that the cases of this case law must have occurred. Given no case, there can never arise a law of cases; and given no precedent, there can never be a precedent to quote. But apart from an actual historical incident there can be neither case to adjudicate, nor judgment thereon, to abide as a precedent to guide either the present or the future.

The Theory assumes that there may be Regulative Precedents destitute of any Historical Basis.

Applying this, the author's own analogy, to the case in hand, how, it may be asked, can the narrative of the consecration of Aaron and his sons be regarded as furnishing *precedents* to regulate future consecrations, if no such consecration of Aaron and his sons ever took place? If it did not take place, it cannot be regarded as a precedent; and if it did take place at all, it must have taken place in Aaron's day; and if so, then the theory of "the newer criticism" is subverted; for while that theory contends that the Aaronic distinctions of the Levitical Torah were of gradual development, attaining their perfection under Ezra, this narrative, which is represented as furnishing ritual precedents, presents the system as complete at the very outset, as it came from the hand of Israel's lawgiver. If, then, the consecration of Aaron as high priest, and of his sons as priests, with their respective distinctive dress and functions, be regarded as a precedent, it must be regarded as a precedent from the hour in which it occurred; and if high priests and other priests were ordained in conformity with it in the days of Ezra, their ordination but serves to prove the pre-exilic origin of the Aaronitic priestly distinctions, which "the newer criticism" would have us believe came into existence, or at least reached its full development only in post-exilic times.

The Theory attempts to shake Confidence in the Historical Character of the Narrative.

It is manifestly impossible to reconcile this theory with the narrative of the consecration of Aaron and his sons, and therefore the only hope of the so-called critical school is to shake confidence in its veritable historical character. One or two examples of the way in which this is attempted by our author are very instructive. The first instance given is Ex. xxxiii. 7, "which is non-Levitical." Here "we read," he says, "that Moses took the Tabernacle and pitched it outside the camp, and called it the tent of meeting. But the Levitical account of the setting up of the Tabernacle, with the similar circumstance of the descent of the cloud upon it, does not occur till chap xl. (comp. Num. ix. 15)."

Now, in the first place, it would seem impossible for any writer of any goodly measure of intelligence, and certainly impossible for any writer possessing the intelligence exhibited in this Book of Exodus, to make the historical mistake attributed to him by our author; for, at the time Moses is said to have pitched the Tabernacle outside the camp, *the* Tabernacle had not yet been made. At the time referred to, Bezaleel and Aholiab, and their fellow-workmen, had not yet entered upon their work, nor had the people as yet begun to bring the ordained material for its construction. One would conclude, if he were not a hostile critic, that there must be an explanation by which the two apparently contradictory passages may be reconciled.

The Tent pitched by Moses was not the Tabernacle.

This explanation is not far to seek. Moses was Israel's judge, and it was necessary that he should have a judgment-seat, or place for the administration of justice. It was also necessary that one who sought counsel in difficult cases immediately from Israel's LORD and Lawgiver, should have his judgment-seat near to the manifested presence of Jehovah. These considerations indicate the solution of the apparent discrepancy between Ex. xxxiii. 7, which speaks of Moses pitching the Tabernacle before it was made, and Ex. xl., which speaks of his pitching it after it was made. The solution is simply this, that the Tabernacle of chap. xxxiii. is not the Tabernacle of chap. xl.

The former is the magisterial tent of Moses, where God met with him to counsel and guide him in the government of Israel; the latter is the Tabernacle of Jehovah, erected for His own dwelling-place in the midst of the congregation of Israel. Such an explanation is perfectly legitimate; for one occupying the position of Israel's lawgiver, and meeting publicly with God before the congregation, must have had a tent for that specific purpose, distinguished above all the tents, even of the chief of the fathers and princes of the people. And it is a noteworthy fact that the Septuagint translation proceeds upon this assumption; for its version of the passage is: "And Moses took *his* tent (τὴν σκηνὴν αὐτοῦ), and pitched it outside the camp, afar off from the camp, and called it the tent of testimony." Here, then, the version by which our author would correct the Hebrew text itself, teaches that the tent pitched by Moses, on the occasion referred to, was the tent of Moses himself, and consequently must be regarded as distinguishing it from the Tabernacle properly, or strictly so called.

Besides, it is obvious from the context that this tent was different from the historic Tabernacle of Israel; for the sole minister of it is Moses, who is attended within its precincts, not by Aaron or his sons, but by Joshua, "who departed not out of the Tabernacle." The contrast between this arrangement and that of the tent in which Aaron and his sons ministered with such glory, and in which Joshua held no office, bespeaks an entirely different structure.

Nor does the reference to Num. ix. 15 confirm the view of the author. That passage simply states over again *in brief*, what is stated *in extenso* in Ex. xl., that "on the day that the Tabernacle was reared up, the cloud covered the Tabernacle." This statement is perfectly consistent with the explanation now given, for the Mosaic tent of judgment was the provisional place of meeting with Jehovah until the Tabernacle proper was reared. And as the divine presence and sanction of the Mosaic administration were indicated by the pillar of cloud, it was to be expected that the cloud should mark out and signalize the tent in which the lawgiver of Israel was holding communion with Israel's covenant God. The argument based upon this reference to the passage in Numbers seems to assume that the pillar of cloud could not descend at one time upon the provisional tent, and descend also, at a different time, upon a different tent, erected for a different or more comprehensive purpose.

The Context confirms this View.

But, reverting to the fact mentioned at the outset, the whole context in Exodus proves that the Mosaic economy, at the time in which Moses pitched this tent outside the camp, was simply in process of institution, and as yet in the earlier stages of its development. The historical statement is, that Moses had been up in the mount with God, receiving the law written on tables of stone and the ceremonial law, embracing a pattern of the Tabernacle, with minute instructions respecting the material and style of its several parts, together with a detailed ritual for the consecration of Aaron and his sons to the office of the priesthood. Whilst Moses is thus engaged with God, the people become weary with waiting, imagine that their leader is lost, and commit the dreadful trespass of "making for themselves gods of gold." God informs him of their sin, threatens to consume them, and to make of Moses himself a great nation. True to his mediatorial office, he loses sight of himself, and intercedes for his rebellious brethren, and averts the threatened doom.

On nearing the camp, and witnessing their idolatry before the golden calf, he casts the tables of the law out of his hands, and breaks them beneath the mount. After chastising them for their sin, he returns to the mount, and intercedes for them again. His appeal is only partially successful, and under a deep sense of the impending wrath entertained toward Israel by their offended God, he returns to the camp and reports the "evil tidings." Now, it is just at this juncture we are told that "Moses took the tent and pitched it without the camp, afar off from the camp, and called it the tabernacle (or tent) of the congregation." If ever there was history written, this seems to be history; and if we are to accept it as being what it professes to be, it is impossible to regard this tent as the Levitical Tabernacle. The lawgiver had received instructions to make the latter, but he had not as yet had an opportunity of putting his instructions into execution. The very tables of stone, which are to be its most sacred deposit, lie broken beneath the mount, and have not as yet been replaced by God; and the congregation of the children of Israel have not as yet been called upon to contribute the "gold and silver and brass, and blue and purple and scarlet, and fine linen and goats' hair," etc. etc., for its construction, and Bezaleel and Aholiab have not as yet begun to work. How, it may well be asked again, could any intelligent writer, especially any writer of the intelligence displayed in this narrative, or even any "final redactor," if you will, who possessed any common sense at all, without the slightest break in the continuity of the narration, pitch the Levitical Tabernacle into the midst of such a context? God, with whom all duration is present, can call the things that are not as though they were, but it is not so with man. It is not within the compass of the possible to take, as an actually existing thing, a tent not yet in existence, and pitch it anywhere. It is surely not too much to claim that the theory which requires for its support the assumption of such historical incapacity, or intentional historical inversion, effected by a Levitical conspiracy one thousand years after the history was written, and imposed as true history upon a whole nation, merits unqualified and instantaneous condemnation, by all men who have any regard for the Bible as an authentic record of the history of redemption.

The Charge of Falsifying the Record preferred again.

As an additional proof of this Levitical tampering with the original history, we have the following:—
"Again in Num. x. we have first the Levitical account of the fixed order of march of the Israelites from Sinai with the ark in the midst of the host (vv. 11–28), and immediately afterwards the historical statement that when the Israelites left Sinai the ark was not in their midst, but went before them a distance of three days' journey (vv. 33–36). It is plain that though the formal order of march with the ark in the centre, which the author sets forth as a standing pattern, is here described in the historical guise of a record of the departure of Israel from Sinai, the actual order of march on that occasion was different. The same author cannot have written both accounts. One is a law in narrative form; the other is actual history. These examples," it is added, "are forcible enough, but they form only a fragment of a great chain of evidence which critics have collected. By many marks, and particularly by extremely well-defined peculiarities of language, a Levitical document can be separated out of the Pentateuch, containing the whole mass of priestly legislation and precedents, and leaving untouched the essentially historical part of the Pentateuch, all that has for its direct aim to tell us what befell the Israelites in the wilderness, and not what precedents the wilderness offered for subsequent ritual observances. As the Pentateuch now stands,

the two elements of law and history are interspersed, not only in the same book, but often in the same chapter. But originally they were quite distinct" (pp. 319, 320).

Extravagant Claim advanced in behalf of "the Newer Criticism."

This passage has been given at length because of the light it sheds upon the author's estimate of Pentateuchal history, and the means by which alone he can hope to subvert its testimony against his post-exilic theory of the origin or final development of the Levitical system. It will be seen that the charge here preferred against the integrity of this portion of the Pentateuchal record is a very serious one. If it be true, the Church of God is at the mercy of the critics; for we are told that it is by certain marks and peculiarities of language that the Levitical document can be separated out of the Pentateuch, and discriminated from the essentially historical parts. As these marks are of an order of which none save critics can take cognizance, it is out of the question for ordinary people, such as Christ addressed (John v. 39), to "search the Scriptures" until the critics have made the necessary Pentateuchal revision. When this revision shall be accomplished it were difficult to conjecture, as no two of the critics are agreed, all along the line, as to what is historical and what is Levitical post-exilic interpolation. In the meantime, the whole record is before the public, arraigned on a charge which, from its generality, may be applied, as its accusers list, to almost any part of it.

The alleged Historical Discrepancy examined.

But let us look at the grounds advanced in proof in the present instance. In one section of Num. x., which gives an account of the march from Sinai, we are to understand that the ark is represented as carried in the midst of the host, while in the section *immediately following*, it is represented as not in the midst of the host at all, but as preceding them "a distance of three days' journey."

In the first place, in the former section the ark is never mentioned. After the camp of Judah set forward, the sons of Gershon and the sons of Merari followed bearing the Tabernacle; and after the camp of Reuben set forward, the Kohathites followed bearing the sanctuary. This is all that is said in the former section which can have any bearing on the point at issue. In the section *immediately following*, we are informed that "the ark of the covenant went before them in the three days' journey" (not a distance of three days' journey, as our author absurdly translates, an arrangement which would put their guide out of sight of the camp altogether), "to search out for them a resting-place." Where is there any ground for the alleged discrepancy between these two narratives? What is there in the former, as distinguished from the latter, to create the suspicion that it was concocted by the Levites and inserted in the actual history? Is there such evidence of Levitical tampering with the actual history as warrants any man, much less a critic, to say that " it is plain that though the formal order of march, with the ark in the centre, which the author sets forth as a standing pattern, is here described in the historical guise of a record of the departure of Israel from Sinai, the actual order of march on that occasion was different," or to say that "the same author cannot have written both accounts"? There is no real discrepancy between the two sections of the narrative. The former, like the first chapter of Genesis, gives the general statement; and the latter, like the second chapter, furnishes information in detail regarding the most important item in the previous general historical sketch. The ark was in the history of Israel's march what man was in the history of creation, and is therefore singled out, as man is, for special notice. It appears from the sequel of the order of march, that when all was ready the ark set forward first, and that there was a formal, though a very brief, liturgy observed, both when it set forward and when it rested. "When the ark set forward, Moses said, Rise up, Lord, and let Thine enemies be scattered, and let them that hate Thee flee before Thee. And when it rested, he said, Return, O Lord, unto the many thousands of Israel" (Num. x. 35, 36). All, therefore, that any critic can fairly deduce from the second section, which our author represents as being irreconcilable with the first, is that it gives an item of information respecting the position of the ark in the order of march which is not furnished in the general account given in the first section; and it is only on the principle that additional information is necessarily contradictory, that anything bordering upon contradiction or discrepancy can be made out.

The Assumption necessary to make out the Charge of Discrepancy.

The only ground on which any plausible case against the historical integrity and harmony of the narrative, as given in the two sections, can rest, must be the assumption that the ark was inseparable from the other portions of the furniture of the sanctuary. If this were true, then, as we are told in the former section that the sanctuary was in the midst of the host, it might seem reasonable that, in a strictly accurate narration, the ark, which was inseparably connected with the sanctuary, could not be represented as moving in advance of the whole line of march. But is this assumption itself historical? Is it in accordance with the history of the ark that it was never separated from the sanctuary, and carried separately in advance of the host of Israel? A reference to the closing march of their desert journeyings will decide this question. When the children of Israel removed from Shittim, and came to Jordan, we are told that after lodging there for three days, the officers went through the host and commanded the people, saying, "When ye see the ark of the covenant of the LORD your God, and the priests the Levites bearing it, then ye shall remove from your place, and go after it. Yet there shall be a space between you and it, about two thousand cubits by measure: come not near unto it, that ye may know the way by which ye must go; for ye have not passed this way heretofore. . . . And Joshua spake unto the priests, saying, Take up the ark of the covenant, and pass over before the people. And they took up the ark of the covenant, and went before the people" (Josh. iii. 1–17). This passage proves two things: first, that the ark was sometimes separated from the sanctuary, and borne before the host of Israel; and, second, that one of the objects of such an arrangement was to show Israel "the way they must go."

Now, all that is necessary to the solution of the apparent discrepancy which our author is so careful to point out to "the Scottish public," is simply to assume that the arrangement made by Joshua on the plains of Moab over against Jericho, was also made in the wilderness, whenever the way had to be pointed out for the guidance of the host. This separation of the ark from the sanctuary, which we know as an historical fact, from this and other instances, was sometimes made, proves that the sanctuary might remain in its position next in order after the camp of Reuben, and yet the ark of the covenant not remain with it. Where an explanation, at once reasonable and in accordance with historic fact, can be given, there is no warrant for such critical impeachment of the sacred record. Nor is it unworthy of notice, that the cloud which accompanied and guided Israel abode upon that part of the Tabernacle which took its designation from the sacred law contained in the ark, and which was, for that reason, called "the tent of the testimony." Is it too much to assume that when this symbol of the divine presence moved to the front of the host as they were about to march, the ark, with which it was so closely associated, moved along with it? It would thus, as it moved along their wilderness pathway, illumined or shaded by the cloud of the divine glory, become a most expressive symbolic embodiment of the sentiment of the psalmist, "Thy word is a lamp unto my feet, and a light unto my path."

Consequence of the Failure of this Impeachment of the Record.

The historic integrity of the impugned record, therefore, abides despite the allegations of its adversaries; and the consecration of Aaron and his sons must be regarded as an unquestionable historical fact. There is no possibility of getting rid of this fact, except by denying the truthfulness of the record; and there is no way by which its truthfulness can be successfully challenged, save by proving that its parts are incongruous or contradictory. This "the newer criticism" has tried, at every point in which it could cherish any hope of success, but it has failed. Aaron and his sons still hold their place on the pages of the pre-exilic record as consecrated priests,—as priests consecrated by divine ordination to minister in the priest's office before the covenant God of Israel. From these first-born of the Aaronic order the Levitical system, in all its perfection, is inseparable; and the critical system which teaches that it was a thing of gradual development, reaching its maturity only in post-exilic times, must be regarded as irreconcilable with the central institution of the Mosaic economy.

The New Testament endorses this Impugned Record.

But this is not all. It is not saying all, to say that this post-exilic theory is inconsistent with what is taught in the Pentateuch regarding the Aaronic or Levitical priesthood and its sacrificial system; for besides doing, or threatening to do, violence to the plainest and most unquestionably established facts of the Pentateuchal history,—in fact, endeavouring absolutely to disintegrate and invalidate the entire record, a record which is unreadable when despoiled of its priestly Torah,—it must, if it hopes to succeed, deal in the same spirit of irreverence with the New Testament, which is correlative to this same Pentateuch, and especially to those very portions of it which " the newer criticism" has singled out as the object of its most determined onslaughts and its deadliest hostility. The New Testament not only recognises the Levitical system, but it recognises that system as Aaronic. In proving that Christ was duly called to His office as our High Priest, the author of the Epistle to the Hebrews argues from the appointment of Aaron. "No man taketh this honour unto himself, but he that is called of God, as was Aaron. So also Christ glorified not Himself to be made an High Priest; but He that said unto Him, Thou art my Son, this day have I begotten Thee" (chap. v. 5, 6). Could there be a stronger testimony to the divine authentication of the Aaronic priesthood than this? The call of Aaron is the norm and pattern of the appointment of Christ Himself to the mediatorial function of His own glorious high-priesthood. The doctrine of this epistle, therefore, gives no countenance to the theory that would relegate the Torah by which a high priest is distinguished from other priests to the days of the Babylonish exile. The high priest it fixes upon, as furnishing, in his appointment, the type and pattern of Christ's vocation, is Aaron himself; and this selection of Aaron, for this purpose, proves that the Levitical priesthood, with its priestly distinctions, was, from the days of Aaron, an institution as truly sanctioned of God as was the priesthood of our Redeemer. Aaron's priesthood has been challenged before now. "Korah and his company" held the very same views respecting the eligibility of all Israelites to the office of the priesthood as are advocated by Kuenen and his company, and were opposed, as these men are, to the Aaronic monopoly of priestly functions. They thought, as these newer critics do, that all the congregation were holy, every man of them entitled to act as a priest. The gainsaying of the latter is as ambitious and irreverent as the gainsaying of Korah; and as it is impossible to separate irreverent treatment of the type from irreverence done to the Antitype, the theory which would strip the priesthood of Aaron and his sons of the authority of a positive divine institution, striking, as it must, if carried to its logical issues, at the divine authentication of the priesthood of Christ, cannot but be exceedingly offensive to Him who called Him to suffer, and raised Him to intercede.

CHAPTER XII.

THE NEWER CRITICISM AND THE PRIESTLY OFFICE.

ONE of the things which gives peculiar force to this argument from the divine authentication of the high-priesthood of Aaron, as distinguished from, and yet carrying along with it, *pari passu*, the priestly status of his sons, is the fact, so clearly revealed in the Epistle to the Hebrews, that priesthood is correlative to sacrifice, and that they are not priests at all who have no sacrifice to offer. Its doctrine is, that " every high priest is ordained to offer gifts and sacrifices ; " and the argument is, that inasmuch as every high priest is set apart to this, as the leading function of his office, " it is necessary that this *high priest* also " (the Lord Jesus Christ, who was called to this office) " have somewhat to offer " (Heb. viii. 3). It is therefore a fundamental, that a high priest be a sacrificing priest. A priest without a sacrifice were a misnomer. Such is the doctrine which lies at the basis of the argument in this epistle in exposition and defence of Christ's Messianic claims, and it is manifest that it links sacrifice to the priesthood of Aaron and his sons from the very hour of their consecration. In other words, the Levitical system, with its grades of priests, its exclusive priesthood, and its sacrifices, is as old as the Mosaic economy, under which it was introduced by the typical mediator of that economy himself. All, therefore, that is advanced by these lectures in support of the position that the sacrifices and ritual of the Levitical system were not, in pre-exilic times, " of positive divine institution," or that " the Levitical system was not enacted in the wilderness " (p. 288), turns out to be, not simply contradictory of the so-called " traditional theory," but of the Pentateuchal theory itself, as interpreted by the Holy Spirit in the Epistle to the Hebrews. As our author says, in speaking of the views of the prophets on the relation of Jehovah to the Levitical system, so may the friends of " this traditional theory " say of the views of the author of this epistle regarding his theory—" it is impossible to give a flatter contradiction " to the theory which denies that the Levitical system was enacted in the wilderness. He may say that " the theology of the prophets before Ezekiel has no place for the system of priestly sacrifice and ritual," but the Epistle to the Hebrews places both the sacrifice and the ritual under the shelter of the Tabernacle erected by Moses after the pattern given him in the mount.

The Relation of the Priestly to the Prophetic Office.

One of the gravest errors of " the newer criticism," as set forth in this book, is the doctrine it inculcates respecting the relation of prophecy to priesthood in pre-exilic times. As the author himself says (p. 284), "the account of prophecy given by the prophets themselves," as he interprets them, "involves, you perceive, a whole theory of religion, pointing in the most necessary way to a New Testament fulfilment." A whole theory of religion is undoubtedly involved in his views of prophetic teaching on the subject of priesthood and sacrifice. The prophetic doctrine, he alleges, "moves in an altogether different plane from the Levitical ordinances, and in no sense can it be viewed as a spiritual commentary on them. For under the Levitical system Jehovah's grace is conveyed to Israel through the priest; according to the prophets, it comes in the prophetic word. The systems are not identical; but may they at least be regarded as mutually supplementary?" (p. 285).

Author's View of the Relation of Priesthood to Prophecy.

Having raised this last question, the author proceeds to supply an answer; and to this answer attention is now directed. "In their origin, priest and prophet are doubtless closely connected ideas. Moses is not only a prophet but a priest (Deut. xviii. 15; Hos. xii. 13; Deut. xxxiii. 8; Ps. xcix. 6). Samuel also unites both functions; and there is a priestly as well as a prophetic oracle. In early times, the sacred lot of the priest appears to have been more looked to than the prophetic word. David ceases to consult God when Abiathar the priest joins him with the ephod. (Com-

R

pare 1 Sam. xiv. 18, xxii. 10, xxiii. 9, xxviii. 6 with xxii. 5.) Indeed, so long as sacrificial acts were freely performed by laymen, the chief distinction of a priest doubtless lay in his qualification to give an oracle. The word which in Hebrew means a priest is in old Arabic the term for a soothsayer (*Kôhen, Kâhin*), and in this, as in other points, the popular religion of Israel was closely modelled on the forms of Semitic heathenism, as we see from the oracle in the shrine of Micah (Judg. xviii. 5; comp. 1 Sam. vi. 2; 2 Kings x. 19). The official prophets of Judah appear to have been connected with the priesthood and the sanctuary until the close of the kingdom (Isa. xviii. 7; Jer. xxiii. 11, xxvi. 11; comp. Hos. iv. 5). They were in fact part of the establishment of the Temple, subject to priestly discipline (Jer. xxix. 26, xx. 1 seq.). They played into the priests' hands (Jer. v. 31), had a special interest in the affairs of worship (Jer. xxvii. 16: *supra*, p. 114 seq.), and appear in all their conflicts with Jeremiah as the partisans of the theory that Jehovah's help is absolutely secured by the Temple and its services.

" But the prophecy which thus co-operates with the priests is not spiritual prophecy. It is a kind of prophecy which the Old Testament calls divination, which traffics in dreams in place of Jehovah's word (Jer. xxiii. 28), and which, like heathen divination, presents features akin to insanity, that require to be repressed by physical constraint (Jer. xxix. 26). Spiritual prophecy, in the hands of Amos, Isaiah, and their successors, has no such alliance with the sanctuary and its ritual. It develops and enforces its own doctrine of the intercourse of Jehovah with Israel, and the conditions of His grace, without assigning the slightest value to priests and sacrifices. The sum of religion, according to the prophets, is to know Jehovah, and obey His precepts. Under the system of the law enforced from the days of Ezra onwards, an important part of these precepts are ritual" (pp. 285, 286).

Analysis of the foregoing Assertions.

On so important a question it is but due to the author that he should be permitted to speak for himself at full length. The passage just quoted, beyond all doubt, places his views fairly before the reader. The doctrine avowed is: 1. That prior to the days of Ezekiel or Ezra, during what is generally designated by "the newer criticism" pre-exilic times, Jehovah's grace was conveyed in the prophetic word, and not through the priest. 2. That from Ezra and onwards, and not earlier, an important part of Jehovah's precepts, which it is necessary to obey, are ritual, or, as it is put (p. 304), where the conclusion on this point from the whole argument is stated, "The ritual element which the law adds to the prophetic doctrine of forgiveness became part of the system of God's grace only after the prophets had spoken." That is, before the exile God's grace was administered through the prophets; after the exile it was administered through priests. Enough has been said already upon the incongruities of the economies as thus sketched, and of the marvellous wisdom ascribed to what is here called Semitic heathenism, which, according to this theory, must be credited with a full pre-exilic forecast of the essential features of the economy of redemption—a forecast so accurate and so instructive, both in regard to the earthly and the heavenly manifestations of an economy which reveals to the principalities and powers in the heavenly places the manifold wisdom of God Himself, that God, who had previously stood aloof from it, and often through His prophets denounced it, eventually changed His entire attitude towards it, and adopted it as the type and shadow of the gospel of His Son, as administered by Him both in the estate of humiliation and exaltation. It does not seem to be too much to assume that this feature of the theory needs no further exposure to enable any one, who is at all acquainted with the nature and design of the economy of redemption, to see that it is altogether at variance with both.

Is the Primary Function of a Priest Oracular?

Passing from this aspect of the subject, therefore, the point now to be considered is, How does priesthood stand related to prophecy? Is it true that the primary function of a priest is oracular? This seems to be what our author wishes to teach when he dwells so much on the fact that the priests delivered oracles, and that "in early times" (he always knows exactly what took place in early times) "the sacred lot of the priest appears to have been more looked to than the prophetic word;" and when he alleges that "so long as sacrificial acts were freely performed by laymen, the chief distinction of a priest doubtless lay in his qualification to give an oracle." It is for this reason he argues from the etymological kinship between the Hebrew word (*Kôhen*) for a priest, and the old Arabic word (*Kâhin*) for a soothsayer. Such, unquestionably, is the doctrine taught in this extract; but such is not the doctrine of either Jew or Gentile, or of the Church of God, either in pre-exilic or post-exilic times, in regard to the leading function of a priest or of the relation of the priestly to the prophetic office. Reverting to the etymology, it becomes the ablest scholars to speak with modesty on this point. Lexicographers who rank among the foremost Hebraists tell us that the etymology of *Kôhen* is doubtful. Hitzig, quoted in Robinson's Gesenius, supposes *Kâhan* is equivalent to *Kûn*, to stand, whence *Kôhēn*, properly one who stands by, an assistant. The same author also cites Mauer as in favour of deriving it from *gâchan*, to incline, to bend, *i.e.* to bow down, as is done in worship, *Kôhēn* thus signifying one bowing down, making prostrations. Where the etymology of a word is so dubious, we must rely upon the usage of the best writers, and, in this case, chiefly upon the usage of the sacred writers; and in the interpretation of the Old

Testament writers, in this as in all other cases, we must be guided by the teaching of Christ and His apostles. Taking this ground,—ground which must commend itself to all Christian people, as well as to all sound scholarship,—whatever collateral aid we may derive from the use of terms of like or kindred radicals in other cognate languages, we must take our departure from the New Testament definitions, wherever these are given. In the present case, as we have already seen, we have a definition. The Epistle to the Hebrews defines a high priest as one "taken from among men, and ordained for men in things pertaining to God to offer both gifts and sacrifices for sins." Referring to the high-priestly office of Christ, the same epistle (chap. ii. 17) embraces, in its description of its functions, "the making of a propitiation for the sins of the people." Contrasting Christ as a High Priest with the high priests that were under the law (chap. vii. 26, 27), the author of the same epistle says: "For such an High Priest became us, who is holy, harmless, undefiled, separated from sinners, and made higher than the heavens; who needeth not daily, like those high priests, to offer up sacrifices, first for his own sins, and then for the *sins* of the people: for this He did once for all, when He offered up Himself." So also again (chap. viii. 3): "Every high priest is appointed to offer both gifts and sacrifices: wherefore it is necessary that this *high priest* (as the new version gives it) also have somewhat to offer."

The True Ideal of a Priest.

Now, if our views regarding the Scriptural ideal of a high priest are to be ruled by the express teaching of the New Testament revelation, there can be no difference of opinion regarding its fundamental, essential conception. A high priest must be what he is appointed to be and to do, and he is appointed to act on behalf of men before God, and to offer on their behalf "both gifts and sacrifices for sins." Whatever else may pertain to his office, or, rather, whatever other functions he may have been called upon to execute from his acquaintance with the law of his God, which others could not know as he did, his business, as a high priest, did not consist in the performance of these, but in the presentation before God of "gifts and sacrifices for sins." He differed from a prophet in two respects: 1. While a prophet represented God, and dealt with men on behalf of God, a priest represented men, and dealt with God on their behalf. 2. While a prophet had to do with the divine word, and was the ordained messenger of God to bear it to men, a priest had to do with the gifts and sacrificial offerings of men, and was the ordained medium through whom these gifts and offerings were presented before God. A prophet, as a prophet, could bear to men a message of peace or a message of wrath; could utter a promise or proclaim a threatening; but to the office of the priest alone it pertained to avert, by atonement, the threatened vengeance, and to open up the way for the message of peace. The keynote of the Mosaic economy is, "The priest shall make an atonement for him, and it shall be forgiven him." The doctrine of that economy, as stated in the Epistle to the Hebrews (chap. ix. 22), is that "apart from shedding of blood there is no remission." The priestly function, therefore, lies at the foundation of the prophetic, and conditions it.

Definition not to be determined by mere Etymology.

It is not therefore by mere etymology that the functions of the priest, as distinguished from those of the prophet, are to be discovered. What though the *Kôhen* of the Hebrew were not only of kindred, but of identical, meaning with the *Kâhin* of the Arabic, and that the latter meant a soothsayer and not a priest? Would it follow from this, that when these terms became the vehicle for the communication of a divine revelation, they retained, unmitigated and unmodified, their heathenish import? To take this ground were to inaugurate a new era in Biblical criticism, and to sacrifice to the merciless Molech of a rationalistic theory some of the most unchallengeable facts in the history of classic literature. While the radical meaning of a word makes itself felt throughout the various meanings it assumes in the course of its history, it is scarcely necessary to remark that the naked root import of a word is largely overborne and lost sight of in the wear and tear of social change and human progress. Especially true is this when a language employed by heathen is made the vehicle for the communication of a divine revelation. The transfusion of such ideas into any such language renders a new lexicon of that language an absolute necessity. For example, when the Septuagint translators proceeded to transfuse into the language of the Greeks the religious conceptions of the Jews, as given in the Hebrew of the Old Testament, they had no alternative but to select such religious terms as were in use among the Greeks, limiting and explaining such terms by other terms so as to prevent misapprehension.

Special Illustration from the Practice of our Missionaries in India.

This, of course, is a matter of necessity in all such cases. It is just what our missionaries to the heathen are compelled to do, when they endeavour to communicate the truths of Christianity through the medium of languages which have never before been made the vehicle of such ideas. They seize upon such terms as the heathen employ to express their ideas in regard to religious subjects, and so expand, or limit and modify them as to express the truths of the gospel. This fact determines the rule of interpretation in all such cases, whether the new vehicle be the language of Natal or of Greece, of Ur of the Chaldees or of the sons of Araby. The old term, consecrated to the new service, is never to be interpreted exclusively by the meaning attached to it prior to its consecration. In a word, a purely classical lexicon of any language, prior to its impregnation with the truths of the Old Testament or the New, however valuable it may be as an aid, can never serve as the sole standard of interpretation after that language has been leavened with these new ideas.

The bearing of these facts upon a large portion of this book is obvious. If these facts be unchallengeable, as they are beyond all doubt, then it must follow that it is not by an exclusive reference to the root of *Kôhen*, or of any other term, that we are to ascertain its actual historical import. It is not by referring to the roots of the Gujarati terms for the Supreme Being, *Ishwar, Parameshwar, Prābhu*, or of the corresponding Hindustani and Persian term *Khuda*, or to the root of the terms *Dév, Dévi*, employed to designate an object of worship, that we are to learn what meaning these terms have when used by our missionaries as vehicles of Christian thought. These terms in the mouth of an unevangelized native have a very different meaning from what they have as employed by a native who has learned to associate with them what the sacred Scriptures reveal concerning the attributes, prerogatives, and relations of the God and Father of our Lord Jesus Christ. The missionaries have set these terms in a context which renders it impossible to attach to them those degrading conceptions with which they were wont to be associated in the heathen mind. And so it is with the Hebrew term *Kôhen;* it is not by referring to its root, or to the import of the cognate Arabic term *Kâhin*, that we are to find out the idea it was employed by the great lawgiver of Israel, or the sacred penmen, to convey. They have placed it in such an environment as to render its meaning, irrespective of its etymology, clear and unmistakable. In its technical sense, it is always used to designate one who offers on behalf of men " both gifts and sacrifices for sins."

The Nature of the Priestly Function determines its Relation to the Prophetic.

Such is the strictly technical sense of the term *Kôhen*, and this fact must, to the minds of all men acquainted with the relations subsisting between men in their fallen, sinful, guilty estate, and a holy, righteous God, determine the relation which the priestly office sustains to the prophetic. If it be the great function of a priest to make atonement for sin, and if there stand between God and men such an obstacle to intercourse as the guilt of sin implies, then before the prophet can bear a message of peace, the channel of communication, closed up by sin, must be reopened by an act of expiation, which pertains to the office of the priest alone. And if such be the natural estate of man, and such his relations Godward, it would follow that, whether the oracular function were exercised by the priest himself, or by the prophet, it must always have been a subordinate function to that of expiation. It is very likely that it was owing to this dependence of the prophetic upon the piacular function that the heathen sought to ascertain the mind of their gods by the inspection of the entrails of animals. But however this may be, the Scriptures plainly teach that the priestly is the primary, fundamental function, and that on it the prophetic as well as the kingly rests. Our author may say, as he does (p. 285), that prophecy can in no sense be viewed as a spiritual commentary upon the Levitical ordinances, and may further represent the priestly and the prophetic functions as not even mutually supplementary; but the Scriptures give a very different account of the relation subsisting among these great functions of the one great mediatorial office of our Redeemer, as shadowed forth under the Old Testament, and realized and executed under the New.

Relation of Christ's Priestly Functions to His Prophetic and Kingly Functions.

Both in the word of God, and in the estimation of God's people, the work performed by Christ as priest underlies and sustains all He has done, does now, or shall yet do as a prophet or king. It was on the ground and condition that He should bear the iniquities of His people as a priest that He was to have the right of teaching them as a prophet, or of exercising toward them, and on their behalf, the prerogatives of a king. "Through His knowledge (as a prophet) shall my righteous servant justify many;" but He shall do so only on the condition that as a priest "He shall bear their iniquities." As a victorious king He was to obtain a portion with the great, and divide the spoil with the strong; but this spoiling of principalities and powers is ascribed to the pouring out of His soul unto death, His being numbered with the transgressors, and His bearing the sins of many (Isa. liii. 11, 12). He comes as a prophet preaching peace both to Jews and Gentiles, to those who were afar off, and to those who were nigh; but He has the right to execute this prophetic function because He has made peace by the blood of His cross (Eph. iii. 15–18). And as He takes His mediatorial stand upon the basis of His priestly work, so do His servants in the execution of their prophetic functions. They receive commission from Him as prophets, messengers, ambassadors, but it is Christ in His priestly office they pre-eminently proclaim. Christ and Him crucified is the great theme of Moses and all the prophets. "Ought not Christ to have *suffered* these things, and to enter into His glory?"

Relation of these Functions as foreshadowed in the Mosaic Legislation.

Fully to elucidate this relation of the priestly to the prophetic and the kingly offices would require a treatise of no ordinary dimensions. It may be sufficient to refer to the fact, very pertinent in the present case,—a fact which must be patent to almost all who have read the Old Testament,—that the prophetic and kingly offices, in their leading functions, were correlative to the Mosaic legislation, which centred in the work of the Aaronic priesthood, whose work culminated in those priestly acts which characterized the great day of atonement, when by typical sacrifices the ceremonial guilt of Israel was expiated, and the true Israel pointed forward to a higher priest and a nobler sacrifice—a priest by whose mediation the guilt arising from the transgression of the moral law should be fully and truly expiated. In a word, the Mosaic economy, with its sacerdotal system, as illustrated by prophets and maintained by kings, points to the all-important truth that the priestly office of the Messiah is the basis of all His other mediatorial functions, as it is the anchor of faith and the foundation of hope.

Argument from the Experience of God's People.

In accordance with this representation is the experience of the Church of God. From the hour in which the sinner is convinced of sin, until he is finally delivered from it, he cleaves to Christ, especially in His priestly character. He looks to Him as a prophet to instruct him, and to Him as a king to subdue, deliver, and defend him; but the look of faith that brings peace is turned on Christ as an atoning and interceding high priest. The message which inspires confidence, and awakens hope in the tempest-tossed soul, is the message in which Christ is proclaimed as the crucified. It was this that the apostles preached —Christ and Him crucified; and of it the Apostle Paul affirms that it is the power of God unto salvation—the power of God and the wisdom of God. On this great truth, pre-eminently the Church of God is sustained here, and on it she shall ever feed. Her Shepherd feeds her and leads her now, and will ever feed and lead her as her prophet and king; but in what character soever He acts, and under whatsoever guise He appears, He will stand forth pre-eminently as a priest. The horns symbolical of His kingly office, and the eyes symbolical of His qualifications for His prophetic office, we must not forget, belong to Him as the Lamb that was slain. It is because He was slain that He occupies the throne, and it is for the same reason He is entitled to receive power, and riches, and wisdom, and might, and honour, and glory, and blessing, and has the right to feed His redeemed, leading them ever to fresh fountains of the waters of life.

Importance and Gravity of this Question.

These sayings are faithful and true, and the great truth they inculcate is fundamental to the economy of redemption. If, as we have now seen, the priesthood of Christ is the fundamental function of His mediatorial office,—the function on whose exercise all other functions depend, and to which all others are correlative; the function for whose illustration and foreshadowing the Mosaic economy was instituted; the function to which the convicted sinner and the entire Church, both in her militant career and triumphant estate, ever turn,—it must be a serious matter to treat it as the author of this book has done. If such be the relation of Christ's priesthood to the economy of grace, there must be a grave responsibility attaching to any man, whether he occupy the position of a minister, or a professor, or a private member of the Church, who gives to the public a course of lectures professedly prepared and published in the interests of the science of Biblical criticism, but whose chief object, as well as entire scope, is to remove from the Old Testament every trace of this essential priestly function, as a function divinely authenticated prior to the captivity of Judah in Babylon; while, at the same time, the author gives to a system of unauthorized popular religion, common to the heathen as well as to Israel, the credit of having embodied the essential elements of this same function, and represents God as accepting and perfecting this offspring of the religion of nature, as the type and pattern of an economy which is to make known to the principalities and powers in the heavenly places His own manifold wisdom! The difference between putting Christ out of the Old Testament for over three thousand years, and putting out of it, for the same period, the fundamental function of His mediatorial office, is so difficult of estimation, that very few of God's people will believe that there is between these two things any difference at all. It will be difficult to bring evangelical Christendom to believe that for more than three thousand years men were saved, if they were saved at all, on *quasi* Socinian principles, and that from the time of the return from Babylon the way of life was changed from the Socinian to the evangelical.

"*The Newer Criticism*" *and Development.*

"The newer criticism," as represented by our author, claims to hold by a scientific doctrine of economic development; but the science of the theory, as it is set forth in this book, seems to be very questionable. Scientists, even of the Darwinian school, are wont to hold that the essential elements of the existing organism of the present day were contained in the original primordial germ, ere the process of development began. According to this theory of the development of the economy of redemption, however, the redemptive element, which is of the very essence of the economy,—an element without which there can be no remission of sin or deliverance from its thrall and bondage,—was not to be found in it during the first three thousand years of its history! But the old doctrine of the economy, which our author discards as merely a tradition, and as an unscientific conception, claims that at every stage of its history, from the hour of its annunciation to our first parents, the redemptive element has had its place. We find it in the primordial germ of the economy as given in Gen. iii. 15, in the bruising of the heel of the woman's seed as he triumphs over and crushes the head of the adversary. We find it in the offerings of Abel, and Noah, and Abraham; and, in strict accordance with the development of the redemptive purpose of Jehovah, on the theatre of its actual enactment, we find those essential elements, which gave character to the economy in antediluvian and patriarchal times, gathered up and organized in an economy, for whose exhibition in pre-exilic times a whole nation was called into existence, and kept and guarded by special interpositions of Jehovah, in signs and wonders wrought in the land of Egypt, and in the field of Zoan, and at the Red Sea, and in the wilderness, the whole process culminating in their settlement in the promised land, and in the erection of a Temple, in which the redemptive element from day to day, and feast to feast, and year to year, was ever kept before the covenant people by typical atoning victims offered by a typical priesthood. Such is the so-called traditional theory; and the reader is asked to look upon this picture and then on that, and say which of the two accounts of the history of redemption has the higher claims to rank as scientific. According to the theory which our author rejects, the slain Lamb, whose blood alone can wash men from their sins, whether in pre-exilic or post-exilic times, appears in the typical sacrificial victims which bled and burned before God until He Himself took up the mighty burthen of our guilt, and blotted out the handwriting that was against us, nailing it to His cross. According to the theory which he has advocated in this book, and for which he claims scientific rank, the Messiah, as the sinner's atoning substitute, is unrepresented to the mind of the Church by any type or symbol, for which divine sanction could be claimed, for more than three thousand years! Of such a view of the Messiah's office, as the Saviour of men, the pre-exilic prophets knew nothing, and of it Israel never heard until Ezekiel, during the exile, had a vision of the Levitical system on a mountain in the land of Israel, or, perhaps, until Ezra brought to the children of the captivity at Jerusalem a copy of the law of his God! If any one who makes this comparison of the two sketches of the economy of grace, even on the score of their respective scientific claims, decides in favour of "the newer critical" theory, all that needs be said is, that he must have strange notions of what constitutes a science. The proper analogue of such an attempt at a scientific exhibition of the economy of redemption would be a scientific exhibition of the solar system with the sun left out, or a sketch of the theory of La Place with the central generative incandescent sphere introduced into the system after all the planets and their satellites had been developed and arrayed in their respective orbits. What the sun is to our solar system, what the central incandescent sphere is to the La Placean theory, such are the priestly functions of Christ to the economy of redemption. They are indispensable to it now, and have been essential to it throughout all the stages of its wondrous evolution.

"The newer criticism" may call this view of the economy of redemption a tradition; but it is not the less Scriptural for being traditional. There are traditions which we have apostolic authority for holding fast; and if there be a tradition to be held with all tenacity, it is the tradition which makes Christ, and Him crucified, its Alpha and its Omega. Such is the tradition assailed in this book—assailed, it is to be hoped, unwittingly; but it is the tradition of apostles and prophets, of martyrs and confessors, of the whole brotherhood of the Reformation, and of all that is truly evangelical in Christendom in whatsoever Church. With this tradition, in its essential priestly element, the mysterious drama of man's redemption opens, and with it, as fully developed in the exaltation of the Lamb that was slain to the throne of the Father to preside over the fountain of the water of life, which is to gladden eternally the city of God, the mystery of the cross is finished. It is a tradition for which, on many a moor and in many a glen, our Scottish forefathers laid down their lives; and the prayer of the author of this present vindication is, that the sons of these heroic sires may refuse all compromise with its rationalistic rival, and contend for its every jot and tittle as for the citadel of our common Christianity.

CHAPTER XIII.

STRICTURES ON THE ARTICLE "BIBLE."[1]

GENERALIZATION upon the basis of questionable or imperfect *data* is one of the most fertile sources of error in the fields of science and philosophy. The author of this article has caught the spirit of the age, and has carried it into the department of Biblical criticism. The first manifestation of its influence is seen in the opening of the second paragraph: "The pre-Christian age of the Biblical religion falls into a period of religious productivity, and a subsequent period of stagnation and merely conservative traditions." This generalization, besides being entirely too sweeping, proceeds upon a false assumption regarding the relation between religion and revelation, making piety the basis and condition of revelation, and thus, in accordance with one of the rationalistic schools, assuming that the religious consciousness is the source of theology. So far is this representation from being in harmony with the fact, the reverse relation is the one taught in the Bible. Both under the Old Testament and the New, religion was originated and maintained

---

[1] Slightly altered from an article by the author of this Reply in the *British and Foreign Evangelical Review* for April 1880

by supernatural interpositions occurring at sundry times and in divers manners. The knowledge communicated was not the offspring of the religion, but the religion was the offspring of the knowledge. The order has ever been, faith cometh by hearing, and hearing by the word of God. It was just as true of Isaiah as it was of Balaam, that it was not by reading the record of his religious consciousness that he discovered the glories of the coming Messiah.

Nor was the Biblical religion left to depend upon one impulse which operated during a period of productivity, and then vanished away, leaving the Church to spiritual stagnation and conservative traditions. The diverse estates of action and stagnation have alternated throughout the history of the Church, divine communications always preceding religious revival. This fact forbids the generalization with which the writer has opened the discussion. The Biblical religion, so far as the Old Testament is concerned, cannot be classified under the two heads specified in this article. A glance at the history as given in the Bible itself is sufficient to justify this stricture. Entering on life in the image of God, with knowledge and holiness supernaturally communicated, and not left to acquisition or development, man lapsed and lost both. By a supernatural and gracious interposition he was brought again into covenant relation. Under this covenant the seed of the woman, whilst having his own heel bruised, was to bruise the head of the serpent. In the one family the enmity is revealed, and the apparent triumph of the serpent's seed terminates the first period of the covenant of grace. God interposes again, and by the gift of Seth in the room of Abel renews the conflict. The next great epoch is marked by the deluge, by which God avenges Himself upon an ungodly race, and delivers the only family in which the true religion was found. But as there was a Cain in the family of Adam, so was there a Canaan in the family of Noah. And even the descendants of Shem became so corrupt, that God, to preserve His truth, found it necessary to call out and separate Abram from amongst them. To illustrate this point fully would be to re-write the Bible. The true religion was maintained, if we are to accept the testimony of Scripture, by a series of supernatural impulses given at different epochs, and distributed all along the history of the covenant people, and not by an impulse operating for a period continuously, and then waning into feebleness and spiritual stagnation.

The writer is aware of this, and hence represents the period of productivity as also a period of contest. This is true. It is true of the life of the body taken as a whole, and true of the spiritual life of its individual members. There cannot, therefore, be any warrant for a generalization which assigns religious productivity a place at the beginning and religious stagnation a place at the end. The fact is, these estates have alternated from the beginning, and, if we are to credit the New Testament, will alternate to the end.

The period assigned for the beginning of the struggle

between the spiritual principles of the religion of revelation and polytheistic nature-worship, and unspiritual conceptions of Jehovah, is singularly inconsistent with the facts. It is alleged that the struggle began with the foundation of the theocracy by Moses. We are to infer, therefore, that there was no polytheistic nature-worship nor unspiritual conception of Jehovah among the covenant people prior to the foundation of the theocracy by Moses! This is a very questionable position. That polytheism had prevailed among the descendants of Shem before the call of Abraham is put beyond question by the express testimony of Joshua (chap. xxiv.), and that they continued to serve false deities is proved by the fact that Rachel, on leaving Padan-aram, took her country's gods with her. Surely we are not to assume, with Kuenen, the alternative that at that stage there was no monotheistic religion.

In this same paragraph it is stated, as a matter of course, that "it was only the deliverance from Egypt and the theocratic covenant of Sinai that bound the Hebrew tribes into national unity." What warrant is there for this statement? None whatever. During the lifetime of Jacob his sons were under his government, and recognised his authority. After his death till the time of Moses, there is little known of their tribal relationship. It is evident, however, that Moses was divinely commissioned to them as one people; for when he and Aaron went into Egypt they gathered together all the elders of the children of Israel, and when the people heard that the Lord had visited the children of Israel, and that he had looked upon their affliction, then they bowed their heads and worshipped. They were visited as being already Israel; they were redeemed as one people. It was neither the deliverance from Egypt nor the theocratic covenant that bound them into one nationality. On the contrary, it was as the one seed of Abraham that they were delivered, and their deliverance as a nation was in pursuance of the previously existing Abrahamic covenant. From the fact that Moses and Aaron gathered all the elders together, it is manifest that they were governed by an eldership which represented the whole nation.

The gradual development of the religious ideas of the Old Testament is spoken of as if it were a discovery of criticism, while the fact is that the doctrine of development is expressly taught in the New, and has been held by the people of God under both Testaments.

Separating the sacred ordinances from the religious idea,—a most unwarrantable procedure,—the writer alleges that their subjection to variation was less readily admitted. The passages cited prove, notwithstanding, that from the very inception of the Mosaic economy, the position taken was that variation was contemplated, and, within certain limits, was to be allowed. How this should affect our views in regard to the authorship of the Pentateuch one is at a loss to determine. Does it prove that Moses was, or was not, the author, to cite passages extending as far back as the 20th chapter of Exodus, which prove that sacrifices might, so far as the earlier legislation of the Pentateuch is concerned, be offered elsewhere than at the centre of worship, and then prove that Deuteronomy limits sacrifices to one centre? Well, the argument advanced is: that we find a practice of sacrificing in other places sanctioned by Ex. xx. 24 ff., followed by Samuel, and fully approved of by Elijah, forbidden by a written law-book found in the Temple in the days of Josiah (2 Kings xxii., xxiii.), and it is assumed that the legislation of this book does not correspond with the old law in Exodus, but with the book of Deuteronomy. The answer is obvious: 1. The book found is not described as "a written law-book," but as *the* book of the law. It is true the article is wanting before book, but it is before the noun "law," with which it is in construction, where it ought to be, and the phrase is properly rendered "the book of the law." This usage is in harmony with the rule that "the article is not prefixed to a noun in construction with a definite noun." 2. There is no need for the new hypothesis that Deuteronomy alone was found, because the old hypothesis assumes that it was embraced in the Torah along with the other books. 3. It is as easy to reconcile Deuteronomy with Exodus, on the old assumption that both were written by Moses at different stages in the development of the revelation, as on the new assumption that they were composed by different writers living at different epochs. The question is not how Moses could consistently write one law in Exodus and another law in Deuteronomy; but how God could authorize one, whether Moses or any other, to write diverse laws? It only enhances the difficulty to sever Deuteronomy from its historic position, and ascribe it to a date as late as the days of Elijah or Josiah. If God, by whose inspiration the Scriptures were written, could consistently issue, in the days of Elijah or afterwards, the law as it appears in Deuteronomy, could He not, with equal consistency, after a period of nearly forty years, and when His people were about to enter upon Canaan, authorize His servant Moses, whom He was about to remove from among them, to issue a more restrictive law? The force of this consideration is all the more manifest when one examines the Book of Deuteronomy, which contains the alleged diverse law, and finds that it endorses Exodus, from which it is said to differ. 4. The Book of Deuteronomy itself professes that the things written therein were spoken by Moses before the Israelites crossed the Jordan: " on this side Jordan, in the land of Moab" (chap. i. 5). No theory of the time of the issuing of the law in question, inconsistent with this claim, can be accepted by any man who believes in the inspiration of the Book of Deuteronomy.

And, finally, the assumption on which the whole argument proceeds is utterly destitute of foundation. It is alleged that "the legislation of the book" (found in the Temple) "corresponds not with the old law in Exodus, but with the Book of Deuteronomy." The reason for this statement is, that the reformation inaugurated by Josiah finds its sanction and authority, not in Exodus, but in Deuteronomy. Now, here two questions arise—(1) "What was the character of Josiah's reformation?" and (2) "Is the authority for it to be found in the Book of Deuteronomy alone, and not in Exodus, or elsewhere in the Pentateuch?" As to the former of these questions, the answer is furnished by the narrative of what the good king did, as given 2 Kings xxii., xxiii. From beginning to end the work of reformation was an overthrow of the instruments and symbols of idolatry, and the abolition of idolatrous practices both within and without the Temple, and the re-inauguration of the pure worship of Jehovah. With regard to the second, which is the vital question in this controversy, both elements of the reformation have their full sanction and authority in the Book of Exodus: "Ye shall not make with me gods of silver, neither shall ye make unto you gods of gold" (Ex. xx. 23). And this is, of course, but a reiteration of the second commandment: "Thou shalt not bow down to their gods, nor serve them, nor do after their works; but thou shalt utterly overthrow them, and quite break down their images" (Ex. xxiii. 24). "Ye shall make you no idols nor graven image, neither rear you up a standing image, neither shall ye set up any image of stone in your land, to bow down unto it: for I am the Lord your God" (Lev. xxvi. 1). These prohibitions of idolatry, both in Exodus and Leviticus, are followed by threatenings as severe as are to be found in Deuteronomy. (See the reason annexed to the second commandment, and the outburst of the divine vengeance against Israel for their sin in the matter of the calf which they importuned Aaron to make, and the whole of Lev. xxvi., and the wrath revealed against Israel in the matter of Baal-peor, Num. xxv.) So far, therefore, as the questions raised by the reformation of Josiah are concerned, there is no need for seeking a new book diverse from Exodus, or a new law diverse from anything found in the Pentateuch outside the Book of Deuteronomy. All that Josiah wrought has full warrant in and was demanded by the law as given in the Decalogue itself, and as reiterated and illustrated by terrible judgments in Exodus, Leviticus, and Numbers.

If, however, the position taken is that the reformation consisted not merely in the overthrow of idolatrous shrines and practices, but also in the abolition of other places of sacrificing to Jehovah than the single central one at Jerusalem, the reply is: (1) Granting this to be true, the doctrine of "a single sanctuary" can claim the support not only of the Book of Deuteronomy, but of the whole tenor of the Mosaic legislation. The doctrine is interwoven with the whole Mosaic economy. It is inseparable from the structure of the sacerdotal system, which restricted the priesthood to Aaron and his sons, and their successors. The invasion of the office by Korah and his company was visited by a fearful manifestation of the divine displeasure, and the record of it is found in Numbers, and not in Deuteronomy.

As there was but one priesthood, so also there was but "a single sanctuary." Moses was not enjoined to make several tabernacles, but one, and David did not receive the plan of several temples, but of one. The rule from the inauguration of the priesthood and Tabernacle in the wilderness, throughout the history of Israel, was a single sanctuary for all Israel. But (2) the assumption that the reformation effected by Josiah had exclusive, or even chief, reference to the erection of other sanctuaries or places of sacrificing to the true God cannot be granted. As already shown, the leading characteristic of the great revival of religion by the hand of the good king was the destruction of idolatrous instruments and practices. According to the words of Huldah the prophetess, the reason assigned for the wrath of God threatened against Judah was their forsaking of Jehovah and their burning incense unto other gods (2 Kings xxii. 17). These words were the keynote of both the wrath and the reformation, and it is only incidentally that reference is made to the characteristic which has been singled out as distinguishing the national reform.

However viewed, therefore, the generalization is both groundless and gratuitous, and there is no need for the assumption of a book of law so peculiar as to demand at the hands of a Biblical critic a theory such as is here advanced. There is no need for assuming that Deuteronomy alone was found, for there was nothing done that was not fully authorized in other parts of the Pentateuch, and there is no need for the assumption that Deuteronomy is anything else than what its name implies—a reiteration of the law. Hence the author of the narrative of this reformation, in winding up the history of king Josiah, sums up his character as follows: "And like unto him was there no king before him, that turned to the Lord with all his heart, and with all his soul, and with all his might, *according to all the law of Moses;* neither after him arose there any like him" (2 Kings xxiii. 25). He who penned these words took a broader view of the characteristics of both Josiah and his reformation than the author of the article in question has done. He represents his standard of action as the whole law of Moses, and does so in such connection and in such terms as to leave no room for doubt that he attributes the thoroughness of the reformation to the fact that the king ordered it according to the whole law.

It is not, then, "an obvious fact," as our author alleges, "that the law-book [the reader will mark that 'law-book' is a translation in the interest of the theory] found at the time of Josiah contained provisions which were not up to that time an acknowledged part of the law of the land." Could any theory be more absurd? On such a theory, how account for the wrath threatened against Judah by Huldah the prophetess, speaking in the name of Jehovah? What ground could there be for wrath against a people for not obeying a book hitherto unknown? The wrath of God, we are told, has its law, and is revealed against those "who hold (or repress) the truth in unrighteousness;" but here, if we are to credit the author, the wrath of God is revealed against Judah for not obeying a book of which they had never heard before! If the provisions of the book in question were not, up to that time, a part of the law of the land, Judah could not be held as guilty of any sin respecting it, and the discovery of it could not have awakened in the heart of Josiah such conviction of sin as caused him to rend his clothes. So far is Josiah from regarding this book as containing provisions hitherto unknown to Judah, that he recognises it as containing *an old law which had been neglected by their fathers.* His words on hearing it read are: "Great is the wrath of the Lord that is kindled against us, because our fathers have not hearkened unto the words of this book, to do according unto all that which is written concerning us" (2 Kings xxii. 13). Surely such language implies the existence of this book in the days of the fathers, and assumes their knowledge of it, and their refusal to obey it. The penalty dreaded by Josiah was the penalty incurred by the sin of departed fathers, which, according to the law, not only as given in Deuteronomy, but in Exodus, a jealous God was about to visit upon that generation. This reference to the fathers stamps the book with an antiquity which negatives the theory of its novelty, for the innovations abolished in purging the sin of these fathers embrace idolatries dating as far back as the days of Solomon and Jeroboam the son of Nebat. In fact, the good king purges the land of Judah and Israel of the symbols of idolatry introduced by the kings of Israel and Judah, throughout their whole history from the time of the degeneracy of David's successor—a period of about 380 years.

Nor is it to be overlooked in this discussion, that the law according to which the reformation was conducted, as stated in the article " Bible,"—the law of a single sanctuary,—was a " positive" enactment. For the violation of laws founded in our moral nature, or in the nature of things, we may be justly held responsible, and visited with punishment, without any revelation beyond the light of nature ; but it is not so in the case of laws founded simply on the will of God. In such cases, those alone are responsible to whom the divine will has been made known. Tested by this rule, the theory is disproved, for according to it the special sin condemned in the newly discovered book—the sin for which the wrath of God was kindled against Judah—was the multiplication of sanctuaries and worshipping elsewhere than at the single sanctuary. Now the law prohibiting this was obviously a positive law. No one could have discovered it by the light of nature, whether internal or external. It rested simply and solely on the divine will, and was a mere temporary provision, to be abolished for ever on the introduction of that coming dispensation when the true worshippers should worship the Father neither at " Jerusalem, nor in this mount," but anywhere in spirit and in truth. In order that Judah should have been held responsible for this law, it was absolutely necessary that they should have been made acquainted with it. This, however, if we are to credit the *Encyclopædia Britannica*, was not done; and thus we are conducted to the fearfully immoral conclusion, that for breach of an unknown positive enactment the descendants of the breakers of it are constituted the objects of the great wrath of Jehovah! Any theory leading to such a conclusion is *ipso facto* condemned (Rom. v. 13); "sin is not imputed when there is no law."

As additional arguments in support of this theory, there are adduced (p. 637) the refusal of Gideon (Judg. xiii. 23) to rule over Israel, and the answer of the Lord to Samuel (1 Sam. vii. 7), when he prayed to Him respecting the request of Israel to have a king. On these passages the writer remarks that, "if the law of the kingdom in Deut. xvii. was known in the time of the Judges, it is impossible to comprehend" these texts. To this it were sufficient to reply, that if the law in Deuteronomy was not in existence till, as the author teaches, after the days of Elijah, it is impossible to comprehend it. Let us glance at the preface to this law of the kingdom. It is as follows: "When thou art come unto the land which the Lord thy God giveth thee, and shalt possess it, and shalt dwell therein, and shalt say, I will set a king over me, like as all the nations that are about me; thou shalt in any wise set him king over thee whom the Lord thy God shall choose" (Deut. xvii. 14, 15). Now, according to our author, this law was issued after the days of Elijah, and therefore issued at least 550 years after Israel had come into the land, nearly 200 years after the kingdom had been set up, after it had been rent in sunder, and after the two kingdoms had been ruled over by several kings! If the book dates from the days of Josiah, when it was discovered, these figures must be greatly enlarged, and the theory become all the more manifestly absurd. If it is difficult to comprehend Samuel's hesitation and Gideon's refusal, on the assumption that these men knew of the existence of the law of Deut. xvii., it is absolutely impossible to comprehend this law viewed as an *ex post facto* enactment. What could be the object of issuing a law to regulate the election of the first king of Israel after the days of Elijah, yea, after the kingdom of the ten tribes had been carried into captivity? Biblical criticism does not demand from any man the sacrifice of his common sense, and common sense pronounces such projection of a law five or six centuries beyond the events it was designed to regulate an utter absurdity. Besides, if Samuel did not know of this law respecting the rise of the king, he must have known less than his own mother (1 Sam. ii. 10), and less than Eli (1 Sam. ii. 35), and less than the elders who, in their request for a king, quote the very words of Deuteronomy (1 Sam. vii. 5).

But this theory is embarrassed with something worse than anachronism and absurdity: it involves a charge of gross immorality against the author of the Book of Deuteronomy. Our author felt that it was not unnatural to raise this objection, for on p. 638 he anticipates it, and tries to fortify the theory against it: "If the author," he says, "put his work in the mouth of Moses, instead of giving it, with Ezekiel, a directly prophetic form, he did so, not in pious fraud, but simply because his object was not to give a new law, but to expound and develop Mosaic principles in relation to new needs. And as ancient writers are not accustomed to distinguish historical data from historical deductions, he naturally presents his views in dramatic form in the mouth of Moses." One, on reading this attempt to disembarrass the theory of the charge of immorality which it necessarily involves, instinctively reads it over again to ascertain whether he has not made a mistake in his interpretation of the language which the author has here put in print. But beyond question there it is. The defence is, that although Moses did not use the words put into his mouth by the author of Deuteronomy, he taught the principles which that author has simply expounded and developed in relation to new needs.

On this defence it may be remarked: 1. That the slight degree of plausibility attaching to it arises from its abstractness. It is perfectly true that any rule of action deduced by just and necessary inference from Mosaic principles may be represented as a part of the Mosaic legislation. This, however, is a very different thing from what the author of Deuteronomy has done. He has not deduced principles from the teaching of Moses, and put these principles in the mouth of Moses, but he has formally given us discourses uttered by Moses, and has told us when and where Moses uttered them. The moment one passes from the abstract defence to the concrete work for which it has been devised, all its plausibility vanishes. The actual work with which the theory professes to deal, and which it pronounces a drama, professes to be a *résumé* of the history of Israel throughout their wanderings from Horeb to the plains of Moab. The words recorded, and not the mere principles of the Mosaic legislation in their relation to new needs, the author represents as the words spoken by Moses. He tells us when they were spoken, for the events recorded in the third chapter fix the time, viz. "after he had slain Sihon the king of the Amorites, which dwelt in Heshbon, and Og the king of Bashan, which dwelt at Astaroth in Edrei;" and he tells us where the words were spoken, viz. "on this side the Jordan, in the land of Moab" (ch. i. 4, 5). The preface is manifestly historical, and it pledges the truthfulness of the author, not for the accuracy of historical deductions about to be drawn, but for the accuracy of the historical representation of words uttered and deeds performed. There is no more reason for regarding the book thus introduced as a post-Mosaic drama than there is for regarding Genesis, or Exodus, or Leviticus, or Numbers, as post-Mosaic romances. It were just as plausible to say that the previous books of the Pentateuch were *ex post facto* compositions written after the settlement in Canaan, for the purpose of justifying the Israelites for taking possession of other people's property, and instituting a peculiar system of national worship. It could be urged, as our author has pointed out, and as has often been pointed out by others, that even in Genesis, as in the other books, there are names of places which were not in use till after Israel had possessed the land. If the fact that Samuel and Gideon *seem* to have been unaware of the existence of the law respecting the king and the kingdom, found in Deut. xvii., necessitates the device of a theory which transforms Deuteronomy into a legal or ceremonial drama, and strips it of perhaps more than eight centuries of its antiquity, surely the reference to places under names which they did not bear till after the Israelitish occupation of the land must necessitate, not only the transference of the composition of these parts of the Pentateuch to a corresponding date, but, for the reason assigned by our author in the case of Deuteronomy, the transportation of them from their traditional character of veritable histories into historical dramas, in which we are presented with historical deductions instead of historical facts.

2. These considerations acquire additional force in view of the principle avowed by our author, to wit, that "ancient writers are not accustomed to distinguish historical data from historical deductions." If this principle be applied to Deuteronomy, who will forbid its application to Genesis, or Exodus, or Leviticus, or Numbers? May we not, indeed, regard the argument for such application *a fortiori*, as these books are on the hypothesis in question much more ancient? In his recent lectures this extension of the principle has been carried out.

3. If a composition couched in historical terms, and cast in historical form, as Deuteronomy is, without a single hint given to put the reader on his guard, and without a single expression from which one could infer that the writer was not putting on record actual historical occurrences, can, by the magic wand of criticism, be converted into a delusive drama, there is not only an end to all history, but a suicidal termination of all criticism. On such critical principles one must become not only an historical sceptic, but sceptical of all historical criticism, and find himself unable to determine whether the critic is in earnest, or whether he is not, as in Whately's *Historical Doubts* respecting Napoleon Bonaparte, turning a particular school of criticism into ridicule. There is no more reason for regarding Deuteronomy as belonging to the class of compositions to which our author has assigned it, than there is for assigning his article "Bible" to the class of the witty archbishop's famous critical *jeu d'esprit*.

4. But it is surely but fair to inform us what is meant by the expression "ancient writers." Without some temporal limitation, such phraseology must set our author's disciples completely adrift. Are we to understand, as he says, that it is customary with ancient writers not to distinguish historical data from historical deductions? If this be the common usage —the use and wont—of ancient writers, how are we to draw the line between the dramatic presentation of principles under the garb of history and actual

veritable historical compositions? On such an hypothesis, how much of ancient history, whether sacred or profane, will remain history, one is at a loss to determine. If the rule laid down by our critic be valid, it is questionable whether we have any ancient history at all, either inside the Bible or outside it. The critical genius that can turn Deuteronomy into a drama, can, with equal facility, turn any ancient composition, indeed any composition, whether ancient or modern, into anything embraced within the domain of literary composition.

5. Nor are we to overlook the fact that what is said of "ancient writers" is true only of writers of the fabulous period. Only of such writers can it be said that they were "not accustomed to distinguish historical data from historical deductions." Are we to understand him as teaching, by this reference to the use and wont of ancient writers, that writers such as the author of Deuteronomy and his predecessors (for if the expression embraces the one it must embrace the others) belonged to the fabulous period and to the class of fabulous writers? If he does not mean to place these ancient Biblical writers in this class, he has certainly been most unhappy in the selection of his terms; for he assigns this custom, which belongs to the period referred to, as a reason for stripping Deuteronomy of its historical character. If so, then it must follow that the author of Deuteronomy, and at least all his predecessors and contemporaries, belong to a period whose use and wont was unhistorical!

As this period embraces not only the Pentateuch, but all the books of the Bible as far as the books of the Kings and the Chronicles, and probably (for he refers Deuteronomy to the eighth and seventh centuries B.C.) the larger portions of these national records, we have no guarantee that the first half of the Old Testament (for fully that amount of it must, according to our author, be assigned to this undiscriminating period) is veritable history! Surely a criticism leading to such conclusions is self-condemned. It is reckless beyond all apology. Let its verdict be accepted, and the Scriptures are divested of all claim to be treated as the word of God. Men will not long regard a book as composed under the inspiration of the Holy Ghost, which represents a man as speaking what he never uttered, and doing so with every detail of time, and place, and occasion, and this in order to acquire for it an authority to which it is entitled only on the assumption that these representations are true.

6. And this leads to the very obvious remark, that from this wholesale reference to the use and wont of ancient writers, it is natural to infer that our author does not distinguish ancient writers into inspired and uninspired. He who infers from the literary usage of the age in which a book of Scripture was composed, what the character of the composition must be, does, *ipso facto*, treat the writer as an ordinary *littérateur*, and overlooks the grand fact that the writers are represented in the Bible itself as moved by the Holy Ghost. However others may deal with the sacred

record, no Christian critic can thus treat it. Christian criticism can admit of no theory which classes the sacred writers of any period with profane writers of the same period, and treats their compositions as if they were the products of mere uninspired genius, determined, as to form, and style, and phrase, not by the indwelling Spirit, but by the use and wont of the age. The Apostle Peter places the writers of the Old Testament beyond the pale of any such classification, for he affirms that they "spake as they were moved by the Holy Ghost," and not as they were moved by the Zeit-Geist or spirit of the age in which they lived. The fact that they spake in the language of their country and age, and availed themselves of existing modes of presentation, such as the parable and other literary devices, as vehicles for the communication of the truths they were commissioned to proclaim, is far from warranting the sweeping conclusion that they were so ruled by the literary use and wont as to confound historical deductions with historical data. The principle laid down by the Apostle Peter (and it is a principle which holds true of all "the ancient" sacred "writers") excludes any such conclusion. To say that men, under the inspiration of the Holy Ghost, writing seven or eight centuries after the entrance of Israel on the land of Canaan, and after the captivity of the kingdom of the ten tribes, drew up rules to be observed by Israel respecting the election of a king, is nothing short of imputing folly to the Most High. The sacred writers are not to be so confounded with their profane contemporaries as to ignore their relation to the Holy Ghost, under whose all-determining agency they were borne along and guided, and by which they needed to be infallibly directed even to the words they employed in communicating truths of whose signification they themselves had very imperfect conceptions.

Besides, what evidence have we, so far as the great body of the sacred writers are concerned, that they were so familiar with their profane contemporaries as to adopt them as literary models? Christian apologists have been in the habit of saying that it was *largely* the reverse—that the Gentile sages were *largely* indebted to the Jews. The author is much nearer the truth when he says that "the way in which a prophet, like Amos, could arise untrained from among the herdsmen of the wilderness of Judah, shows how deep and pure a current of spiritual faith flowed among the more thoughtful of the laity." Even here, however, there lurks a false theory of inspiration, by which the religious consciousness is made the source or medium of revelation. Well, it would seem that Amos at least was independent of the use and wont of ancient writers outside the wilderness of Judah, for it is not very likely that there was a circulating library embracing works of profane authors established among the herdsmen of Tekoa. To the same effect is the sentence which immediately follows. "Prophecy itself," says our author, "may from one point of view be regarded simply as the brightest efflorescence of the lay element in the religion of Israel, the same element which in subjective form underlies many of the Psalms, and in a shape less highly developed tinged the whole proverbial and popular literature of the nation; for in the Hebrew commonwealth popular literature had not yet sunk to represent the lowest impulses of national life." Assuming that the last remark was not intended to apply to anything embraced within the canon of the Old Testament, the passage may be accepted as a much more reasonable account of the literary influences which were ever at work on the Hebrew mind, than that which represents the sacred writers as subject to a certain *ab extra* influence, which may be designated the use and wont of ancient writers. If it were allowable to assume such familiarity with the actual procedure as characterizes this article, one might say that it was just in the way described that the Old Testament writers were raised up and endowed, so far as their literary culture was concerned, for the agency with which they were honoured as the instruments and vehicles of the Holy Ghost. It is more than likely that even Moses himself was more indebted to his home training by his Hebrew mother than he was to the culture received at the hands of the sages of Egypt. It is eminently true of all the sacred writers—with, perhaps, the exception of the author of the Book of Job—that they were nursed in the lap of Israel's piety, and nurtured on the word of Jehovah as it existed in their day. Thus trained at home, and by the very spirit and genius of their religion separated from the Gentiles and their literature, they acquired the national style—a style Hebraic in every instance, and utterly removed from anything that can be pointed out in the literature of any other nation under heaven, except those nations which have become acquainted with the sacred treasures of the chosen race. It is therefore difficult to imagine a more thoroughly baseless argument than that which infers the alleged dramatic form of Deuteronomy from the literary usage of ancient writers.

But we have now a very grave question to raise, and one which is peculiarly grave on the writer's theory. How came this unpublished book—for unpublished it must have been, if we are to credit our author,—how came this hitherto unpublished book to be in the house of the Lord? Is there a single instance in the previous history of the Mosaic economy of "a written law-book," with its legal prescriptions all formally written out, being employed as the medium for communicating the will of God to His people, prior to the oral communication of its contents from time to time, as the providence of Jehovah furnished the occasion? It was in this way the contents of Exodus and Leviticus and Numbers were introduced to Israel. The record containing the Mosaic legislation is so characterized by this peculiarity, that it has been called a legislative journal. The order of procedure is set forth in the opening words of Leviticus: "And the Lord called unto Moses, and spake unto him out of the tabernacle of the congregation, saying, Speak unto the children of Israel, and say unto them," etc. etc. Very different, however, if we are to accept the theory of our author, was the procedure in the case before us. Here is a book unheard of by priest or Levite, prophet, scribe, or king, until the days of Josiah, when some peculiar incident brings its existence to the knowledge of Hilkiah the priest, who gives it into the hands of Shaphan the scribe, who reads it before the king. Neither Hilkiah, nor Shaphan, nor the king seems to have doubted its divine origin or authority. It is at once recognised as the law of God, and its words produce in the mind of the king such a sense of Israel's sin and danger that he rends his clothes. Why should a book thus introduced produce such effects? How came it to pass that no one ever doubted its claims to the obedience of the king and his people? If our author's theory be true, it was destitute of the wonted authentication, for what he regards as its central doctrine was never heard of before, and yet as soon as it is read its claims are recognised! There is no possibility of accounting for its recognition and effects except on the assumption of its being a copy of the law given by Moses, or perhaps the autograph itself, which Moses after writing had commanded the Levites to put in the side of the ark of the covenant, for a witness against Israel (Deut. xxxi. 26). If it be asked, How could so sacred a book as this, and one so carefully laid up, pass out of sight and memory? the answer is to be found in the same chapter in which the account of the discovery of it is found. The corruptions of which Josiah had purged Judah and Jerusalem could never have been introduced had not the book of the law been neglected and cast aside. If Judah and her priests could permit the house of the Lord to become a partial ruin, if they could introduce idolatry, not only into the high places, but into the very precincts of the Temple itself, it is not to be wondered at that they permitted the sacred book of the law to share in the general neglect, and to be hidden among the rubbish until it was unearthed by the workmen who repaired the breaches of the house. Why, the marvel is that any one acquainted with the narrative of the universal decay of religion, and cognizant of the desecration of the Temple, and the state of dilapidation to which it had been reduced, should think any theory necessary to account for the effects produced by the discovery of the book, much less the extraordinary theory that the book could not have been the Book of Exodus, as its characteristic laws are not found therein! The state of religion and of the house accounts for the loss of the law of Moses laid up there, and the revival of religion and the repair of the house account for the finding of it; and there is no need for the hypothesis of a hitherto unknown book, which, if brought in at all, must have been introduced surreptitiously. His critical canon, that the non-observance of a law implies its non-existence, is the sprite which has allured our author into all this critical blundering.

Passing to the general question respecting the date and authorship of the Pentateuch and the earlier prophetical books, we find the old objections, raised by Spinoza and others his successors, urged once more by our author. The facts enumerated are, the fact that "the limits of the individual books are certainly not the limits of authorship;" the fact "that the Pentateuch as a law-book is complete without Joshua, but as a history is so planned that the latter book is its necessary complement;" the fact "that the Pentateuch uses geographical names which were not known till after the occupation;" the fact that in one place it even "presupposes the existence of a kingship in Israel;" the fact that "the last chapters of Judges cannot be separated from the Book of Samuel, and the earlier chapters of Kings are obviously one with the foregoing narrative." "Such phenomena," it is alleged, "not only prove the utter futility of any attempt to base a theory of authorship on the present division into books, but suggest that the history as we have it is not one carried on from age to age by successive additions, but a fusion of several narratives, which partly covered the same ground, and were combined into unity by an editor"! In reply to these old objections, it were sufficient to copy out of Horne's *Introduction* the conclusive answers so well summarised by that able apologist more than forty years ago. The resurrection of them in the present day, however, may serve as a partial apology for a fresh examination of their claims.

And first of all, it may be asked, "On what authority is it assumed that the traditional theory of

Biblical authorship is based upon the present division into books?" The contrary is the fact. The theory was the cause of the division, and not the division the cause of the theory. It was owing to the fact that both Jews and Gentiles, friends and foes, regarded Moses as the author of the Pentateuch that it has been regarded as a distinct book, the work of one author.

In the next place, it may be asked, "What is there in the systematic and orderly consecution of the books in question to necessitate the theory of one editor to combine them into unity?" Suppose it to be true that God had a plan of redemption, and that the history of His people was intended and designed, before its actual enactment on the stage of time, to be a systematic unfolding of that plan—suppose this to be the fact, would it not follow that the incidents, when placed on record, would fall in as consecutive, orderly arranged parts of the one plan devised and administered by the One Mind? And, on the other hand, to take the instance mentioned, would it not awaken suspicion, and lead us to conclude that the history could not be a history of the administration of such a plan, if it were found that Joshua was not "the necessary complement of the Pentateuch"? And would not this fact preclude the possibility of interjecting Deuteronomy after the history of the kingdom of the ten tribes, or at any point later than the death of Moses, and prior to the history of Israel under Joshua? Our author not only admits the existence of such a plan, but argues from it, and claims for Biblical criticism the discovery of its development. Granting, which we do not, that this discovery was never made till the Deborah of criticism arose in Israel, and holding, as we do, that the plan is developed in the history of the chosen race, does it not inevitably follow that the historical facts recorded do, by their character as a revelation, and the progressive development of this plan, determine their own position in the inspired narrative? In a word, does not the development theory held, as we have already seen, throughout the history of the Church, forbid the resurrection of Moses from his undiscovered tomb in the land of Moab, to deliver his farewell address to an Israel which must have been raised from the dead to hear it, 250 years after Elijah himself had gone to heaven, and 100 years after Israel had ceased to exist as a nation? Whensoever Deuteronomy was written, there is no place for it but that given it by both Jew and Gentile. Nowhere else can it be placed without marring the history of the development of the economy of redemption. And if this be the only place, the time is *ipso facto* determined, for it were truly preposterous to suppose that, after the economy had been developed to the point reached in the days of the kingdom of Judah, an inspired writer should write a book of which Joshua is the necessary complement. Let any one make the experiment suggested by the theory, and transfer Deuteronomy to the position assigned to it by this novel criticism, and if we have not overrated his claims to intelligence, he will feel shocked at the work of his own hands. Indeed, the principle of development itself furnishes a safe guide in all questions pertaining to the time and place of any part of the revelation. If, despite the lapses of the chosen seed, there is no lapse or retrogression in the revelation of which they were the ordained channel, if their very sins become the occasion for fresh disclosures of the plan of redemption, and its infinite resources of pardoning grace, we have in this fact a rule to which our Biblical critics would do well to take heed. If this be a law of the economy, then the books naturally arrange themselves along the pathway of the divine Logos, as He has unfolded, in His sovereign wisdom, the mystery which, from the beginning of the world, was hid in God. On this principle it would be just as preposterous to place Deuteronomy after Joshua, or after Judges, or after Samuel, or the Kings, as it would be to transfer Joshua to any of these places.

Nor are we to lose sight of the confession made by the author, to wit, that " a good deal may be said in favour of the view that the Deuteronomic style, which is very capable of imitation, was adopted by writers of different periods." This is a considerable abatement of the pretensions of Biblical criticism as an instrument by which the age of a given composition may be determined. If the style of a book may be imitated, and that " by writers of different periods," may not " a good deal be said in favour of the view " that the style of a book is not an absolute criterion of its authorship, and that genuine criticism implies much more on the part of a critic than a knowledge of the language in which the book has been written, or of the literature in which that language has been developed? In saying this, there is no intention to disparage such acquirements. On the contrary, it is held that they are among the most important of the many qualifications which the high functions of criticism demand. All that is here contended for is, that, on the author's own confession, a Biblical critic cannot determine the time or canonical place of a book by virtue of his linguistic or literary lore. In addition to all this, it is indispensable that the critic have a thorough acquaintance with the structure of the economy whose closely correlated provisions have been revealed through the agency of the sacred penmen, whose writings furnish, not merely grammatical exercises, but theological problems, which are immensely the profoundest with which the human mind has to deal. As already seen, the economy admits of no retrogression, and therefore, in this the norm of its evolution, furnishes one of the most reliable of all criteria for the determination of the times and canonical *loci* of the accumulating increments of a predetermined revelation.

But whilst the ordinary *apparatus criticus* furnishes, and can furnish, no safeguard against literary imposture, and is confessedly incompetent to detect an existing literary fraud, there are in the character of the economy and its author the highest of all guarantees against any such procedure. "Let God be true, but every man a liar." No man, whether learned or unlearned, can, without incurring great guilt, attempt to make the truth of God abound through his lie. And certainly no man, speaking by the Spirit of God, would put into the mouth of a well-known historical character words never uttered by him, and this, too, in constructing a book of law, whose whole drift and tenor render it altogether impossible to regard it in any other light than that of a veritable historical sketch, with additional legal enactments or expositions, suggested by experience, or demanded by the approaching demise of the legislator, and the settlement of those he had been appointed to lead, in the inheritance promised to their fathers.

On p. 638 the author neutralizes, to a very large extent, all that he had previously advanced in support of the late date of the composition of Deuteronomy:—

"The Levitical laws," he says, "give a graduated hierarchy of priests and Levites; Deuteronomy regards all Levites as at least possible priests. Round this difference, and points allied to it, the whole discussion turns. We know, mainly from Ezek. xliv., that before the exile the strict hierarchical law was not in force, apparently had never been in force. But can we suppose that the very idea of such a hierarchy is the latest point of liturgical development? If so, the Levitical element is the latest thing in the Pentateuch, or, in truth, in the historical series to which the Pentateuch belongs; or, on the opposite view, the hierarchic theory existed as a legal programme long before the exile, though it was fully carried out only after Ezra. As all the more elaborate symbolic observances of the law are bound up with the hierarchical ordinances, the solution of this problem has issues of the greatest importance for the theology, as well as for the literary history, of the Old Testament."

On reading this passage it is difficult to resist the conclusion that the writer has taken alarm at his former critical deliverances, and is here endeavouring to tone them down by pointing out the weakness of the grounds on which they mainly rest, and the lack of unanimity among the critics regarding the date of the Pentateuch—the question on which he has already delivered a final authoritative judgment. If the question be as here stated, and if, in the determination of it, we are dependent "mainly" on Ezek. xliv., which teaches that "before the exile the strict hierarchical law was not in force, and apparently had never been in force," it is no wonder his confidence should give signs of abatement. Leaving the contending critics to counterbalance one another, is there any one who has any regard for his reputation as a reader of the Bible, who will venture to base any theory in regard to "liturgical development," before the exile or after it, upon Ezekiel's vision of the Temple and its priesthood? From that vision it is impossible to find out what the liturgical law was either before the exile or after the restoration. The house seen by Ezekiel, and the priesthood which was to take part in its services, have never had, and were never intended to have, a literal realization. Whilst the vision was vouchsafed in order to cheer the hearts of his fellow-exiles, by the assurance of the restoration of the Temple, and city, and land, its chief object was to foreshadow the spiritual temple, by which all local centres of worship were to be superseded, and a dispensation under which the waters of the sanctuary were to flow forth to regenerate and fertilize the moral wastes outside the bounds of the land of Israel. If the vision is to be taken literally—and it is only on the assumption that it is to be so taken that it can serve the end to which the author has turned it,—if it is to be taken literally, there is no possibility of stopping short of the conclusion reached by the advanced premillennial school, who, on the ground that it has never been fulfilled, look for the restoration of the Jews to the land of Palestine, the rebuilding of the city of Jerusalem and the Temple, the restoration of the priesthood, and the re-inauguration of animal sacrifices — who, in fact, make Christianity a sort of interlude in the Mosaic economy. It is difficult to see how any one can seek for the law of liturgical development in this marvellous vision, and stop short of the singular theory which looks forward to a time when the waters which Ezekiel saw issuing from under the threshold of the house shall burst forth in reality, and continue to flow as a symbol of the Holy Ghost!

Equally manifest must it be that no theory in regard to the relative positions of Leviticus and Deuteronomy in the sacred canon can be based upon the alleged diversity of their laws respecting the position of the Levites. The facts alleged may be accepted, while the theory may be rejected. The Levites may be regarded as excluded from the priesthood by the law as given in Leviticus, and as possible priests according to the Deuteronomic legislation, and yet our views as to which of these books should have the precedence remain unaffected, and the question be undetermined. In order that the alleged diversity of legislation should have any weight in the determination of the question of chronological precedence, it is necessary to assume that a graduated hierarchy bespeaks an earlier or a later stage in the process of liturgical development.

But are we in a position to say which of these assumptions is true? Might not a good deal be said in favour of the view that the law of Deuteronomy on this point, which, it is alleged, regards all Levites "as possible priests," denotes an earlier stage? This much might be advanced with considerable force in its favour, viz. that a law limiting the priesthood to a tribe would naturally precede a law limiting it to a family. Prior to the Mosaic economy, and during an unquestionably earlier stage, there were no tribal distinctions in regard to the priestly office. All the tribes and all the families of Israel exercised the functions of the priesthood. Now, it would surely seem more reasonable, if we are to make assumptions at all, to assume that the first limitation in a process of development would be from the nation to a tribe, rather than from the nation to one of the families of a single tribe. As the goal of the economy was the typifying of the one priesthood as held by the one Priest, would it not seem as if the first step towards the attainment of it should be less definite than the subsequent ones, and that the graduated hierarchy, of which the Aaronic priesthood is the crown and consummation, should mark the close of the whole typical evolution? And, on the other hand, might it not be urged with equal force, in favour of the view that the law of Leviticus indicates an earlier stage, that in an economy which was not only to prefigure the Christian dispensation, but give way to it, and wax old and give signs of vanishing away, it might be expected that all along the track of its administration there would be introduced changes premonitory of a final dissolution? On general principles, therefore, it is very questionable whether any rule can be arrived at by which a critic may determine what is or what is not an earlier or a later stage *in this particular element* of the liturgical development. This much, at least, may be assumed, that this point, around which the author alleges the whole discussion turns, is one on which there is no warrant for critical dogmatism, and one which can give no key for the solution of questions of priority among the sacred books.

Under the head of "Fusion of Several Elements into One Narrative," the writer gives us his views respecting the composition of the sacred books—if anything composed in the way alleged deserves to be styled sacred. The substance of the whole matter is this:—

"The Semitic genius does not at all lie in the direction of organic structure. In architecture, in poetry, in history, the Hebrew adds part to part instead of developing a single notion. The temple was an aggregation of small cells, the longest Psalm is an acrostic, and so the longest Biblical history is a stratification and not an organism. This process was facilitated by the habit of anonymous writing, and the accompanying lack of all notion of anything like copyright. If a man copied a book, it was his to add and modify as he pleased, and he was not in the least bound to distinguish the old from the new. If he had two books before him to which he attached equal worth, he took large extracts from both, and harmonized them by such additions or modifications as he felt to be necessary. But in default of a keen sense for organic unity, very little harmony was sought in points of internal structure, though great skill was often shown, as in the Book of Genesis, in throwing the whole material into a balanced scheme of external arrangement. On such principles minor narratives were fused together one after the other, and at length in exile a final redactor completed the great work, on the first part of which Ezra based his reformation, while the latter part was thrown into the second canon. The curious combination of the functions of copyist and author, which is here presupposed, did not wholly disappear till a pretty late date; and where, as in the Books of Samuel, we have two recensions of the text, one in the Hebrew and one in the Septuagint translation, the discrepancies are of such a kind that criticism of the text and analysis of its sources are separated by a scarcely perceptible line."

Here, then, is our author's account of the way in which those books which Christians have been wont to style the word of God have come into existence! In the first place, it is laid down as an unquestionable axiom, that the sacred writers had no genius for anything but literary patchwork. In proof of this assertion reference is made to the architecture of the Temple, to the acrostic structure of the 119th Psalm, and to the longest Biblical history! From the first of these references we are, of course, to infer that the architecture of the Temple was simply the offspring of Semitic genius. The Bible itself gives a somewhat different account of the authorship of the temple architecture. If we are to credit the book itself, God Himself was the architect of both the Tabernacle and the Temple. It was not left either to Moses or to David, as representatives of Semitic genius, to determine what the fashion of the dwelling-place of Jehovah should be. The great symbol and type of Messiah's body, personal and mystical, was far too important a matter to be marred by the untowardness of any order or class of human genius, whether of the Gentile or the Jew. Speaking on this point, David says: "All this the Lord made me understand *in writing* by his hand upon me, even all the works of this pattern" (1 Chron. xxviii. 19). The Chronicles will not be accepted as authentic history by "the newer criticism," but we have the authority of the Epistle to the Hebrews (chap. ix. 8) for regarding the Tabernacle, which was the Temple in miniature, as designed by the Holy Ghost. The charge therefore of incapacity to develop a single notion, or to achieve an organic structure, if it lie at all against any one concerned in the authorship of the Temple, must lie against God Himself.

Equally irreverent and inconclusive is the second reference. It is not true that because the 119th Psalm is an acrostic its structure is not organic. It is not an impossible achievement, to write an acrostic in which a "a single notion" is developed. And certainly it is one of the slenderest and most partial of inductions, to infer what Semitic genius could achieve in poetry from the fact that the 119th Psalm is an acrostic.

What our author means when he says that "the longest Biblical history is a stratification and not an organism," we do not clearly comprehend; for the distinction between "stratification" and "organism," in such connection, is not very transparent. But taking his own account of the distinction, to wit, that in stratification "part is added to part," while in organization "a simple notion is developed," there is no ground for the assumption that the one is exclusive of the other. There is such a thing as organization by stratification, and that too as a mode of development. Teleologists have been in the habit of arguing that our earth is an organized whole, and have cited in support of their position the correlated strata composing its crust. These strata are not haphazard deposits, but, on the contrary, reveal in their mutual relations, and in their common subordination to the wants and purposes of man, the presence and control of an infinitely wise and beneficent Mind.

In like manner, we are told by physiologists and biologists, that whilst the architecture of the body is of the cellular order, it is none the less an organism. Whilst "part has been added to part," as if outlined by some "Semitic genius," there is nevertheless a common consciousness in this wonderful "aggregation of small cells," which bespeaks an organic unity and demonstrates "the development of a single notion." And surely it is not necessary to refer to the *flora* of our world to confirm the position that stratification is not the antithesis of organic structure. What are the rings disclosed when a tree of the forest is felled, but so many elements of a stratification which is confessedly organic? In a word, it is not "the adding of part to part" that determines the character of the resultant aggregate, but the presence or the absence of a determining purpose to the achievement of which the parts are made, or are not made, to contribute. Wherever parts are so added to parts as to contribute to the attainment of an end, we pronounce the arrangement an organization. This judgment we pronounce instinctively, whether the parts be the cells of the human body, or the rooms of a house, or the rings of a tree, or the companies, or regiments, or columns, of an army moved on the battlefield by the commander-in-chief, or the paragraphs, or chapters, or books, of a work.

But not only is the distinction groundless, it is peculiarly inapplicable to the actual products of "Semitic genius" given us in the Bible. Christian apologists have been wont to argue the divine authenticity of the Bible from its organic unity. Of course, if it be a stratification, as the writer would have us believe, and if, as he tells us, stratification is the very antithesis of organic structure, the doctrine of organic unity, and with it this apologetic position, must be given up. Besides, Biblical criticism itself must lose one of the tests by which it judges of the claim of any of the sacred books to a place in the sacred canon. If, as critics say, in addition to all other proofs, "the organic function" of a book must be taken into account, that is, the manifested fitness of the book to fill its place as a part of one organism, it must be clear that no book of the Bible could, on the principle of our author, stand the trial. If the author were within reach he would foreclose the inquisition, and dismiss the inquisitors, telling them that no men of intelligence would sit down to test the fitness of a stratum, or any number of strata combined, to perform organic functions, as the ideas of stratification and organization were mutually exclusive.

It is true the "Semitic genius" sometimes all but shook itself loose from the trammels of stratification, and somehow or other managed, as in the Book of Genesis, "to throw the material into a balanced *scheme* of external arrangement;" but, of course, a balanced *scheme* of external arrangement is not an organic structure; at least a writer, by using this nicely-balanced phrase, can, for the moment, avoid the appearance of self-contradiction, while, at the same time, he admits a fact subversive of his theory. As a matter of fact, the Book of Genesis reveals a "*scheme*" balanced both externally and internally. It contains a brief but most comprehensive history of the *development* of the *protevangelion* as displayed in the conflicts of the two seeds—the seed of the woman and the seed of the serpent — for a period of more than two thousand years. Our author may, if it please him, deny that the development of the first promise is "the development of a single notion," but most people will regard the denial as an additional illustration of the way in which a pet theory may blind the intellect and warp the judgment. What our author styles "a balanced scheme of external arrangement," is a living organization — an organization of living men brought into existence in order that through them the promise of the Messiah might be developed towards its fulfilment. To speak of the history of this organization as if it consisted of a congeries of incongruous elements, brought into a sort of external harmony by some *ex post facto* copyist, or final redactor, who, from the untowardness of the materials, felt it necessary "to add and modify," and not to be too precise about distinguishing the old from the new, is as unfair and as unphilosophical as it is irreverent. Of "the curious combination of the functions of copyist and author which is here *presupposed*," and which, we are told, "did not wholly disappear till a pretty late date," it is difficult to speak with calmness, or to think without feelings bordering on indignation. Here is a young man talking about the way in which one of the most ancient of books was composed, with as much confidence as if he had lived throughout the 1500 years occupied in the writing of it, and had looked over the shoulders of the writers as from age to age they plied their marvellous task; and when he has told us just how the work was done, turns round and tells us that he was merely *presupposing* it had been composed in this way! *Presupposing!* and presupposing all this about the genesis of the word of God, that cannot be broken, and which abideth for ever! Let rationalistic, destructive critics utter and give currency to such hypotheses regarding the origin of our Bible, but, "O my soul, come not thou into their secret; unto their assembly, mine honour, be not thou united."

Conclusion.

Notwithstanding the extravagant claims put forth on behalf of the scholarship of "the newer criticism," the fact is, it has failed in its assault upon the traditional theory of the gospel of pre-exilic times. When it has done its worst, the remnant record, on which it has not as yet ventured to lay its hand, rises up to witness against it, and presents each of the cherished doctrines of the analogy of the faith, against which it has directed its attacks, in its immemorial historical position. Despite its irreverent, ruthless attempts, the citadel of Truth stands secure, presenting on its foundation, and on every course of its superstructure, the hope-inspiring inscription, "Christ and Him crucified." This inscription, and the stones which bear it, "the newer criticism" has tried to efface, or remove, from all that part of the building which precedes the Babylonish exile, but, like the name of the sculptor inwrought in the shield of Minerva, it resists deletion so long as any part of the structure remains. When the analytic instruments of Nöldeke are laid down, and the battering-rams of Kuenen and Wellhausen are withdrawn, the inscription τὸ ἀρνίον ἐσφαγμένον ἀπὸ καταβολῆς κόσμου,—the Lamb slain from the foundation of the world,—still abides, irradiating the building from basement to battlement, and assuring its inmates that the fortress in which they have taken refuge is impregnable.

APPENDIX.

Supplementary to the Argument, Chapter V., pp. 107-115.

Even though it were true, as our author assumes, that the scribe had before him the six naked consonants, HMMTTH, his liability to mistakes in the transcription would be much less than if he had, besides, to transcribe their attendant vowel-points, as supplied afterwards by the Massorets. But our author's assumption is not warranted by the facts of the case. It is not true that the naked text, as it stood prior to the Massoretic punctuation, presented in the case adduced, or in like instances, or in any instance, two consonants where the Massoretic text has but one, with a *daghesh forte* in its bosom. The naked, unpunctuated text, in the case submitted, instead of the six consonants with which the lecturer credits it, exhibited to the eye of the scribe simply three radical letters and the article, thus—HMTH. It is needless to point out the bearing of this unquestionable fact upon one's estimate of the critical competency of the leader of "the newer criticism" in Scotland, or to speak of the additional force it lends to the vindication of the scribes against his most uncritical assumptions.

INDEX.

AARON and his sons; their consecration historical, 236-240; history of, endorsed in New Testament, 252-254.
Abel's offering commanded of God, 125, 126.
Achilles prays without sacrifice, 199.
Agamemnon, 197.
Ahaz, 17, 18.
Altar of the God of Israel, 9; Damascene, 17, 18.
Ancient writers; comprehension of term, 295-298.
Annals of the kings of Israel and Judah, 3.
Apollo, 197-199.
Ark; reason of its sacredness, 213, 214; ceremonies connected with, unsanctioned until it was lost, 227, 228; references to, in Epistle to Hebrews, 228; necessary from time the law was given, 229; special difficulties owing to loss of, in the exile, 232-234.
Artaxerxes; his decree, 8.
Article "Bible," 277-320.
Asham, 18-20.
Ashtaroth, 34, 39.
Atonement; ignorance of, in pre-exilic times, 78; difficulties of this theory, 78-80.

Atreus, 198.
Azariah, argument from his rebuke, 30.
BABYLON, 4.
Balaam, 278.
Berosus, 3.
Bridge; trustworthiness of the old, questioned, 4-6; Deuteronomic and Esdrine arches do not furnish a complete bridge, 159.
CAPTIVITY; children of, 10.
Carmel; Elijah's sacrifice on, 27.
Chataoth, 19.
Chronological difficulty, 3, 4.
Chryses, the priest's prayer to Apollo, 197, 198.
Confession of Faith; author's doctrine contrary to, 94-96, 148-154.
Covenant of Sinai reduced to a covenant of works, 129-133.
DARIUS, 8.
Deuteronomic theory; difficulties in the way of, 42-44; solution unsatisfactory, 68-72; code pronounced unsacrificial, 73, 74; Deuteronomy not the sole standard of Josiah's reformation, 283-295; consequences of dating Deuteronomy from a post-Mosaic period, 291-301; how came this book to be accepted ?

302, 303; style easily imitated, 307, 308; argument for late date from change of laws, 311–313.

Development; theory of, demands what author cannot admit, 168, 169; "the newer criticism" and, 273–276; not a discovery of "the newer criticism," 281.

Discrepancy, alleged, 247; examined, 247–249; assumption necessary to make out charge of, 249–251; alleged, between Exodus and Deuteronomy, 283–289.

EGYPT, 4.

Elijah, argument from his sacrifice on Carmel, 27.

Eusebius, 3.

Exodus, had the writer of, common sense? 240, 241.

Ezekiel and Jeremiah brought into conflict, 52, 53; Ezek. xliv. main reliance for argument in support of late date of Pentateuch, 309–313.

Ezekielian hypothesis of the origin of Levitical Torah, 14 seq., 45, 46; Ezekiel's new ordinances, 47–51.

Ezra, his law and the Pentateuch, 7–13; knowledge of its contents before Ezra's visit to Jerusalem, 8 seq.

FORGIVENESS of sin, author's theory of, in pre-exilic times, 138–145.

Fraud; charge of, 170, 231, 234, 291–299.

GENERALIZATION, author's faculty of, 105, 106; adverse, 177, 180; from imperfect *data*, 277, 278.

Gideon, his refusal to rule over Israel, 290, 291.

God's attitude towards sacrifice, 116–118.

Grace; author's theory of, in pre-exilic times, determines the date of the Pentateuch, 147, 148; contradicts the Confession of Faith, 148–154.

HEATHEN; views of ancient, on prayer, 195–199.

Hebrew; sacred writers Hebraistic, 299, 300.

Holy Spirit; doctrine of His relation to God's ancient people, 94–96; Romish cast of doctrine, 98 seq.

Homer; prayer and sacrifice in his day, 197–199.

Horne's *Introduction* answers author's objections, 304.

Hypotheses respecting the origin of sacrifice, 182–186.

IMPEACHMENT of record a failure, 251.

Index Expurgatorius; author's, 55.

Isaiah, 18; his denunciation of sacrifice, etc., explained, 83–90.

JASHER, Book of, 3.

Jehoash, 20.

Jehovah; theory charges Him with changeableness, 200, 201.

Jeremiah's restoration implies a priestly Torah, 67, 68.

Jeroboam; argument from the sin of, 26, 27.

Jeshua, 9.

Jonah; argument from book of, 195, 196.

Josephus, 3.

Josiah; argument from his reformation, 30–42.

Jozadak, 9.
KUENEN, 11, 13, 44, 237, 321.
LAMB ; slain from the foundation of the world, 321.
Law ; argument from distinction between moral and positive, 33, 289 ; meaning of term law in Romans, 154, 155 ; case-law needs cases—precedents imply history, 236-239.
Levites, 8.
Literature, Old Testament, 2, 3 ; New Testament, 2.
MAIMONIDES, 13.
Manetho, 3.
Massorets ; their competency, 112-114.
Mediation, still found in record, however reduced, 220-223.
Minchah, 24-26.
Minerva, 321.
Moabite stone, 3, 4.
Moral law ; anti-economic separation of, from ceremonial, 207, 208; states condition of life under all dispensations, 209 ; ceremonial correlative to, 210, 211 ; bearing of this fact on character of Christian dispensation, 215 ; on post-exilic theory, 218-220.
Mosaic economy ; design of, 202 seq. ; typology of, 216, 217.
Moses, 8, 9, 12, 16, passim ; how known to have been a priest, 165-167 ; " the newer criticism " must get rid of Moses as well as of his authorship, 223, 224 ; what he owed to his mother's training, 300 ; according to the author's theory, addresses an audience in wilderness in the days of Josiah, 306.
NATIONAL unification of Israel ; when effected, 280, 281.

Nineveh, 4.
Noah's sacrifice ; argument from, 126-128 ; Noachian revelation, 199.
Nöldeke, 166, 167, 321.
'OLAH, 24-26.
'Olah tamîd, 25.
Organization and stratification, 314-320.
PASSOVER ; theory in conflict with, 53, 56, 57 ; places Jeremiah in conflict with, 58-60 ; was passover boiled ? 59 seq.; symbolic import of, 203, 204 ; sacrificial character of, 205-207.
Pentateuch ; date of Samaritan, 104, 105.
Peter the Apostle and the Zeit-Geist, 298.
Polytheism, origin of, in Israel, 279, 280.
Prayer ; author's views of, under Old Testament, 187-195.
Priesthood, inseparable from Jeremiah's prophecy, 66 seq. ; a sign of God's favour, its loss a sign of His displeasure, 65, 66 ; inseparable from sacrifice, 255, 256 ; priestly office related to the prophetic, 256 ; author's views of this relation, 257-259 · true ideal of a priest, 263 ; not derived from mere etymology, 264-267 ; nature of, determines its relation to prophecy, 267, 268 ; relation of Christ's priestly to His prophetic and kingly functions, 268, 269.
Principles, first critical, 1 ; applicability of, 2 ; gravity of, at stake in this discussion, 171-174.
Prophets, pre - exilic, arrayed against post-exilic, 83 seq.

Psalm, argument from 51st, 91, 94; difficulties of "the newer criticism" remain even when last two verses are left out, 93 seq.

Psalm cvii.; adverse to author's theory of prayer, 196, 197.

QUESTION, a crucial one for the author, 182–185.

RABBINS; the Jewish, and their learning, 5, 6.

Reformation; argument from relation of, to a Torah, 29 seq.; argument from Josiah's, 30 seq.

Religion in pre-exilic times, 74–78; how related to revelation, 277, 278; Biblical, not left to one impulse, 279, 280.

Romish cast of author's doctrine of the relation of the Holy Spirit to the Church, 98, 99.

SACRIFICE; boiling not inconsistent with, 61–63; origin of, 120–130.

Salvation; author's theory of, in pre-exilic times, 141–147.

Samuel; his hesitation to appoint a king, 290, 291.

Scholarship; extravagant claim in behalf of, 246.

Scribes, the, and the selection and transmission of the Hebrew text, 5, 6; author's accusations of, met by himself, 106–115.

Semitic genius not organic, 314–320; plan of Tabernacle and Temple not dependent on, 315, 316.

Shealtiel, 9.

Shelamim, 24, 25.

Solomon, 17 seq.

Spinoza, 13; author's theory traced to, 303, 304.

Stratification not inconsistent with organization, 316–319.

Syllogism, author's, retorted, 86, 87.

TABERNACLE; the tent pitched by Moses (Ex. xxxiii.) not the Tabernacle of chap. xl., 240–244.

Tekoa; its herdsmen not acquainted with the use and wont of ancient writers outside Israel, 299.

Temple; argument from history of the first, 21 seq.

Text; a vowelless, easier of transmission, 109–115.

Theory, author's, unreasonable, 174–177.

Thetis, mother of Achilles, 199.

Torah; origin of the Esdrine, 7–14; deductions from the Mosaic Torah, 157, 158; can a ceremonial Torah be developed from a moral Torah? 161–165.

Transmission of Pentateuch; have scribes acted faithfully in? 101–115.

Typology of sacrifices, how accounted for, 202–207.

URIJAH, 17, 18.

VARIATION; contemplated in the Mosaic economy, 281–283.

WARS of the Lord, Book of, 3.

Wellhausen, 11, 13, 167, 321.

Whately; his *Historical Doubts*, 295.

Worship by sacrifice, uncommanded before the exile, 117–119; uncommanded worship unconfessional, 133–137; a breach of the Sinaitic covenant, 134, 135; author's theory of, under Old Testament, 187–193.

ZERUBBABEL, 9.

The following notices are extracted from Reviews which, among many others, have appeared of the previous Editions of this Volume :—

'Dr. Watts not only points out that Professor Smith's view is incompatible with the teaching of the New Testament, and the result of a purely arbitrary method of criticism, but is quite contradicted by portions of the Old Testament, which the "New Criticism" admits as historical. Dr. Watts' book is a thoroughly learned, fair, and convincing refutation of Mr. Robertson Smith's teaching on the Old Testament.'—*Church Bells.*

'A masterly exposure and refutation of the Lectures of the Aberdeen Professor. . . . The volume bears ample evidence of patient, scholarly investigation, careful criticism, and close, logical reasoning, and is throughout a lucid display and satisfactory vindication of Scripture doctrine, against loose, unsupported theories and plausible sophistical reasoning. . . . The work well deserves a careful perusal, and deserves to be extensively circulated.'—*Reformed Presbyterian Witness.*

'We think that even the warmest admirer of the Aberdeen Professor, if he be candid, will admit that Professor Smith's views and arguments for the post-exilic origin of the Torah get sadly mangled in the mouth of his Belfast antagonist. We can in all sincerity commend Professor Watts' book to our readers.'—*Edinburgh Courant.*

'The church at large, especially young men—students of God's word—will owe a debt of gratitude to the author for the thoroughness with which he has met the criticisms of Robertson Smith, and demonstrated their utter good-for-nothingness.'—*New York Observer.*

'We have read with great interest Dr. Watts' masterly polemic; . . . we have never read anything from his pen that pleased us so well. . . . Dr. Watts deserves the thanks of the various evangelical churches for his manly, scholarly, and seasonable treatise.'—*The Presbyterian Churchman.*

'An earnest, forcible refutation of the lectures delivered by Robertson Smith, in Edinburgh and Glasgow, against the decision of the Free Church Commission in 1880. . . . Any scholar who wants evidence of the unsatisfactoriness of a good deal of the "Newer Criticism" will find materials in these pages.'—*Freeman.*

'Answers to Professor Smith's sometimes subtle, but oftentimes extremely rash, reasonings have cropped up here and there; but we have nowhere met with so complete and exhaustive a reply as that which Dr. Watts' admirable volume contains.'—*Baptist Magazine.*

'Dr. Watts shows very ably and conclusively in these pages that the principles advocated by Mr. Robertson Smith are unsafe guides in Biblical criticism, and subversive of all confidence in the Old Testament as a divine revelation, as well as of all faith in the fundamental doctrines of Christianity. . . . This work will be of immense value to all who are interested in refuting the attempts made in so many quarters to invalidate the divine origin of the Old Testament revelation.'—*English Churchman.*

'Those who care to follow Professor Smith in his discussions cannot do better than carefully study this able reply.'—*Clergyman's Magazine.*

'This book will cast to the winds a good deal of the sophistical reasonings of the champion of the new doctrine.'—*Christian Union.*

'We can commend this work; and it is only fair that those who have read the attack should also read the defence.'—*Rock.*

'Dr. Watts has come forward with a brave, earnest, and scholarly examination of Professor Smith's criticism. He does not make a sweeping and general condemnation of the "New Criticism," but, taking each and every one of the Professor's attacks on the received opinions of the Church, examines them in detail, and with such references and comparison of passages as to convict the critic of extraordinary errors of fact, and consequent errors of opinion.'—*New York Observer.*

'The theories which for a time filled with alarm the friends of orthodoxy have received, at the hands of the Belfast Professor, the *coup de grace*, and will not, we are convinced, show face again before the "Scottish public," to whom the lectures were originally addressed.'—*Daily Review.*

'Our distinct judgment is that no reader should omit to acquaint himself with the work of Dr. Watts, if he really wishes to know what an undoubtedly penetrating intellect has to urge against the "Newer Criticism." . . . Dr. Watts has acquitted himself with noble ability.'—*Fountain.*

'We commend it most cordially, and are satisfied that it is well fitted to deepen the conviction that the more the Bible records are examined, the more fully will the accuracy of the ordinary view of their history and legislation be established.'—*North British Daily Mail.*

'Professor Watts, by his book, has rendered an important service at a very serious juncture; and we think no one should read Mr. Smith's lectures without also studying this reply.'—*British Messenger.*

'This reply of Dr. Watts is a most seasonable and able exposure of theories adverse to the authority of Old Testament revelation, and which, therefore, discredit much of the New, and is at the same time a defensive reassertion of truths most firmly believed amongst us.'—*Belfast News Letter.*

www.ingramcontent.com/pod-product-compliance
Lightning Source LLC
Chambersburg PA
CBHW032358230426
43672CB00007B/737